THE 20 MOST SIGNIFICANT EVENTS OF THE CIVIL WAR

THE
20 MOST
SIGNIFICANT
EVENTS OF THE
CIVIL WAR

A RANKING

ALAN AXELROD

Skyhorse Publishing

Skyhorse Publishing books may be purchased in bulk at special discounts for sales promotion, corporate gifts, fund-raising, or educational purposes. Special editions can also be created to specifications. For details, contact the Special Sales Department, Skyhorse Publishing, 307 West 36th Street, 11th Floor, New York, NY 10018 or info@skyhorsepublishing.com.

Skyhorse® and Skyhorse Publishing® are registered trademarks of Skyhorse Publishing, Inc.®, a Delaware corporation.

Visit our website at www.skyhorsepublishing.com.

10 9 8 7 6 5 4 3 2 1

Library of Congress Cataloging-in-Publication Data is available on file.

Cover design by Rain Saukas
Cover photo credits: Library of Congress

Print ISBN: 9781510715202
Ebook ISBN: 9781510715226

Printed in the United States of America

My thanks to Mike Lewis, who had this idea and who thought of me when he wanted to make a book out of it, and to Veronica Alvarado, who edited the manuscript.

CONTENTS

INTRODUCTION

For the Sake of Argument and Understanding

T HERE IS A story from World War II about a pilot and co-pilot who flew C-47 Skytrains as part of the extremely hazardous India-China Ferry across the Himalayas, a mission popularly known as "Flying the Hump." The pilot always carried with him into the flight deck the makings of a gin martini—gin, vermouth, some olives, and a shaker. After a few flights, his co-pilot finally asked: "What's with all the martini stuff?"

"If we gotta bail out somewhere over these mountains, beyond rescue, in the middle of nowhere, I'm going to take all this 'stuff' and start making a martini as soon as I hit the ground," he explained. "I guarantee you that, within two minutes, somebody will show up to argue with me that whatever I'm doing is no way to make a martini. Then you'll be happy I took this gear with us."

It may be that the only surer way of starting an argument than this is to express an opinion about the Civil War. To those as passionate about their history as they are about their martinis, the causes, course, events, outcomes, personalities, and what-ifs relating to America's deadliest war still pack the urgent punch of current events, even more than 150 years after Appomattox. There is a pleasure and a fascination about Civil War disputes, but there is also a sense of earnestness and a genuine importance. As many historians have pointed out, the American Revolution may have won our independence from Britain, but it was in the Civil War that an enduring nation was finally, and painfully, born. We Americans—along with everyone in every other part of the world who had any interest in the United States—continue to share a stake in that war. It is important that each of us creates an understanding of it.

Toward that end, I want to start, or in certain cases restart, some arguments about the Civil War—minus the violence of the war itself, of course—by offering my ranking of the twenty most significant events in (and leading up to) the bloodiest and most consequential conflict fought on American soil. I present the events ranked in order of their significance rather than in their chronological order (which you will find, however, in the timeline that follows this introduction), and I do so with the intention of persuading you that what I have included and the order in which I have included it is spot-on accurate.

That is my intention. It is not, however, my expectation.

No, like that World War II "Hump" jockey, I expect an argument, and, if it is a good one, I expect that everyone involved will learn a lot more than any of us would from memorizing a chronological history.

We learn the most from arguments that are made not just from a basis of verifiable fact, but also from clear criteria rather than mere opinion or gut feeling. The criteria I have consulted for inclusion and ranking of the top-20 most significant events include the following:

1. The event's effect as cause or trigger of the war.
2. The event's decisiveness—Was it a war-winning/war-losing event (both in military terms and in terms of public opinion, morale, and support)?
3. The event's magnitude and scope—for instance, the size and cost of a battle.
4. The event's enduring postwar significance in American history, politics, society, culture, and/or in military history and technology.

My objective has been to adopt as fresh and unfiltered a perspective on the war as possible and to narrate each of the twenty events as if they were accounts being given for the very first time. This said, the discussion of each event also elaborates on the rationale for the choices made and how these choices account for the origins, conduct, and outcome of the Civil War.

"Twenty events" is like the game of Twenty Questions. The first question the very concept should prompt is "Why not twenty-one or sixteen or just about any other integer?" The truth is that, for this question, there is no good answer. Twenty is one fourth of four score—a convenient number. Other than that, it is an arbitrary number. So this book concludes with a twenty-first chapter, which contains about ten more events for your consideration, each of which *might* have been included in the twenty, but wasn't.

A Civil War Timeline

T HIS TIMELINE LISTS the twenty most significant events of the Civil War in chronological order, together with an additional, unnumbered, ten discussed in Chapter 21.

1856, MAY 22

#1 The Gentleman from South Carolina Canes the Gentleman from Massachusetts

South Carolina's Representative Preston Brooks assaults abolitionist Charles Sumner, senator from Massachusetts, at his desk in the Senate chamber.

1859, OCTOBER 16–18

#19 John Brown Raids Harpers Ferry

Radical abolitionist John Brown seizes the federal arsenal and armory at Harpers Ferry, Virginia—today, West Virginia—with the intention of inciting and arming a slave rebellion.

1860, DECEMBER 20

South Carolina Secedes from the Union

1861, MARCH 4

#2 "Black Lincoln" Is Inaugurated

While not an avowed abolitionist, Abraham Lincoln is opposed to the expansion of slavery, and his inauguration as the sixteenth president of the United States is sufficient to make secession and civil war inevitable.

APRIL 12

#3 General Beauregard Opens Fire on Fort Sumter

After Major Robert Anderson, commanding the US Army garrison at Fort Sumter, refuses the demand of South Carolina's governor that he surrender, P. G. T. Beauregard, the Confederacy's first general, directs an artillery siege against the fort. This is the first battle of the Civil War.

JUNE 8

The United States Sanitary Commission Is Authorized

JULY 21

#10 The Rebels Win at Bull Run

Confederate forces under Generals P. G. T. Beauregard, Joseph E. Johnston, and Thomas J. Jackson rout a Union army commanded by Irvin McDowell at the First Battle of Bull Run, near Manassas, Virginia, a short march from Washington, DC. It is the first major battle between the armies of the North and the South.

NOVEMBER 8

Confederate "Diplomats" Mason and Slidell Are Seized from the British-flagged *Trent*

1862, MARCH 8

#20 The Ironclads Clash at Hampton Roads

The revolutionary proto-battleships CSS *Alabama* and USS *Monitor,* iconic products of innovation in industrialized warfare, fight to a stalemate.

APRIL 8

#14 Shiloh Creates a New American Reality

Both the Confederate and Union public are appalled at the level of carnage in North American combat on an unprecedented scale.

MAY 20

#15 Congress Passes the Homestead Act of 1862

Locked in a Civil War that is not going well, the Lincoln administration champions legislation designed to strengthen the Union along its East-West axis.

JUNE 1

#11 Lee Rises to Top Command in the Confederacy

Robert E. Lee replaces a wounded Joseph E. Johnston as commanding general of the Army of Northern Virginia, the flagship force of the Confederacy.

JULY 22

The Dix-Hill Prisoner Exchange Is Signed

AUGUST 17

The Great Santee Sioux Uprising Begins in Minnesota

AUGUST 24

CSS *Alabama* Is Commissioned by the Confederate States Navy

AUGUST 28–30

#18 Lee Divides and Conquers at the Second Battle of Bull Run

In a demonstration of his military genius and daring, Robert E. Lee purposely violates tactical convention by dividing his forces in the presence of the enemy—and achieves victory.

SEPTEMBER 22

#4 Lincoln Issues the "Preliminary" Emancipation Proclamation

President Lincoln issues an executive proclamation that effectively makes the permanent abolition of slavery one of the objectives of the Civil War.

NOVEMBER 7

#17 Lincoln Chooses Burnside to Lead the Army of the Potomac

Desperate to find a general who will bring the Union decisive victories, President Lincoln presses Ambrose Burnside into leadership of the premier force in the Union army—with disastrous results.

1863, MAY 2

#16 Stonewall Jackson Falls to Friendly Fire at Chancellorsville

In the middle of a battle that would be called "Lee's masterpiece," Lee's indispensable general, Thomas "Stonewall" Jackson, is mortally wounded by his own men.

JULY 4

#12 Vicksburg Falls to Grant

Overshadowed by the victory at Gettysburg the day before, the fall of Vicksburg to Union general Ulysses S. Grant divides the Confederacy east and west and deprives it of vitally important Mississippi River navigation.

JULY 13

#8 New York Draft Rioters Set Fire to the Orphan Asylum for Colored Children

Hard-pressed New Yorkers riot to protest conscription into an army to liberate slaves they fear will take their jobs.

JULY 18

The 54th Massachusetts Infantry Regiment Assaults Fort Wagner

NOVEMBER 19

#6 Two Minutes at Gettysburg

Lincoln's masterfully brief "Gettysburg Address" defines what is at stake in the Civil War.

1864, APRIL 12

Nathan Bedford Forrest Leads the Fort Pillow Massacre

MAY 7

#13 Defeated, Grant Advances

Ulysses S. Grant becomes a strategic juggernaut, even in defeat, during his Overland Campaign.

JULY 2

Congress Passes the Wade-Davis Bill, Mandating a Punitive Reconstruction Policy

SEPTEMBER 27

Bloody Bill Anderson Leads the Centralia Massacre

1865, APRIL 9

#5 Lee Surrenders to Grant at Appomattox Court House, Virginia

Robert E. Lee surrenders the Army of Northern Virginia to U. S. Grant, precipitating the end of the Civil War.

APRIL 14

#9 John Wilkes Booth Assassinates Abraham Lincoln

By killing President Abraham Lincoln, John Wilkes Booth deprived a shattered America of the single political leader most capable of healing the wounds inflicted by four years of the Civil War.

1

May 22, 1856

The Gentleman from South Carolina Canes the Gentleman from Massachusetts

Why it's significant. The first battle of the Civil War opened on April 12, 1861, when P. G. T. Beauregard fired the first of some 4,000 cannonballs against Fort Sumter. The war itself, however, may have started five years earlier, not with an artillery bombardment, but with a battery of blows from a Southern congressman's gold-headed walking stick rained down upon the head and body of a Northern senator. South Carolina Representative Preston Brooks beat Massachusetts Senator Charles Sumner nearly to death in the US Senate chamber because the Northern abolitionist had made speech denouncing "slave power." That political debate should be preempted by violence—one lawmaker against another, within the very heart of the national Capitol—foretold the coming war between the states.

T HE BEATING SEEMED to erupt from a rage of the heart, the product of a violent impulse. It was the afternoon of May 22, 1856. Massachusetts Senator Charles Sumner was writing at his desk in the Senate chamber. South Carolina Representative Preston Brooks approached him, spoke to him in a calm, low voice—the tone and volume of voice that, in some people, precedes a whirlwind of violence.

Confronted, Sumner began to stand. Before he could straighten himself, however, Brooks gripped his cane just below its gold head. The walking stick was made of black lacquered gutta-percha, a thick, rigid, heavy natural rubber, a material just flexible enough to resist breaking. Brooks brought it down upon the senator's head, shoulders, back, and body time and time again, as if by irresistible reflex.

As if by reflex as well, the beaten man responded. By his own recollection, everything went dark after the first few strokes of the cane. Sumner no longer saw his assailant, or anyone or anything else for that matter, in the hallowed chamber. "What I did afterwards was done almost unconsciously, acting under the instincts of self-defense," he later reported.

Reeling beneath the machinelike blows, Sumner slid under his desk. It afforded no protection. The desk was bolted to the floor, the chair that went with it ran back and forth on a track laid into the floor. As he sat or lay in a semi-conscious heap beneath the desk, the chair effectively imprisoned him yet still left ample room for Brooks to continue wielding his cane. Blinded by the effusion of his own blood, Sumner managed to get to his feet. In doing so, he tore the desk from the floor in an animal effort to evade the bludgeoning.

He staggered into the aisle, sightless, arms outstretched either to fend off the cane or to substitute for the sense of sight. Released from his trap beneath the desk, however, Sumner only made an easier target. Brooks was not finished with him. Using what he later admitted was the "full extent of [his] power," the South Carolinian struck him in fresh places, across the face, the shoulders, and the head. At length, the gutta-percha, as if weary of bending, broke, snapping in two. Brooks retained the end with the golden head and continued to ply it, even as it shattered into even more pieces.

"Oh Lord," Sumner was heard to gasp as he at last lost consciousness—as he faded, bellowing (Brooks subsequently mocked him) "like a calf."

The Southerner would not let him lie, but, before his victim crumpled fully to the floor, he took hold of his lapel, in one hand gathering a fistful of the cloth, pulling the unconscious man partially upright before him. He now used the much-shortened stick to continue the beating at face-to-face range.

* * *

An act of passion—dreadful, awful, ungovernable, unstoppable. But hardly spontaneous. In fact, the force that drove the muscle that wielded the walking stick had been decades in gathering. Its accumulation began when the architects of American independence failed to face, let alone resolve, the issue of slavery. In his original draft of the Declaration of Independence, Thomas Jefferson (a slave owner himself) condemned slavery, but other hands deleted the condemnation in subsequent drafts. When the Constitution was being drawn up in 1787, there were calls to include the abolition of slavery, but those voices were neither very loud nor very enthusiastic. In the end, the conservative voices prevailed. Yet the Constitution did not entirely ignore the subject of slavery. By stipulating that the importation of slaves—that is, the slave trade—was to cease by 1808 (Article I, Section 9), the framers (some have insisted) seem to have implicitly acknowledged an inherent wrong in the institution of slavery. At the same time, however, those same men created a document that both recognized and explicitly protected slavery. Article IV, Section 2 specified that slaves who escaped into a free state were not thereby freed; on the contrary, the government of a free state into which a slave escaped was obligated to ensure that the fugitive would be "delivered up on claim of the party to whom such labor may be due."

In the end, the Constitution was all but silent on slavery, and when it did speak, it spoke both ambiguously and ambivalently, implying that slavery was an evil, yet also protecting it—in those states that did not outlaw it. These were all in the South or along the border between South and North, places where plantations were a form of agribusiness, enterprises that did not merely furnish food for subsistence or local consumption, but cultivated crops for widespread domestic sale and export—chiefly cotton, rice, and indigo dyestuffs. All of these were labor-intensive crops, and the cheapest form of labor was that of slaves. Economic conditions and matters of climate ensured that slavery in the United States would be regional. By protecting slavery wherever it existed, the Constitution unwittingly fostered a deepening divide between South and North, slave states and free states.

As moral objections to slavery—an abolition movement—developed in the North, the South feared that this more populous and more generally prosperous region, if it ever gained control of the federal government, would amend the Constitution to abolish slavery, an institution central to the Southern economy and way of life. The South's only legal defense against abolition was to block passage of any anti-slavery legislation in the Senate, where federal representation was independent of population. There, whether large or small, each state had two senators. Thus, as the nation grew following the American Revolution, the addition of each new state became an event of utmost anxiety over which way the new state would tip the balance—toward preserving slavery in the United States or toward abolishing it. The prospect of a civil war was never very remote, and it was renewed each time a US territory petitioned for statehood.

In 1836, Texas, home to many slave owners, won its independence from Mexico. Since 1821, the United States had been balanced between slave and free states, and there was great reluctance to upset this equilibrium. Congress therefore repeatedly put off the petitions of Texas for annexation and eventual statehood. Instead, Congress remained impassive while an independent Texas continued to exist as a republic. When France and Britain showed interest in colonizing that republic, however, Congress was at last moved to action. Texas was annexed to the United States in 1845 and, at the end of that year, was admitted as a state, bringing the slave/free ratio to 15:14.

The annexation and statehood of Texas triggered a US-Mexican War (1846–48). During the war's first year, Congress was eager to bring the conflict to a quick end and therefore debated a bill to appropriate $2 million to compensate Mexico for what the lawmakers euphemistically termed "territorial adjustments." Seizing opportunity where he saw it, Pennsylvania Congressman David Wilmot, an ardent abolitionist, introduced an amendment to the proposed appropriation legislation. Called the Wilmot Proviso, it would have barred (had it been enacted) the introduction of slavery into any territory acquired as a result of the Mexican War. Everyone knew that this potentially represented several new states, the addition of which would suddenly throw the slave/free balance significantly in favor of the North. The Wilmot Proviso therefore prompted Senator John C. Calhoun of South Carolina to propose four resolutions:

1. That all territories, including those acquired as a result of the war, be regarded as the common and joint property of the states.
2. That Congress, acting as agent for the states, could make no law depriving any state of its rights with regard to any territory.
3. That enacting any national law regarding slavery would violate the Constitution and the doctrine of states' rights.
4. That the people have the right to form their state governments as they wish.

Calhoun warned that failing to accept his resolutions would upset the balance between the demands of the North and the South and would therefore inevitably mean civil war. Wilmot's provocative Proviso and Calhoun's even more provocative resolutions set into motion a three-year debate on how to shore up the existing Missouri Compromise. Enacted in 1820 in response to Missouri's request to be admitted to the Union as a slave state, the Missouri Compromise granted that request but also split off Maine from Massachusetts and admitted it as a free state, thereby maintaining the slave/free balance. As part of the compromise, Congress also passed legislation drawing a line across the former Louisiana Territory, establishing a boundary between free and slave regions that would apply to the creation of future states. In 1850, two years after the war with Mexico ended, California, formerly a possession of Mexico, was admitted into the Union directly, without going through an interim territorial status. Southerners objected, assuming (correctly) that California would vote itself free. So, to stave off the civil war Calhoun had warned of, Senators Henry Clay of Kentucky and Daniel Webster of Massachusetts worked out a new compromise. California was to be admitted as a free state, but the people in the other territories acquired as a result of the Mexican War would be given "popular sovereignty," voting themselves as either "free" or "slave," without interference from the federal government. To appease the South further, Congress passed a strong fugitive slave law, forbidding anyone to aid or harbor escaped slaves. To sweeten the deal even more, the federal government agreed to assume debts Texas (admitted as a slave state in 1845) incurred before it was annexed to the United States.

In 1854, when the territories of Nebraska and Kansas applied for statehood, Congress repealed the Missouri Compromise and passed the Kansas-Nebraska Act. This extended "popular sovereignty"—the right of citizens of a territory to vote themselves free or slave when they became a state—beyond territory acquired as a result of the Mexican War, and it erased the 1820 boundary between free and slave territories. A majority of Nebraskans clearly favored admission into the Union as a free state, but the balance was much closer in Kansas, and the antislavery and pro-slavery factions erupted into a guerrilla civil war so deadly that the territory was dubbed "Bleeding Kansas."

* * *

Charles Sumner was Boston-born, the son of a Harvard-educated lawyer who was not only an early abolitionist, but a pioneering advocate of racially integrated public schools and an opponent of laws barring marriage between the races. Under his father's influence, young Charles grew up hating slavery. He became a lawyer and a Harvard lecturer on law, earned a reputation as a powerful abolitionist orator, and helped found the Free Soil Party, an important precursor of the Republican Party. Until the Seventeenth Amendment was ratified in 1913, senators were elected by state legislatures, not by the people. Running on the Free Soil ticket, Sumner won election to the US Senate by a single vote of the Massachusetts General Court (which functioned as the state's legislature) on April 24, 1851.

On May 19, 1856, with Kansas awash in blood, Sumner began to deliver on the floor of the Senate the first part of a speech so long that it had to be carried over into the next day. Known as the "Crime against Kansas" speech, it argued for immediate admission of Kansas as a free state, and it contained an especially incendiary condemnation of so-called "Slave Power," meaning the disproportionate influence slave owners exercised on government and public policy. The speech framed "Slave Power" in especially violent, even sexually charged terms, speaking of a "lust for power" and the "rape of a virgin Territory," which was being forcibly compelled into "the hateful embrace of slavery." The result of such a "depraved desire," Sumner argued, would be the birth a "new Slave State, hideous offspring of . . . crime."

Then Sumner made the speech personal, calling out Senator Andrew Butler of South Carolina. He "has read many books of chivalry, and believes himself a chivalrous knight with sentiments of honor and courage," Sumner declaimed. "Of course he has chosen a mistress to whom he has made his vows, and who, though ugly to others, is always lovely to him; though polluted in the sight of the world, is chaste in his sight—I mean the harlot, slavery."

South Carolina representative Preston Brooks, a committed champion of slavery, was Andrew Butler's cousin. Outraged by Sumner's words, he consulted his fellow South Carolina congressman Laurence M. Keitt on the etiquette of dueling, for he intended to challenge Sumner. But no, Keitt advised. Duels were properly fought between gentlemen of equal social standing. The offensive vulgarity of Sumner's speech had already revealed the Bostonian as no gentleman. Keitt advised instead that the appropriate response for such as Charles Sumner was to administer a beating with that symbol of true gentlemanly status, the walking stick.

And so the fury of Preston Brooks was channeled through a code of chivalry that both he and Keitt believed worthy of Southern gentlemen. Two days after the speech, Brooks entered the Senate chamber in the company of Keitt and Henry A. Edmundson, a congressman from Virginia. The Senate was in session, but the chamber was nearly empty. The trio scanned the galleries, anxious to ensure that no ladies were present to witness the violent retribution about to be meted out. It was, after all, unseemly for a Southern gentleman to cane a man in the presence of the fairer sex.

Brooks was a tall man, thirty-seven years old. He had attended South Carolina College—today the University of South Carolina— but had been expelled because he threatened local police officers with shooting. Later, in 1840, he actually did fight a duel, with Louis T. Wigfall, a future senator from Texas. Wigfall shot his challenger in the hip, which was why Brooks was obliged to walk with the aid of a cane. In contrast to Brooks, Sumner appeared older and frailer than his forty-five years. He certainly had no interest in duels, but was passionate about art and architecture, having traveled as a young man throughout Europe. In Paris in his late twenties, he fell in love with the treasures of the Louvre, the works of Leonardo and Raphael touching his mind, he wrote in his journal on January 19, 1838, "like a rich strain of music." It is surprising that a man of such refined sensibilities could have written so fiery a speech.

Brooks did not approach Sumner with stealth. On the contrary, with his witnesses in tow, he confronted him openly at his Senate desk.

"Mr. Sumner, I have read your speech twice over carefully," he said in a low, calm voice. "It is a libel on South Carolina, and Mr. Butler, who is a relative of mine." With that, the beating commenced.

A number of senators and others attempted to intervene, but Edmundson interposed himself and blocked them. Keitt brandished his own cane at those who approached, and then he drew a pistol.

"Let them alone, God damn you," he menaced. "Let them alone!"

Among the senators who tried to stop the beating was John J. Crittenden of Kentucky. A born peacemaker, he would, on December 18, 1860, offer before the Senate a set of six constitutional amendments designed to protect slavery while simultaneously limiting its spread. It was a desperate, last-ditch attempt to avert civil war, but the so-called Crittenden Compromise never had a chance. For Crittenden's sons, the Civil War proved literally to be a conflict of brother against brother. One son resigned his commission as lieutenant colonel in the US Army to join the Confederate army. Another, who had been a member of a pro-Confederate Kentucky militia, joined the Union army, as did a third Crittenden boy. One

grandson enlisted in the Confederate forces, while another graduated from the US Naval Academy and became an officer in the
Union navy.

But these were things yet to come. Right now, Crittenden
pleaded with Brooks not to kill Charles Sumner. Keitt responded by
pointing his pistol at Crittenden, prompting Georgia Senator Robert
Toombs to admonish Keitt that he must not attack a man who was
not party to the dispute. (As for what Brooks was doing to Sumner,
however, Toombs would later express his full approval.)

At length, New York Senator Edwin Morgan and New York
Representative Ambrose Murray—who had brought with him Senate Sergeant at Arms Dunning R. McNair and a youthful Senate
page—restrained Brooks. Spent by his exertions, the South Carolinian departed the chamber without a word. He left behind the bloody
form of Charles Sumner, writhing on the bloodsoaked Senate floor
along with the shattered remains of Brooks's cane, which had broken into several pieces, some of which were greedily gathered up by
Representative Edmundson. He presented the piece with the gold
head to the House sergeant at arms, and it lives today in the collection of Boston's Old State House Museum. Edmundson apparently
distributed other pieces of the cane to a variety of Southern lawmakers, who fashioned rings out of them and wore them in public on
neck chains. Brooks claimed that his Southern legislative colleagues
fairly begged him for pieces of the walking stick "as sacred relics,"
like fragments of the True Cross.

As Sumner slowly came to, the page and the sergeant at arms
helped him to his feet and guided him to the Senate cloakroom. A
physician was summoned and stitched the worst of his open wounds.
Speaker of the House Nathaniel P. Banks and Henry Wilson, his
fellow Massachusetts senator, accompanied Sumner on a carriage
ride to his Washington apartment. But his recovery proved to be
slow and agonizing. When he failed to appear in the Senate, Southerners condemned him as a coward, but the Massachusetts General
Court reelected him in November 1856. No matter that his chair in
the chamber was vacant. The state legislators believed it a fittingly
shameful monument to Southern barbarism. Sumner did try to return
in 1857, but remained at his seat only a few hours. He traveled to

Europe, and, in 1858, underwent a painful spinal treatment—burning the skin along the spinal cord—administered by a Paris physician. It was 1859 before he finally returned to the Senate, and when he made his first major speech, on June 4, 1860, during the election that brought Lincoln into the White House, it was devoted to the "Barbarism of Slavery." If anything, the oration was even harsher than the speech that had provoked the 1856 attack.

If Preston Brooks had intended to beat abolition out of Charles Sumner, his efforts were in vain. The genteel Bostonian lover of Raphael and Leonardo emerged from his ordeal not just a charter member of the newly formed Republican Party, the party of Lincoln, but a member of its most extreme wing, a Radical Republican, adamantly opposed to any further attempt at compromise with the South. Sumner's radical conversion reflected the hardening divide in the nation itself. The caning of Charles Sumner marked the tipping point that sent the United States hurtling toward war.

* * *

As guerrilla fighting raged in Kansas, talk of compromise was heard less and less everywhere in America. Then, on March 6, 1857, a decision of the United States Supreme Court made compromise constitutionally impossible. That day, Chief Justice Roger B. Taney, native of the slaveholding state of Maryland, handed down the court's decision in the case of *Dred Scott v. Sandford.* Dred Scott was a fugitive Missouri slave who had belonged to Dr. John Emerson of St. Louis. An army surgeon, Emerson was transferred first to Illinois and then to Wisconsin Territory, and he took Scott with him to each of these posts. After Emerson's death in 1846, Scott returned to St. Louis, where he sued Emerson's widow for his freedom, arguing that he was now a citizen of Missouri, having been made free by virtue of his terms of residence in Illinois, where slavery was banned by the Northwest Ordinance, and in Wisconsin Territory, where the provisions of the Missouri Compromise (since repealed, but in force at the time) made slavery illegal. After a Missouri state court ruled against Scott, his lawyers appealed to the United States Supreme Court. The high court's antislavery Northern justices, predictably, sided with Scott, whereas the proslavery Southerners, the court's majority, upheld the Missouri court's decision. Taney wrote the decision, which held that neither free blacks nor enslaved blacks were citizens of the United States and, therefore, had no standing to sue in federal court. This alone would have settled the case, but Taney, intending the case to be a landmark slavery ruling, ruled further that the Illinois law banning slavery had no force on Scott once he returned to Missouri, a slave state, and that the law obtaining in Wisconsin was likewise without force, because the Missouri Compromise was unconstitutional. It violated (Taney ruled) the Fifth Amendment, which barred the government from depriving an individual of "life, liberty, or property" without due process of law.

The Dred Scott decision galvanized the Northern abolitionist movement, but also did much more. The caning of Senator Sumter took the issue of slavery out of the realm of orderly legislative argument and beyond the rule of law. The brutality in the Senate chamber was scaled up in the ugly violence that pervaded Kansas. Both the caning and Bleeding Kansas *implied* that there *would* be no compromise on slavery and, therefore, no alternative to civil war. The Dred Scott decision *implied* nothing. It forthrightly *declared* that there *could* be no compromise. By defining slavery as an issue of property, a Fifth Amendment issue, the decision mandated that slavery had to be protected in all the states, regardless of whether or not a given state permitted slavery. As abolitionists saw it, if the Constitution universally protected the rights of slave holders as long as slavery existed, then, universally, slavery had to be abolished. That would require a constitutional amendment, something the South would never accept—not without a fight, not without a war.

2

March 4, 1861

"Black Lincoln" Is Inaugurated

Why it's significant. Southern champions of slavery believed that, by electing Abraham Lincoln president in 1860, Northerners declared their intention to abolish the institution on which the Southern economy and way of life so heavily relied. That belief was enough to start a secession movement, which ultimately resulted in the creation of the eleven Confederate States of America. At his inauguration, Lincoln tried to stem the secessionist tide with a straightforward pledge that he had neither the "lawful right" nor the "inclination" to "interfere with the institution of slavery in the States where it exists." But he also proclaimed his belief that the Constitution held the "Union of these States [to be] perpetual." Accordingly, he also pledged, "to the extent of my ability," to do "as the Constitution itself expressly enjoins upon me" by ensuring "that the laws of the Union be faithfully executed in all the States." After South Carolina became the first state to secede on December 20, 1860, Lincoln's feckless predecessor, James Buchanan, had reportedly exclaimed, "I am the last President of the United States!" Lincoln was not so resigned. He would demonstrate that *the extent of his ability* included the power to restore the Union, and to do so with iron and with blood. He would take the nation to war.

SPRINGFIELD, CAPITAL OF Illinois, the "Prairie State," was the hometown Abraham Lincoln was about to leave. It was a chilly morning, February 11, 1861, sunless in midwinter, with an icy drizzle that failed to keep the president-elect's friends, associates, and neighbors from gathering to see him off. The victor in the presidential election of 1860 stood—as always, at a raw-boned six-four, head, shoulders, and chest above everyone else—in the waiting room of the Great Western Depot. He shook hands and acknowledged the good wishes all round. Spirits, however, were not high in that room. There was no banter, no laughter, no joy.

On the track alongside the depot, a waiting locomotive hissed, its steam mingling in wisps with the wintry vapor. At eight sharp, the engineer sounded the all-aboard whistle, summoning the president-elect, together with his family and a handful of others, to the steps of the passenger car that would take him on a twelve-day whistle-stop tour ending at Washington. Lincoln stood on the observation platform at the rear of the train and spoke to those who would remain behind. Among them were men and women Lincoln had known for many years, and, so, when he began his farewell speech with the words "My friends," it was more than an oratorical commonplace. They *were* his friends, and Lincoln was by no means confident of finding any in the city for which he was bound. "My friends," he began—

> no one not in my situation can appreciate my feeling of sadness at this parting. To this place and the kindness of these people I owe everything. Here I have lived for a quarter of a century, and have passed from a young to an old man. Here my children have been born, and one is buried. I now leave, not knowing when, or whether ever, I may return, with a task before me greater than that which rested upon Washington. Without the assistance of that Divine Being who ever attended him, I cannot succeed. With that assistance I cannot fail. Trusting in Him who can go with me and remain with you and be everywhere for good, let us confidently hope that all will yet be well. To His care commending you, as I hope in your prayers you will commend me, I bid you an affectionate farewell.

* * *

In his Farewell, he called himself an old man. Doubtless, that iron gray morning, it was how he felt. Yet, the very next day, Abraham Lincoln would turn just fifty-two. He was, at that point in American history, the youngest man to be elected to the presidency.

His election had followed the destruction of the Whig Party, traditional opponent of the pro-Southern Democratic Party. The Whigs had lost credibility among the swelling ranks of anti-slavery voters, who resented their complicity in the 1854 passage of the Kansas-Nebraska Act, which allowed the people of each separate state to vote their state free or slave. As those opposed to slavery saw it, as long as a single US state allowed slavery, the United States was a slave nation. After passage of the act, abolitionists, who had deserted the Whigs for numerous small antislavery parties, joined forces to create a new party, one firmly founded on antislavery principles. The result was the Republican Party.

The Republicans held their first national convention in 1856, two years after the party's founding, nominating the famous Western explorer John C. Frémont as its first presidential contender. Although he was defeated by Democrat James Buchanan, there was still good news; in its maiden election, the party did win more than 100 congressional seats. Two years later, the new party nominated Lincoln to oppose incumbent Democrat Stephen Douglas in the race for Senator from Illinois. Lincoln lost to Douglas, but not before earning a national reputation for his eloquence in an epic series of debates against his opponent and, in particular, for a speech that drew upon the apostle Mark, comparing the United States to a "house divided against itself," unable to "stand . . . permanently half slave and half free."

Yet, on balance, Lincoln's position on slavery in 1858 was not dramatically different from Douglas's. Both men wanted to ban slavery in the territories, but neither believed it constitutionally possible to abolish slavery altogether—not by legal action, at any rate. Nevertheless, as the Republicans drove the wishy-washy Whigs into political irrelevance, radical Southern Democrats claimed with certainty that the election of a Republican in 1860 would—and should—drive the Southern states out of the Union.

Lincoln's reputation grew so rapidly throughout the North after 1858 that the Republicans made him their standard bearer for the White House in 1860. He was, however, eminently beatable—and likely would have been defeated, if the Democrats had not suffered their own internal secession. The party splintered into northern and southern factions, thereby dividing the vote: 18.1 percent went to John C. Breckenridge, the Southern Democratic nominee, and 29.5 percent went to Stephen A. Douglas, nominee of the Northern Democratic Party, with an additional 12.9 percent going to John Bell, nominee of the new Constitutional Union Party, which was made up of Whig diehards. This was a total of 60.5 percent of the vote. Lincoln claimed just 39.8 percent—less than a majority, but more than any other single candidate. So, he was now president.

And with his election, seven Southern states made good on their threat to secede: South Carolina (December 20, 1860), Mississippi (January 9, 1861), Florida (January 10), Alabama (January 11), Georgia (January 19), Louisiana (January 26), and Texas (February 1). On February 8, representatives from these seven states met in Montgomery, Alabama, to declare themselves a new nation, the Confederate States of America. Jefferson Davis of Mississippi was elected interim president—pending a general election—and Alexander Stephens of Georgia as Vice President.

The secessionists called the president-elect "Black Lincoln" and painted him as a radical abolitionist, who not only wanted to end slavery but also to upend the "natural" social order, by which they meant a society founded on the inherent superiority of whites. In truth, Lincoln never called himself or considered himself an abolitionist. True, he was personally and morally opposed to slavery. On a scrap of paper preserved by Mary Todd Lincoln and believed to date from August 1858, Lincoln wrote, "As I would not be a *slave,* so I would not be a *master.* This expresses my idea of democracy. Whatever differs from this, to the extent of the difference, is no democracy." Yet not until he championed the Thirteenth Amendment, when he stood for reelection in 1864, did Lincoln call for ending slavery where it already existed.

As early as 1858, Lincoln did propose banning the further extension of slavery into US territories, and, early in his first term, he even proposed a system of compensated emancipation, whereby slavery would be gradually abolished altogether, but slave owners would be compensated in cash for freeing their slaves. On April 16, 1862, such legislation was actually applied to the District of Columbia. Beyond these views, however, as a candidate and as a president, Lincoln believed that the Constitution protected slavery as a property right. Nor, apparently, did he believe that blacks and whites were inherently equal. In his debates with Douglas in 1858, he spoke of the racial superiority of whites, and he made clear his opposition to African American service on juries and to marriage between blacks and whites. As the war and his own presidency progressed, Lincoln evolved, arguing for the enfranchisement of African American voters—albeit arguing tepidly. In what turned out to be his very last public address, delivered to a crowd gathered outside of the White House on April 11, 1865, two days after Lee surrendered the Army of Northern Virginia to Grant, the president commented on the new constitution Louisiana had drawn up in a bid for restoration to the Union. The document proclaimed emancipation throughout the state, which Lincoln praised, but it did not extend "the elective franchise . . . to the colored man." Gratified by the emancipation, Lincoln nevertheless said that he would "prefer that [the right to vote be] conferred on . . . very intelligent [blacks], and on those who serve our cause as soldiers." By today's standards, the remark is, of course, racist, implying that prospective black voters would have to pass an intelligence test. At least one member of the audience gathered that day believed the president's words were a radical betrayal of the white race. Hearing them, the man vowed that this speech was "the last speech he will make." The offended party was John Wilkes Booth.

No one, including those who founded the Confederacy, could have foreseen, let alone assumed, Abraham Lincoln's evolution on slavery and race. At the time of his election, Lincoln shared the view of the majority of American whites, who found slavery distasteful, perhaps even immoral. Many more believed it an economic threat to free labor for wages. As for racial equality, however, this view was uncommon among whites, who generally believed they were created, by nature and God, superior to the black race. But this did not mean that African Americans were not entitled to justice under the law. In short, Lincoln's point of view was one shared by most Northerners. This further implies that just about anyone the North would have supported for president would have been unacceptable to the South, where slavery was an essential pillar of the economy and the social order.

* * *

Prior to the January 23, 1933 ratification of the Twentieth Amendment, which established January 20 (or January 21, if the 20th fell on a Sunday) as the end of the sitting president's term, Inauguration Day was on March 4. Thus, there was a four-month gap between the election of Lincoln and his installation into office. During this interval, a dwindling handful of lawmakers held onto the hope that the Union could yet be saved. Among these was Senator John J. Crittenden, who, as mentioned in Chapter 1, presented in December 1860 a package of six constitutional amendments intended to explicitly protect slavery while also explicitly limiting its expansion. He hoped this would mollify the South.

Concerning the "Crittenden Compromise," the fifteenth president of the United States, James Buchanan, did what he had done for the previous four years of the growing secession crisis—nothing. It is for his single term of incomprehension and inaction that most historians rate him near or at the bottom of lists ranking the American presidents. Yet President-elect Lincoln also refused to take any public position on Crittenden, the course of secession, or any other matter of significance before he formally assumed office. He even went so far as to instruct a Republican colleague to "entertain no proposition for a compromise in regard to the extension of slavery." The apparent indifference on the part of the incoming chief executive cast the Crittenden Compromise adrift. It was little discussed and largely ignored.

Today, the interval between election and inauguration is much briefer, and that abbreviated time is used to make a transition guided, in part, by the incoming president's dedicated "transition team." There was no such thing in Abraham Lincoln's day. Before he left Springfield, he was silent, and then he spent twelve days, from February 11 to February 23, on a meandering rail journey from his home in the Illinois capital to Washington. He believed it was far more important for as many American citizens to see him than for him to speak out on matters of civil war before he had any legal authority to deal with them. Even after Lincoln learned that Jefferson Davis was offering to negotiate peaceful relations with the United States, he held his tongue and kept traveling. With many stops between the major cities, the journey took him east to Indianapolis, Cincinnati, Columbus, and Pittsburgh. Then it veered northeast to Cleveland, from which the train traveled northeast to Buffalo, due east to Albany, then a sharp turn south to New York City.

From New York, the train was scheduled to head toward Philadelphia via Trenton. Then from Philadelphia, it was supposed to stop at Harrisburg, the Pennsylvania capital, before going on to Baltimore. But there was a potentially cataclysmic problem with the Lincoln itinerary.

Before the president-elect set off from Springfield, railway officials hired the Scottish immigrant who had, for all practical purposes, invented the American profession of private detective, Allan J. Pinkerton, to investigate a rash of apparent sabotage against railway property in and around Baltimore. Maryland was a border state. It had not seceded from the Union, but it nevertheless was a slave state, and many of its citizens had greater sympathy for the Confederacy than for the Union. Baltimore was regarded as a hotbed of dissension and anti-Union conspiracy. Investigating the attacks on railroad property, Pinkerton was rapidly persuaded not only that a plot to assassinate the president-elect was afoot, but that the murder was being planned as the curtain raiser on an invasion of Washington, DC. The objective was to so stun and demoralize the North that the federal government would abandon any effort to force the South to bend to its will and would simply allow the disgruntled Confederate states to leave the Union.

Pinkerton understood that Lincoln presented an especially soft target in Baltimore. Coming from Harrisburg, a rail passenger would not only have to change trains, but also change stations, to continue the journey to Washington. Lincoln, of course, was no ordinary passenger. The plan was to uncouple his private railway car from the inbound train when it stopped at the Northern Central Railway station on Baltimore's Calvert Street. The car would then be pulled to another train waiting at the Baltimore and Ohio's Camden Street Station for the ride to Washington. Pinkerton believed that assassins were plotting to ambush the car as it made its way slowly from one station to the other. He therefore dispatched one of his "female operatives," Kate Warne, from Baltimore to New York, where she met the president-elect's train and conveyed the details of the assassination conspiracy to Norman Judd, a member of the inaugural party traveling with Lincoln. Warne and Judd decided to lay all the facts before the president-elect when he arrived in Philadelphia on February 21. According to recollections published in Pinkerton's memoirs, Lincoln received the news not with fear, but sorrow. Through Warne, Pinkerton advised the president-elect to cut short the rest of his itinerary and head immediately to Washington. Lincoln protested, however, that he had promised to raise the flag over Independence Hall in Philadelphia and then to visit the Pennsylvania legislature at Harrisburg in the afternoon.

Pinkerton proposed another alternative, to which Lincoln agreed. After the president-elect addressed the legislature at Harrisburg, a special train consisting of a baggage car and one passenger coach would secretly carry Lincoln back to Philadelphia. There Pinkerton would meet the train and personally escort Lincoln from one Philadelphia depot to another, where the two would board a regularly scheduled 11 p.m. passenger train bound for Baltimore. The next day, the official inaugural train, which the assassins were expecting, would leave Harrisburg for Baltimore as scheduled—but minus the president-elect. To ensure that no telegraph message could reach the conspirators to advise them of the change, George H. Burns, the American Telegraph Company's confidential agent, was assigned to see to it that the line between Harrisburg and Baltimore was cut and any messages sent were intercepted and delivered directly to Pinkerton.

At 5:45 p.m. John G. Nicolay, Lincoln's private secretary, handed the president-elect a note while he and his traveling party were in the dining room of a Harrisburg hotel. The men abruptly rose, and the president-elect changed out of his dinner clothes and into a traveling suit. According to Joseph Howard, Jr., a reporter for the *New York Times,* Lincoln, acting on Pinkerton's instructions, carried a plaid shawl upon one arm, as if he were an invalid, and had a soft felt hat—apparently, a distinctly unpresidential tam o'shanter—tucked into his coat pocket. Lincoln was spirited into a coach, which took him to the depot. The special train arrived in Philadelphia shortly after 10:00 p.m. Lincoln, now in the care of Pinkerton, was transferred by coach to the other depot. Kate Warne had already booked the entire rear half of the Baltimore-bound sleeping car to accommodate (she explained to the ticket agent) "her invalid brother." At the depot, Warne approached the president-elect (who, according to the *New York Times* reporter, still carried the shawl over one arm) and greeted him loudly as her brother. Together with Pinkerton and Lincoln's longtime friend Ward H. Lamon, who had accompanied the president-elect all the way from Springfield, she entered the sleeping car by its rear door.

The train pulled into Baltimore at 3:30 in the morning of February 23. Lincoln did not leave the sleeping car. Ordinarily, a small locomotive would could be used to pull the car from the President Street Station to the Camden Street Station, where it would be coupled to the Washington-bound train. However, a Baltimore city ordinance prohibited night rail travel through the central city, so the sleeping car was drawn by a team of horses over the horse-car tracks. Pinkerton had heard a rumor that, despite all his efforts at secrecy, this car might be attacked as it moved slowly through the downtown streets. He kept a wary lookout, but the car arrived at the Camden Street Station without incident, whereupon Pinkerton sent a brief telegram to the president of the Philadelphia, Wilmington, and Baltimore Railroad: "Plums delivered nuts safely."

As it turned out, the arrival of the Washington-bound train to which Lincoln's car was to be coupled was delayed nearly two hours. The occupants of a railway car without a locomotive were wracked by anxiety—all except Lincoln, who settled back in his berth, cracking jokes with his nervous companions. Even at so early an hour, the depot was active, and Lincoln and the others caught snatches of "rebel" tunes, including *Dixie*, a song introduced by the popular minstrel entertainer Dan Emmett in 1859 and taken up by secessionists as an unofficial anthem. "No doubt there will be a great time in Dixie by and by," Lincoln dryly quipped.

On the afternoon of February 23, the *official* inaugural train pulled into Baltimore. Lincoln's wife, Mary Todd, and their children had been on board—but they left the train when it made an unscheduled stop a number of blocks before reaching President Street Station. Thus, when the train pulled into that station, the waiting crowd—perhaps assassins among them—were supremely disappointed.

Well before this—shortly after six in the morning—Lincoln's train arrived in Washington. As journalist Howard reported it, the president-elect, once again wrapped in his "invalid shawl," left the sleeping car with Lamon and Pinkerton. The crowd in the depot did not recognize him. That was just what Pinkerton had hoped. Doubtless, he breathed easier, having delivered his man safely to the nation's capital.

But there was a price to pay. Cartoons depicting Abraham Lincoln absurdly disguised as a sickly grandma were published in hostile newspapers on both sides of the Mason-Dixon line, including Baltimore. It remains a subject of debate, however, whether Lincoln ever actually appeared in this get-up. Historians widely believe that the story was entirely fabricated by Joseph Howard, Jr., the *Times* reporter.

* * *

Lincoln lodged at Willard's Hotel, on 14th and Pennsylvania Avenue, where he was soon joined by his family. They would live there until the inauguration on March 4. Elsewhere at the Willard, the Washington Peace Conference of 1861 had been underway since February 4. Convened under the sponsorship of the state of Virginia, it was a quasi-official gathering of 131 delegates from twenty-one states (including Southern states, but none of the seven seceded states) groping for one final compromise to stave off civil war. Presided over by seventy-one-year-old former president John Tyler, they were old men,—so old that one of their number dropped dead shortly after the conference convened, and the press mocked the entire proceedings as the "Old Gentlemen's Convention." Lincoln did not acknowledge the gathering publicly, but he did confide to one friend that "no good results would come out of it." Nevertheless, at nine in the evening of February 23, he invited the delegates to his Willard's parlor. A number of the delegates, including Tyler, accepted the invitation. But the meeting was none too cordial. When one Pennsylvania delegate testily proclaimed that there was no alternative to compromise, which "must be done sooner or later," Lincoln replied, "Perhaps your reasons for compromising the alleged difficulties are correct, and that now is the favorable time to do it; still, if I remember correctly, that is not what I was elected for!" After a fruitless hour, the meeting broke up, the president-elect sending off the delegates by affirming that there would be no compromise involving the extension of slavery. The South, he said, "must be content with what it has." And then he added the strongest condemnation of slavery he had yet uttered: "The voice of the civilized world is against it. . . . Those who fight the purposes of the Almighty will not succeed. They have always been, they always will be, beaten."

On March 1, the Peace Convention presented a handful of proposals to Congress, which simply refused to consider them. As for the Crittenden Compromise, it was narrowly defeated in the Senate on March 2, two days before the Inauguration. On that same day, Congress passed the Morrill Tariff Act, sponsored by Vermont Representative Justin S. Morrill, one of the founders of the Republican Party. It was a tariff intended to protect the industries of the North by blocking importation of manufactured goods. As the Vermonter well knew, the Southern economy relied on trade with Europe. The region exported its produce—especially cotton—in exchange for European manufactures. To the South, nothing could have been more punitive or inflammatory than the Morrill Tariff Act. It may be seen as the final nail in the coffin holding the remains of the *United* States.

* * *

On the morning of March 4, James Buchanan called upon Lincoln at Willard's to escort him, as tradition dictated, to the inauguration platform. The day had dawned fair only to have clouded over before turning sunny again. The ceremony took place on the east portico of the new Capitol building, its still-unfinished dome giving the building an ominously decapitated appearance.

After witnessing the swearing-in of his vice-president, Hannibal Hamlin of Maine, Abraham Lincoln delivered his inaugural address to a crowd of perhaps 10,000. "I have no purpose, directly or indirectly, to interfere with the institution of slavery in the states where it exists," he announced. "I believe I have no lawful right to do so."

Lincoln must have hoped these words would ring with reassurance throughout the South. But he did not—could not—stop there. He continued by pointing out that "no government proper ever had a provision in its organic law for its own termination . . . No state upon its own mere motion can lawfully get out of the Union." With that, he vowed, the "power confided in me will be used to hold, occupy, and possess the property and places belonging to the government, and to collect the duties and imposts."

Having drawn a line in the sand, he did his best to explain the present crisis as he understood it:

> Shall fugitives from labor be surrendered by national or State authority? The Constitution does not expressly say. Must Congress protect slavery in the Territories? The Constitution does not expressly say.
>
> From questions of this class spring all our constitutional controversies, and we divide upon them into majorities and minorities. If the minority will not acquiesce, the majority must, or the government must cease. There is no other alternative; for continuing the government is acquiescence of one side or the other.
>
> If a minority in such case will secede rather than acquiesce, they make a precedent which in turn will divide and ruin them; for a minority of their own will secede from them whenever a majority refuses to be controlled by such a minority . . . .
>
> Plainly, the central idea of secession is the essence of anarchy. A majority held in restraint by constitutional checks and limitations, and always changing easily with deliberate changes of popular opinions and sentiments, is the only true sovereign of a free

people . . . . Unanimity is impossible; the rule of a minority, as a permanent arrangement, is wholly inadmissible; so that, rejecting the majority principle, anarchy or despotism in some form is all that is left . . . .

In your hands, my dissatisfied fellow countrymen, and not in mine, is the momentous issue of civil war. The government will not assail you. You can have no conflict without being yourselves the aggressors. You have no oath registered in Heaven to destroy the government, while I shall have the most solemn one to "preserve, protect and defend it."

Lincoln's logic was impeccable. But he understood that the nation had stepped far beyond reasoning, and so he concluded by appealing to what he hoped was a still-living core of national sentiment:

I am loath to close. We are not enemies, but friends. We must not be enemies. Though passion may have strained, it must not break our bonds of affection. The mystic chords of memory, stretching from every battlefield and patriot grave to every living heart and hearthstone all over this broad land, will yet swell the chorus of the Union when again touched, as surely they will be, by the better angels of our nature.

Having finished his inaugural address, Abraham Lincoln placed his long palm, roughened by a youth lived in frontier labor, on a Bible proffered by the palsied hand of Chief Justice Roger Taney, author of the Dred Scott decision. Lincoln took the oath of office as the sixteenth president of the United States. What manner of nation would be left to the seventeenth, no one knew.

3

April 12, 1861

General Beauregard Opens
Fire on Fort Sumter

Why it's significant. "Black Lincoln," the secessionists called the new president. Yet in his inaugural address, he made it clear: he would not "interfere with . . . slavery in the States where it exists." He had, he said, "no lawful right to do so." But he *had* sworn an oath to uphold the Constitution, which "expressly enjoins upon me, that the laws of the Union be faithfully executed in all the States." This, he said, required "no bloodshed or violence, and there shall be none unless it be forced upon the national authority." As he spoke these words, he and his audience well knew that Fort Sumter, South Carolina, and other federal installations, both military and civilian, were under threat or had already been seized by seceded states. The Constitution, Lincoln said, both required and empowered him "to hold, occupy, and possess the property and places belonging to the Government and to collect the duties and imposts." Lincoln promised that, "beyond what may be necessary for these objects, there will be no invasion, no using of force against or among the people anywhere." The new president wanted no war, but he did mean to govern and act according to his Constitutional oath. To do less was to concede that the Union was at an end. He would make no such concession. If this refusal meant war, then war there would be.

B Y THE TIME of the Civil War, American military forts were of two kinds. In frontier regions, they were mostly lightly fortified enclosures intended to shelter troops who spent most of their time on patrol. Depending on the local availability of building materials, they were constructed either of logs or adobe. Since the principal mission of the US Army throughout much of the nineteenth century was policing "hostile" Indian tribes, frontier forts were not built to withstand cannon fire or prolonged siege. They provided shelter, supplies, and, sometimes, accommodation for soldiers' families.

A very different category consisted of forts built to defend against external threats, which meant attempted attack or invasion by sea. From the end of the American Revolution through the years preceding the Civil War, a system of seacoast forts was slowly built. These coastal defenses were seen as efficient and economical alternatives to maintaining either a large navy or a large field army. The forts were essentially artillery emplacements, which mounted large cannon, aimed toward the water, and capable of being elevated and—to a limited degree—swiveled. Military historians categorize the coastal forts into a First, Second, and Third System. The First System was a set of twenty small but permanent forts built from the 1790s through most of the first decade of the nineteenth century. In 1807–08, President Thomas Jefferson authorized construction of the Second System, which consisted of somewhat larger and better protected forts. In some cases, these mounted two stacked tiers of guns instead of the single tier of First System forts.

Few of the forts planned for the Second System were actually built before a Third System was authorized in 1816, after the War of 1812 proved both the reality of the trans-Atlantic threat and the inadequacy of the First and Second System forts to defend against it. As many as 200 sites were initially identified for fortification, but by 1867 only forty-two had been built—and not all of them completed. Fort construction, which was carried out mainly by civilian laborers under military supervision, typically consumed years. This was certainly the case with Fort Sumter. It was built at the entrance to Charleston Harbor, on a sandbar, which had to be augmented by some seventy thousand tons of granite laboriously transported from New England. Construction began in 1829, but the fort was still incomplete when South Carolina seceded from the Union in 1860. Nevertheless, it was at that time an imposing five-sided bastion, all brick, except for the wooden buildings within the massive brick walls. The left flank wall was oriented toward the west, the left and right faces were oriented northward, and the right flank wall faced east. Each of these was 170 feet long. The rear wall, facing toward the south, was 190 feet long. All five walls were five feet thick and stood fifty feet above water level at low tide. The thickness and elevation were designed to withstand fire from ships, not from the largest land-based artillery. No one anticipated that American soldiers would ever have to fight other American soldiers. Fort Sumter was designed to accommodate a garrison of 650 and was planned to mount 135 guns arranged in three tiers. In its brief active career, however, it would never be manned or armed to capacity.

In 1860, South Carolina was a state known for its "fire-eaters," as the most earnestly committed secessionists were labeled. Of all the Southern states, South Carolina had the most to lose if slavery were abolished. Fifty-seven percent of its population was in bondage—the highest proportion of any state. Nearly half—46 percent—of South Carolina families owned at least one slave. It is not surprising, then, that South Carolina was the first state to secede from the Union, on December 20, 1860. Major Robert Anderson, at the time in command of the US Army garrison at Fort Moultrie on Sullivan's Island, understood that this small collection of fortifications, some of which dated from the era of the First System, could not withstand a land assault. While the walls that stood in 1860 were built mostly of brick, the fort was more famous for the palmetto logs that formed its walls during the American Revolution. In the Battle of Sullivan's Island (June 28, 1776), Patriot General William Moultrie successfully defended Charleston from behind those walls, the cannonballs fired by British men-o'-war bouncing off the stout palmetto. Ever since the Revolution, the palmetto served as the state's proud emblem.

On December 24, 1860, four days after the state's secession, Francis Wilkinson Pickens, governor of South Carolina, dispatched three "commissioners" to Washington with instructions to negotiate the removal of "federal" troops from Fort Moultrie. Unknown to the governor, however, two days later, on December 26, Major Anderson ordered Fort Moultrie's biggest guns to be spiked, and he burned their carriages. He then loaded the smaller artillery aboard boats and stealthily transported these, together with two companies, 127 men, of the 1st US Artillery, to the far more formidable Fort Sumter, which he believed could be more readily defended. His hope was that he could hold out against an attack long enough to receive resupply and reinforcements as well as naval support. The fort, left incomplete after President James Buchannan cut the military budget, mounted fewer than half the guns for which it was designed. The small artillery pieces Anderson had hauled from Moultrie were to be pointed at Charleston and other fortified positions.

The next morning, December 27, local workmen employed at Fort Sumter left their jobs, returned to Charleston, and spread the news: the federals had moved from Moultrie to Sumter. A public outcry arose against Pickens. How could he have failed to anticipate what Anderson had done? The people of South Carolina had already seceded from the United States. In their outrage, they would hardly hesitate to remove their governor. He therefore sent Colonel J. Johnston Pettigrew, his military aide, to meet with Major Anderson at Fort Sumter and "request" that he return to Fort Moultrie. When Anderson politely declined, Pettigrew reported to Pickens, who ordered him to lead a unit of militia to preemptively seize another local fort, Castle Pinckney. Finding nothing more there than a single US Army lieutenant, one private, and a handful of civilian workmen, Pettigrew had no problem capturing the Castle. Later that same day, South Carolina militia occupied the abandoned Fort Moultrie as well.

Pickens telegraphed the news of Sumter's occupation to the three commissioners he had sent to Washington. In the name of the people of South Carolina, they duly vented their outrage against President Buchanan, who they assumed had treacherously ordered the occupation. Clueless as always, Buchanan had no idea of what they were talking about because he had no idea of what Anderson had done. After the indignant commissioners left, the president summoned his cabinet. His inclination was to order Anderson back to Fort Moultrie—nobody having told him that it was now in Confederate hands.

Cabinet members persuaded him instead to let Anderson and his men stay where they were. Quite probably because this fait accompli required no immediate decision on his part, Buchanan agreed.

To his consternation, however, he soon found himself pressed to make a very difficult decision. Should he send reinforcements and supplies to Major Anderson? If he did this, South Carolina—perhaps the whole "Confederacy"—would likely be provoked to military action. If he did not do this, he would be abandoning Fort Sumter and its garrison, and would, in effect, be condoning the dissolution of the Union. On January 2, 1861, the president therefore decided to send supplies and reinforcements—but to do so in what he believed would be the least provocative manner. He would load the reinforcements, 200 troops, and supplies into a chartered, unarmed civilian steamer, the 1,172-ton *Star of the West*. Second, he ordered the soldiers to dress in civilian clothes rather than uniforms. Unfortunately for the president, word of his civilian-looking mission had leaked southward shortly after the vessel left New York. By December 8, when the *Star of the West* anchored at the mouth of Charleston Harbor, Pickens had managed to set up artillery batteries on Morris Island and had recruited cadets from The Citadel, the Military College of South Carolina, to man them. On the morning of December 9, as the vessel sailed into the harbor, the cadets fired. The first shot was a warning across the ship's bow, and although it was quite sufficient to prompt the defenseless captain to turn about and head back toward the mouth of the harbor, the zealous youths fired several more shots, scoring three hits, which did little damage—but did send the *Star of the West* steaming back north to her home port of New York City.

Anderson and his men had witnessed the whole thing from Fort Sumter. Some of the major's men pleaded with him to open fire on Morris Island and, if necessary, on Fort Moultrie as well. Citing his orders from President Buchanan, which directed him to remain on the defensive only, Anderson refused, but he did fire off a letter of protest to Governor Pickens demanding that he disavow the act of shooting at the flag of the United States. Pickens not only refused the disavowal, he ordered as many cannon as could be found to be mounted on every available battery position facing Fort Sumter.

Once he was satisfied that his firepower was sufficiently massive, Pickens sent a note demanding that Anderson surrender the fort. This was on January 11. Anderson refused.

The shots fired by The Citadel boys could accurately be called the first of the Civil War. What followed them, however, was—well, nothing, or at least nothing much.

For his part, President Buchanan again settled into inaction. He made no further attempt to reinforce or resupply Fort Sumter. Pickens sent to the president another emissary, Isaac W. Hayne, bearing a demand that he order Fort Sumter evacuated. Instead of sending Hayne packing, President Buchanan allowed him to "negotiate" until early February. In the end, it was Hayne who gave up. No one, it seemed, could outdo Buchanan when it came to passive noncompliance. In the meantime, of course, the men of Fort Sumter were running out of food. Fearing that he would look inhuman or, worse, ungentlemanly, Governor Pickens ordered, on January 20, some food parcels to be delivered to the fort. Incredibly, Major Anderson returned them, enclosing a message to the effect that he and his command would do without rations until he was allowed to purchase food from local suppliers—just as he always had. Pickens responded by allowing Anderson to send forty-five women and children, the families of some of the garrison, to New York. For more than a week, Pickens had cut off mail to and from Sumter. He now allowed it to resume.

In Charleston, a growing number of fire-eaters insisted that Pickens take *some* action, while a diminishing number of moderates pleaded with him to do nothing. In Washington, President Buchanan was also being pressed, but he decided that he had a way out: just wait out the slow tick-tock of his waning presidency. When he received a new letter from Pickens on January 31, 1861, demanding the surrender of Fort Sumter on the grounds that federal possession of it was "not consistent with the dignity or safety of the State of South Carolina," he simply ignored the missive. When more demand letters followed, he ignored those, too.

So weeks passed. At last, to James Buchanan's unutterable relief, March 4 finally came, and the outgoing occupant of the Executive Mansion welcomed the new inmate. "Sir," he said to Lincoln on the carriage ride back from the inauguration, "if you are as happy entering the White House as I shall feel on returning to Wheatland [the Buchanan residence in Lancaster, Pennsylvania], you are a happy man indeed."

Major Robert Anderson was anything but happy. He sent the new president a report explaining that he was critically low on supplies and that he needed food, reinforcements, and naval support if he was to have any chance of holding the fort. Lincoln consulted with "Old Fuss and Feathers," Major General Winfield Scott, the lavishly bemedaled, over-age, and corpulent general-in-chief of the United States Army. Scott was a gallant soldier, a hero of the War of 1812 and the US-Mexican War, but, in the present situation, he told Lincoln that there was only one thing to do: evacuate Fort Sumter. Lincoln turned next to his cabinet. Every member agreed with Scott, except for Postmaster General Montgomery Blair, who pressed Lincoln to reinforce the fort. Secretary of State William Seward, for his part, met with a fresh delegation from the Confederacy, to whom he implied (without consulting Lincoln, toward whom, early in Lincoln's presidency, he was often condescending) that all of the southern forts would soon be evacuated. As the deliberations and speculations continued in Washington, Major Anderson, waiting in Charleston Harbor at the mouths of Confederate cannon, was kept in the dark.

General P. G. T. Beauregard, who had arrived in Charleston early in March to take command there, used the period of uncertainty to build up the defenses of Charleston and to train more guns against Fort Sumter. The prewar United States Army was small, with 16,367 troops on the rolls, of whom 1,108 were commissioned officers. Those in command in the South knew those in command in the North. General Beauregard knew Major Anderson very well, since it was Anderson who, at West Point, had instructed him in the artillerist's art. Beauregard raised no objection when former US naval officer Gustavus V. Fox requested permission to visit the fort. Perhaps the Confederate thought he could talk some sense into his former instructor. Anderson told Fox that the food would run out by April 15, and Fox reported this to Lincoln, who nevertheless continued to withhold communication from Anderson. Absent word from the president, the major began an exchange of messages with his former student. Between Anderson and Beauregard, the two planned the conditions for the evacuation of the fort.

At last, but without alerting Anderson, Lincoln ordered preparation of a flotilla of Navy vessels, including the brand-new steam sloop-of-war USS *Pawnee,* the older but more heavily armed steam sidewheel frigate USS *Powhatan*, the small-armed screw steamer USS *Pocahontas*, and the Revenue Cutter USRC *Harriet Lane*, together with a civilian steamer, the *Baltic,* to carry supplies and reinforcements to Fort Sumter. The flotilla conveyed about 200 troops and was accompanied by three civilian tug boats to tow troop and supply barges. Although he was no longer an active naval officer, Gustavus Fox was given command (and would, on August 1, be appointed assistant Secretary of the Navy). The vessels of the flotilla set off from various ports beginning on April 6, the very day that a State Department clerk named Robert L. Chew was dispatched to Charleston to inform Governor Pickens that a "resupply convoy" was steaming to Fort Sumter. On April 8, Anderson finally received a letter from Simon Cameron, Secretary of War, informing him of the approaching expedition.

Now, at last, the pace of events accelerated. Pickens informed Confederate President Jefferson Davis that President Lincoln had dispatched warships to Fort Sumter. Davis summoned his cabinet.

Now was the decisive moment for the Confederacy. If secession was real, if it was serious, it required backing by force and payment in blood. Anything less was surrender.

The cabinet unanimously concurred with Jefferson Davis. The approaching warships would be resisted, and Fort Sumter would be taken. Accordingly, Leroy Pope Walker, the Confederacy's first secretary of war, sent a telegram to Beauregard instructing him to demand the surrender of Fort Sumter. If the demand was refused, he was to proceed with the "reduction" of the fort.

Having received the telegram, the Confederate commander delayed sending the surrender demand just long enough to make his final preparations to conduct a prolonged artillery bombardment against Fort Sumter and to fire upon the flotilla, when it arrived. When he was satisfied that all was in place, on the afternoon of

April 11, Beauregard put three men in a boat and sent them to Fort Sumter to formally demand its surrender. They presented an elaborately chivalrous note from General Beauregard: "All proper facilities will be afforded for the removal of yourself and command," the note promised, "together with company arms and property, and all private property, to any post in the United States which you may select. The flag which you have upheld so long and with so much fortitude, under the most trying circumstances, may be saluted by you on taking it down."

Had Beauregard framed his demand as a threat, perhaps Anderson would have indignantly rejected it. But it was instead a proper and respectful request. So Anderson summoned his officers and polled their opinions. To a man, they voiced unconditional opposition to giving up the fort. Personally, Anderson was torn. He was by birth a Kentuckian married to a Georgian, and his nature was more Southern than Northern. But, above this, he prized his vocation as an officer of the army of the United States. He therefore wrote out a refusal to surrender in a note as formal as the demand he had received. The general's demand was one "with which I regret that my sense of honor, and of my obligations to my government, prevent my compliance," he wrote. As he handed the emissaries this message, he commented without a touch of defiance: "Gentlemen, if you do not batter us to pieces, we shall be starved out in a few days."

The rendezvous point designated for the relief flotilla was off the Charleston bar. *Harriet Lane* arrived first, just after sundown on April 11, 1861. As for Beauregard, he read and reread his former artillery instructor's message carefully, and he listened very closely when one of the emissaries repeated Anderson's apparently off-handed comment that he and his command would soon be starved out. This prompted Beauregard to send his commissioners back to the fort. He wanted them to ask Anderson precisely how long it would be before want of food would prompt his surrender.

The emissaries arrived at the fort just after midnight on April 12. Warning Major Anderson that artillery bombardment was imminent, they put the question: When, precisely, will you surrender? Anderson did not instantly return an answer, but retired to confer privately with his officers for a long time. At length emerging, he told his interlocutors that, barring further orders or supply from "my government," he would evacuate the fort by April 15.

It was the very date Anderson had communicated to Lincoln and was therefore a truthful answer to Beauregard's question. The leader of the commissioners, James Chesnut, seems to have taken it as nothing more or less than a play for more time. His tone abruptly changed. It was too long, he said with finality. General Beauregard would open fire in an hour, at 4:30 a.m. With that, the commissioners left.

Tradition long had it that Edmund Ruffin, aged sixty-seven, a rural Virginia newspaper editor and a defender of slavery, pulled the lanyard on the gun that (discounting the four cannonballs fired by The Citadel cadets on December 9, 1860) fired the first shot of the Civil War. He did deliver one of the earliest shots *at* the fort, but firing the very first shot, a signal to commence the general bombardment, was an honor mortar battery commander Captain George S. James offered to Roger Pryor. Pryor had resigned his seat in the US Congress, as a representative from Virginia, to join the Confederate army on March 3, 1861. He was what the divided nation called a "fire-eater," a true believer, who had, on the eve of secession, exhorted the people of South Carolina to "Strike a blow!" Offered the opportunity now to do just that, he gravely shook his head, protesting weakly that *he* "could not fire the first gun of the war." With the appointed hour—4:30—approaching, Captain James turned to Lieutenant Henry S. Farley. It was he who, on schedule, fired a single shell burst over the fort as a signal to open fire.

Exactly 4,003 guns were trained on Fort Sumter that early morning. However, short on ammunition—something that would be true of the Confederate artillery throughout the war—Beauregard was determined to carry out a sustained bombardment but to do so with a minimum of waste. He therefore ordered his guns to fire not in volleys, but one at a time, in a counterclockwise sequence around the harbor. There was to be a two-minute pause between shots. This would allow the Confederate gunners to fire continuously for forty-eight hours.

Major Anderson, of course, was even more critically short of ammunition than General Beauregard, and, undermanned, he could not afford to suffer heavy casualties. He held off for two and a half hours before returning fire, and, when he finally did, he decided that he would use only the guns from the lowest of the fort's three tiers. True, the best artillery was in the upper tier, but that was the most vulnerable to incoming fire, so he left it unmanned. The self-imposed restriction to fire only the cannon of the lowest tier gave Anderson just twenty-one usable guns—against Beauregard's 4,000 plus. The honor of returning the first shot was given to Captain Abner Doubleday, who history remembers far more as the "inventor" of baseball than for anything he did in the Civil War. (This remains true today, despite the fact that virtually all historians agree that Doubleday did not, in fact, create the national pastime. Indeed, Doubleday himself never claimed to have done so.)

As mentioned, Fort Sumter was designed to defend against an assault from the sea, not a barrage from the land. The cannon on naval warships were not capable of firing at high trajectories. This meant they could not lob shells over the fort's fifty-foot-high walls. They could fire into the walls, but the walls' five-foot masonry thickness was enough to withstand most low-trajectory hits. Land-based artillery, however, could easily be elevated sufficiently to get balls and shells over the fort's walls, which meant that the target was highly vulnerable. While the walls and gun tiers of the fort were brick, the buildings within those walls were wooden. Before mid-morning, "hot shot"—cannonballs heated red hot in a furnace before being fired—set the fort's main barracks ablaze, forcing Anderson to divert many men from gunnery duty to instead fight the flames.

Nevertheless, Anderson and his men had reason to take heart, even amid the flames. For now, at least, they saw three ships of the relief flotilla off the harbor bar. The defenders of Fort Sumter had high hopes that resupply and reinforcement would be forthcoming under cover of darkness. They just needed to hold out during the rest of the day.

Fox, commanding the flotilla, awaited the arrival of the largest warship of the flotilla, sidewheel steam frigate USS *Powhatan*. No one in Washington had thought to inform him that Secretary of State William Seward had ordered the ship diverted to relieve Fort Pickens, Florida. Seward had not informed the president, either, and when Lincoln issued a belated countermand, David Dixon Porter, the *Powhatan*'s skipper, refused to honor it because the original order had been signed by Seward, not Lincoln. In Porter's view, only Seward could legally countermand it. The absence of the *Powhatan* was critical, since Fox believed that, without this major warship, he would never make it past the Confederate harbor defenses. Nevertheless, by about six on the evening of April 12, Fox decided that he had to act. He loaded some landing craft with supplies and sent them toward the fort. As he feared, however, heavy Confederate artillery fire soon drove them back.

With neither resupply nor reinforcement, Anderson ceased fire at nightfall. Earlier, he had already ordered a radical reduction in return fire, down to just six guns, because of a shortage of cloth gunpowder bags to hold the charge that fired the projectiles. Anderson improvised to make more, putting his men to work sewing bags out of clothing and bed linen, and even contributing his own spare socks. At nightfall, the Confederates reduced their own rate of fire to one shot every four minutes, but they never ceased firing. At dawn on April 13, Beauregard resumed the original rate of a shot every two minutes, quickly reigniting the barracks. Well trained at West Point by Robert Anderson, Beauregard ordered hot shots to be again used, so that, by noon, his artillery had succeeded in igniting most of the wooden buildings within the fort's masonry walls. As flames crept toward the central powder magazine, Anderson's soldiers began rolling out the first of the 300 powder barrels stored there. Only about a hundred had been removed before Major Anderson ordered the magazine doors closed. Of the hundred powder barrels that had been moved out, those that could not be rapidly moved to safety Anderson ordered to be rolled into the sea. The tide was against the Union, and the barrels kept floating back to the fort, where they were often ignited by incoming rounds. Although Anderson quickened the pace and volume of his return fire, Beauregard's gunners laid down more and more hot shots, intensifying the blazes within the fort.

At one in the afternoon, a cannonball snapped the flagstaff from which the Stars and Stripes flew. The flag was retrieved, and a makeshift staff was quickly erected—but an overeager Texan, former US Senator and now Confederate Colonel Louis Wigfall, seeing the flag disappear, assumed that Anderson was surrendering.

Without consulting any other officer, he rowed himself out to Fort Sumter. Waving a white handkerchief from the tip of his sword, he called out to the defenders, asking if they had surrendered. When the reply was returned in the negative, he was undaunted and asked if he might meet with Major Anderson. The major agreed.

"You have defended your flag nobly, Sir," Wigfall said. "You have done all that it is possible to do, and General Beauregard wants to stop this fight. On what terms, Major Anderson, will you evacuate this fort?"

Surrounded by water and surrounded by fire, low on ammunition and out of food, Major Robert Anderson must have reflected on two remarkable facts. First, he and his men had endured nearly 4,000 incoming rounds—and had endured them nobly. Second, he had suffered not a single casualty.

Whether by design or happenstance, Wigfall had used the verb "evacuate" rather than "surrender." This may have been enough to prompt Anderson to ask for a truce to commence at two. With that, Wigfall removed his handkerchief from his sword and displayed it on the improvised flagstaff that had replaced the one shot away. On his return to Charleston, several Confederate officers indignantly disavowed Wigfall's unauthorized offer of a truce. But General Beauregard saw that white "flag" and, seeing it, sent an *official* delegation, which offered the same terms that had been offered on April 11—withdrawal from the fort with full military honors. In point of fact, those who had been firing on Fort Sumter believed its defenders were worth honoring. They had behaved as men, gentlemen, and worthy adversaries. This gave them reason to believe that the war now begun would be a chivalrous dispute between men of honor.

On April 14, Beauregard proved himself to be as good as his word. Major Robert Anderson was permitted to order a fifty-gun salute to the flag he now lowered and folded and was allowed to take with him. As the *Union* artillery sounded for the last time, a stray ember touched off a nearby powder keg. The resulting blast injured five people and killed one, Union Private Daniel Hough. He was the first soldier killed in the Civil War. No one attending that ceremony could have imagined that, in the next four years, more than 620,000 others would join him.

4

September 22, 1862

Lincoln Issues the "Preliminary" Emancipation Proclamation

Why it's significant. Legalistically cautious in tone and severely limited in application, the "Preliminary" Emancipation Proclamation enlarged the moral dimension of the Civil War, transforming it into both a struggle to make a fractured United States whole and to liberate some four million American slaves.

O<small>N</small> A<small>UGUST</small> 30, 1861, some five months into the Civil War, John Charles Frémont, commanding the Union army's Department of the West, proclaimed martial law over Missouri, warning that the property of those who bore arms in rebellion against the United States would be seized, including their slaves, who would be both removed and emancipated. Fearing that the emancipation would send a deeply divided Missouri into the arms of the Confederacy, President Abraham Lincoln annulled the order. In April of the next year, when Major General David Hunter, commanding the Union army's Department of the South, captured Confederate-held Fort Pulaski, Georgia, he declared free all slaves currently in Union hands. He then expanded the emancipation to all slaves living "within reach" of his military jurisdiction. Once again, Lincoln annulled the orders on the grounds that they authorized an unconstitutional seizure of property without due process of law.

The South feared Lincoln as a bringer of abolition, yet he came into office with an inaugural address disavowing any intention of ending slavery where it currently existed. As late as the summer of 1862, he persisted in defining himself as anything but an abolitionist. On August 19, the influential editor of the *New York Times*, Horace Greeley, published in his paper an open letter to the president on behalf (he claimed) of the twenty million citizens of the loyal states. Among other things, he criticized Lincoln for annulling the orders of Frémont and Hunter and called for immediate emancipation. Three days later, President Lincoln replied in terms so stark that they are still capable of shocking us today: "My paramount object in this struggle is to save the Union, and is not either to save or destroy Slavery. If I could save the Union without freeing any slave, I would do it; and if I could save it by freeing all the slaves, I would do it; and if I could do it by freeing some and leaving others alone, I would also do that."

Lincoln publicly justified his decision to go to war to restore the Union on the basis of his presidential oath to preserve, protect, and defend the Constitution—the very document that unmistakably protected slavery as a property right. In this, he reflected the views of most Northerners and even most Republicans, save the so-called Radical Republicans, who were ardent and uncompromising abolitionists. If he used the war as a convenient occasion for abolishing slavery, he risked making the war itself unconstitutional. If he broke the law, even to achieve a moral purpose, he yielded to the Confederacy the same right to break the law for what they asserted was a moral purpose. Even before taking office, Lincoln wrestled with this conundrum. He groped for alternatives to an executive proclamation of emancipation. What appealed to him was a policy of gradual emancipation, to be carried out within the constraints of the Constitution by compensating slave owners for setting their slaves free. In effect, Lincoln proposed buying their property from them. Moreover, he contemplated instituting this policy of "compensated emancipation" state by state rather than with a federal law. His idea was to begin by approaching law makers in those states where slavery was already weak—border states such as Delaware.

Even after he was inaugurated and the first seven states of the Confederacy had seceded, Lincoln continued to cling to the hope of legislated emancipation. His strategy of not "interfering with" slavery where it existed while blocking the expansion of slavery was a play for time. He hoped that by containing the spread of slavery, he might eventually prevail upon state legislatures to enact compensated emancipation. If this could be made to work, slavery would, in time, wither and die—without civil war and bloodshed.

Not even the eruption of a shooting war ended Lincoln's appeal to the border states (the slaveholding states that had remained loyal to the Union) to adopt compensated emancipation. If he could demonstrate that purchasing the liberation of slaves was possible, perhaps the rebellion would end. Even if the Confederate states were not persuaded, Lincoln believed that the combination of Union military victories and a successful program of compensated emancipation in border states would knock the props out from under the rebellion. As Lincoln saw it, the border states were key. He felt that the best chance for ending slavery while also restoring the Union lay with them, and, for this reason, he dared not alienate them with a forceful, perhaps unconstitutional emancipation policy. If even a single border state fled to the Confederacy, the very idea of a Union might be forever doomed.

Despite the president's efforts, however, every one of the border state legislatures rejected compensated emancipation. Even worse, these rejections came at a time when the war was not going well for the North. The "Young Napoleon," Major General George B. McClellan, on whom Lincoln and the Union staked their hopes for crushing the rebellion, failed to capture Richmond, the capital of the Confederacy. His excessive caution and his delusional belief that his Army of the Potomac was always badly outnumbered by Robert E. Lee's Army of Northern Virginia (quite the opposite was true, of course) led to one draw or defeat after another. Even when the Union managed a victory, it was typically at a grievous cost.

The border states' rejection of voluntary abolition through compensated emancipation, combined with a war fought to bloody stalemate, persuaded Abraham Lincoln that only a decisive combat victory could now drive the abolition of slavery. Winning a major battle would give an executive proclamation of emancipation the force of righteous strength, while such a proclamation would impart to the war a new moral dimension. It would be transformed from a military effort to preserve, protect, and defend the Constitution into a holy crusade to end the abomination of slavery. Fighting the war as a defense of the Constitution was not winning the war. But fighting the war for the moral and spiritual purpose of breaking the chains that held men, women, and children in bondage invited comparison with the Old Testament. Lincoln wanted a holy war.

There were still strategic and legal hazards attached to issuing a presidential proclamation of emancipation. Such a step could well alienate the border states, sending some or all into secession. The proclamation could also be challenged by suit brought in the federal courts, which were conservative and liable to hand down a decision that would not only squelch the proclamation, but also set a legal precedent explicitly protecting slavery forever. For that matter, emancipation might truly be unconstitutional. For all these reasons, Lincoln planned to frame his proclamation in a very limited way as an emergency war measure designed to deprive the rebelling states of the military value of slave labor. In effect, slaves were to be classified as contraband of war, so that the emancipation would liberate only those slaves who lived in parts of the Confederacy that were not yet under the control of the Union army. Elsewhere, where it existed, including in the border states, slavery would continue. Lincoln hoped that its status as a war measure would allow the proclamation to survive or altogether evade legal challenge. He further hoped that its strict limitation, applying only to those states and portions of states actively in rebellion, would prevent alienating the border states and would also avoid provoking renewed fighting in portions of Confederate states occupied by the Union army. Of course, there was no assurance that an executive proclamation occasioned by war would survive the war, even if the Union won. Emancipation would be open to legal challenge on constitutional grounds.

Finally—and this is what so many modern students of history find hard to accept—the border states were not alone in believing that "negroes" were an inherently inferior race. Many citizens, politicians, and soldiers throughout the North, including (at times) President Lincoln himself, also believed this. That many Northerners objected to the injustice of slavery did not necessarily mean that they were eager to sacrifice their lives for the liberation of what they regarded as a lesser race. Moreover, among the Northern working class, particularly recent immigrant laborers, there was great fear that freed slaves, once liberated, would flood the North and "steal" the low-paying jobs on which they depended. Such anxiety triggered racially motivated "draft riots" in New York and other Northern cities and towns during 1863.

Despite all the pitfalls, immediate and potential, President Lincoln decided that the risks were worth taking, if, at long last, emancipation provided a moral and spiritual impetus sufficient to drive a majority of the civilians, soldiers, and commanders of the North to act boldly and achieve victory. Lincoln consulted with William Whiting, a future US representative from Massachusetts who, during the Civil War, served as a solicitor for the War Department. He had just completed a major work of legal theory entitled *The War Powers of the President and the Legislative Powers of Congress in Relation to Rebellion, Treason, and Slavery* (Boston, 1862), and Lincoln now asked him point blank if the president possessed the legal authority to declare emancipation. Whiting responded that, in his opinion, the chief executive's war powers did indeed confer the necessary authority. Seeking further confirmation, the president consulted with his vice president, Hannibal Hamlin, before sitting down to compose an emancipation proclamation designed to seize the moral high ground without alienating the border states or anyone else, without doing violence to the Constitution, and without inviting legal challenge.

On July 22, 1862, the president convened his Cabinet and announced to them his intention of issuing a proclamation freeing the slaves, but only in the unconquered parts of the Confederacy. The response was mixed. Postmaster General Montgomery Blair protested that the proclamation would kick the supports out from under the Republican Party, which, founded in 1854, was still a political toddler. Secretary of State William Seward, however, supported the idea. But he offered a more urgent caveat, which confirmed a concern the president already had. Up to this point, as both Lincoln and Seward well knew, the war had not gone well for the Union. Seward argued that issuing the proclamation on the heels of numerous military defeats would undercut it, perhaps fatally. At best, it would come off as something of an empty gesture. At worst, it would appear to be an act of utter desperation. He strongly advised Lincoln to delay the proclamation until the army could boast a significant military victory.

In some ways, Seward was preaching to the proverbial choir, as this was a concern of the president as well. So far, 1862 had been a year of much heartbreak and some disaster as General McClellan continued to disappoint and even suffered the supreme humiliation of having Confederate cavalry commander J. E. B. Stuart "ride around"—circumnavigate—his entire Army of the Potomac on June 12. Less than a month later, on July 2, McClellan abandoned his advance on Richmond by retreating to Harrison's Landing, his army's point of embarkation. Two days later, on Independence Day, the daring Confederate cavalryman John Hunt Morgan began a three-week sweep through the border state of Kentucky with some 900 raiders, terrorizing the countryside and humiliating the Union's Major General Don Carlos Buell by capturing some 1,200 of his soldiers along with several hundred horses. (He paroled the soldiers, but kept the horses.) Two days after Morgan commenced his raid, another Confederate firebrand, Nathan Bedford Forrest, led a cavalry raid through Union-controlled Middle Tennessee. The next month, on August 26, Stonewall Jackson captured the Union supply depot at Manassas Junction, Virginia, near Bull Run, site of the war's first major battle and the Union's first major defeat. This led to the Second Battle of Bull Run (August 28–30, 1862), in which some 77,000 Union soldiers of the combined Army of Virginia and the Army of the Potomac, all under the command of the insufferably pompous and little-loved John Pope, were trounced by some 50,000 men of Lee's Army of Northern Virginia. Pope lost 14,462 soldiers, killed, wounded, captured, or missing, for Lee's loss of 6,202 killed or wounded.

General Pope, who had supplanted General McClellan, was now himself replaced by McClellan, to whom a desperate Abraham

Lincoln returned full command of the Army of the Potomac on September 2.

"Again I have been called upon to save the country," the "Young Napoleon" wrote to his adoring wife, telling her that, as he cantered his mount among his men, they called out to him: "George, don't leave us again."

On September 4, two days after McClellan was recalled to full command of the army he had created, Robert E. Lee, in a daring and unexpected move, led his Army of Northern Virginia, now with some 60,000 men, into Maryland. The Union was being invaded—and in force.

Although he had been highly successful fighting a defensive war against Union incursions into the South, Lee was convinced that the Confederacy could not prevail in a prolonged defensive war of attrition. The North simply had more of everything than the South—more men, money, and munitions. Lee was convinced that the Confederacy's only hope was to assume the offensive, wrest the border states—of which Maryland was the most important—from the Union's grasp, replenish the Army of Northern Virginia from among the Marylanders, and bring the war farther north. Moreover, if he could win victories in an offensive war, Lee was convinced that he might also win the support of Britain and France. If he could sustain the invasion of the North, he believed that the people of that region would simply lose the will to focus on fighting. Indeed, on September 8, he published an open letter to the people of Maryland, inviting them to secede:

> The government of your chief city has been usurped by armed strangers—your Legislature has been dissolved and by the unlawful arrest of its members—freedom of the press and of speech has been suppressed . . . Believing that the people of Maryland possess a spirit too lofty to submit to such a government, the people of the South have long wished to aid you in throwing off this foreign yoke, to enable you again to enjoy the inalienable rights of freemen, and restore the independence and sovereignty of your state.

Lee had devised an ambitious plan for the opening phase of his invasion, which he detailed in a document known to history as Special

Order No. 191. Rarely has a commander poured so much into a single plan. It was the key to the highest-stakes operation any Confederate general had yet attempted. He gave a copy of the order to Stonewall Jackson, who took it upon himself to copy a set for General Daniel Harvey Hill. Scholars are divided as to what happened next. Some believe that Hill, having already received the orders directly from Lee, carelessly discarded the copy Jackson sent him; others believe it far more likely that the document was not thrown away, but lost, probably dropped by a staff officer. Whatever happened, on September 13, when Union soldiers occupied the campground Hill had just vacated, a Private W. B. Mitchell, of the 27th Indiana, found Order No. 191 lying on the ground, wrapped around a clutch of cigars. Private Mitchell lusted after the cigars, but he took time to glance at the paper and concluded that it was important. He therefore passed it to an officer, who delivered it into the hands of George Brinton McClellan.

At first, the Union commander basked in his unbelievable good fortune. For one thing, he immediately perceived that the daring plan was also an infinitely hazardous one. Lee proposed to split his forces in two. He would send Jackson toward Harpers Ferry, Virginia, and Longstreet toward Hagerstown, Maryland. A conventional military man, McClellan had been taught that to divide your forces in the face of the enemy was to invite certain defeat.

"Here is a paper," McClellan famously exclaimed, "with which, if I cannot whip Bobby Lee, I will be willing to go home."

Victory had been handed him, yet, with a perverse genius for snatching defeat from the jaws of victory, McClellan was suddenly assailed by doubt. For one thing, he was convinced that Lee had twice the number of men he himself commanded—when, in fact, Lee actually had available less than half the Union's strength. For another, McClellan began to suspect that the "lost order" was actually a set-up, a ruse leading to a snare. In any event, on September 14, the Army of the Potomac fought its way through three gaps in South Mountain, near the border of western Virginia. Through these gaps, McClellan was fiercely resisted by D. H. Hill's Confederates, who could not stop but certainly slowed the Union's advance. The delay gave Lee the time he needed to position his army for battle west of Antietam Creek.

Admittedly, McClellan planned carefully and quite competently. He intended to envelop Lee, striking at both of his flanks before releasing his reserves against Lee's center. It was a double-envelopment battle plan that had brought Hannibal victory against the Romans at Cannae in 216 BC. Trouble was, George McClellan was no Hannibal, and when he launched his attack on April 17, it was anything but coordinated, dribbling out in a succession of piecemeal assaults. The Union's "Fighting Joe" Hooker succeeded in driving back Jackson's Corps so far and so fast that Lee was compelled to order up his reserves. But Hooker was alone, unsupported. In the meantime, Confederate units under Daniel Harvey Hill and James Longstreet hit the Army of the Potomac everywhere, in the East and West Woods, in Farmer Miller's cornfield, and around a church belonging to a German pacifist sect called the Dunkards. This blunted Hooker's early success and, by midday, the fighting had shifted to the center, along a sunken farm road forever after called "Bloody Lane." This position was unrelentingly held by Hill's Confederates, and it took a horrific five-hour battle and three divisions under the Union's Major General Edwin "Bull" Sumner to pound the Confederate commander out of position.

It was deep into midafternoon before the entire left wing of the Union army, under Major General Ambrose Burnside, belatedly forced a crossing of the stone bridge that bears his name to this day. Too late to support Hooker or to be supported by him, Burnside managed to pierce the Confederate line, but was quickly overwhelmed and repulsed by a lightning counterattack under A. P. Hill, whose troops were freshly arrived from Harpers Ferry. As Confederate brigadier general John Brown Gordon recalled after the battle, "McClellan's . . . infantry fell upon the left of Lee's lines with the crushing weight of a landslide." Nevertheless, when Lee himself appeared before the wavering soldiers of the line, his troops "re-formed . . . and with a shout as piercing as the blast of a thousand bugles, rushed in countercharge upon the exulting Federals [and] hurled them back in confusion."

In the end, it was the sheer weight of superior Union numbers that prevailed—that and the determination of the individual Union fighting man. Slowly and at great cost, the Confederates were pushed back to the outskirts of Sharpsburg, so that, by the end of the day, McClellan had achieved a great advantage. Yet he himself couldn't see it, even when Lee began to withdraw back toward Virginia. Retreat makes any army vulnerable, and McClellan had a golden opportunity to pursue and quite possibly kill the Army of Northern Virginia. Instead, he let Lee and his army, reduced in number but still intact, cross the Potomac into Virginia.

Antietam was, historians say, the single bloodiest day of the war. Union casualties numbered more than 12,000 killed, wounded, captured, or missing, while Confederate losses were significantly lower, officially tallied at 10,316 killed, wounded, captured, or missing. Because Lee's army had been pushed out of Northern territory, however, the battle must be counted a Union strategic victory—albeit a victory both pyrrhic and limited. While McClellan had driven Lee out of Maryland, he missed an opportunity to destroy the Army of Northern Virginia. Had he pursued, the end of the war would have been hastened by years.

Abraham Lincoln was appalled by the magnitude of casualties on both sides and the fact that Lee and his army had been allowed to withdraw and thereby live to fight another day. Still, he seized upon whatever degree of victory Antietam represented as a sufficiently sturdy platform from which to launch his "Preliminary" Emancipation Proclamation. His secretary of the treasury, Salmon P. Chase, recorded what the president said at a Cabinet meeting on September 22, 1862: "Gentlemen, I have, as you are aware, thought a great deal about the relation of this war to slavery, and you all remember that, several weeks ago, I read to you an order I had prepared upon the subject, which, on account of objections made by some of you was not issued"—referring to Seward's warning that the proclamation must not be introduced against a backdrop of defeat. Lincoln continued:

> Ever since then my mind has been much occupied with this subject, and I have thought all along that the time for acting on it might probably come. I think the time has come now. I wish it was a better time. I wish that we were in a better condition. The action of the army against the Rebels has not been quite what I

should have liked best. But they have been driven out of Maryland, and Pennsylvania is no longer in danger of invasion . . . . I have got you together to hear what I have written down. I do not wish your advice about the main matter, for that I have determined for myself . . . . What I have written is that which my reflections have determined me to say.

The so-called Preliminary Emancipation Proclamation of September 22 did not begin with any mention of slavery, but reasserted what Lincoln had said over and over again, beginning with his first inaugural address. The object of the war was not to abolish slavery, but to restore "the constitutional relation between the United States, and each of the States." Only then did the proclamation continue by reintroducing the idea of compensated emancipation—paying slave owners to free their slaves. Next, it broached a policy of colonizing the freed slaves "with their consent, upon this continent, or elsewhere." These two incentives presented at the outset, the president next proclaimed a significantly limited emancipation:

> That on the first day of January in the year of our Lord, one thousand eight hundred and sixty-three, all persons held as slaves within any State, or designated part of a State, the people whereof shall then be in rebellion against the United States shall be then, thenceforward, and forever free; and the executive government of the United States, including the military and naval authority thereof, will recognize and maintain the freedom of such persons, and will do no act or acts to repress such persons, or any of them, in any efforts they may make for their actual freedom.

The only slaves to be freed on January 1, 1863, were those held by people living within states or parts of states still "in rebellion." Slaves held elsewhere—whether in parts of the Confederacy that were under Union control or in the border states—would remain slaves. Indeed, practically speaking, the "final" Emancipation Proclamation, issued on January 1, 1863, freed not a single slave, since the United States government had no power within most of the Confederacy to enforce this liberation. The president merely *declared* those slaves free.

* * *

Abraham Lincoln was raised in poverty on the frontier, but he prospered as a lawyer, and the Emancipation Proclamation, both in its preliminary and final form, reads like a legal document. It takes a cautious, even tentative tone, which may not be very stirring today, but which was right—just right—for the time and circumstances. The Emancipation Proclamation infused the war with new moral meaning and force, yet it judiciously avoided provoking the occupied South and the border states, and it did not trigger a potentially tragic legal challenge through the federal courts. Moreover, it laid the foundation for the action Congress took even before the Civil War ended. On April 8, 1864, the Thirteenth Amendment to the Constitution was passed by the Senate. After a bitter fight and with much presidential arm twisting, the House followed on January 31, 1865. Within a year, on December 18, 1865, the amendment achieved ratification. In contrast to the Emancipation Proclamation, the Thirteenth Amendment is brief—"Neither slavery nor involuntary servitude, except as a punishment for crime whereof the party shall have been duly convicted, shall exist within the United States, or any place subject to their jurisdiction"—but it was thanks to that cautious and legalistic proclamation, ratified by the blood sacrifice of hundreds of thousands, that the Civil War became truly a war of liberation and social justice.

5

April 9, 1865

Lee Surrenders to Grant
at Appomattox Court House, Virginia

Why it's significant. Following a final twelve-day campaign of gallant resistance, Robert E. Lee surrendered the Army of Northern Virginia, the premier military formation of the Confederacy, to Ulysses S. Grant, general-in-chief of the Union armies. The character of both commanders—Grant in offering generous and humane surrender terms and Lee in accepting them with finality but without bitterness—contributed to ending the war definitively, thereby preventing what could have been a guerrilla conflict that might have lasted for years.

B Y VOCATION, JOSHUA Lawrence Chamberlain was the polymath and multilingual professor of rhetoric at Maine's Bowdoin College. So, when he applied for a leave of absence in 1862 to study languages in Europe—he was already fluent in Greek, Latin, Spanish, German, French, Italian, Arabic, Hebrew, and Syriac—it was readily granted. Instead of sailing across the Atlantic, however, Chamberlain enlisted in the Union army and was soon made lieutenant colonel and then colonel of the 20th Maine Regiment.

At least twice in the Civil War, Chamberlain found himself in precisely the right place at the right time. On day two of the Battle

of Gettysburg, as we will see in Chapter 6, his 20th Maine was positioned at the extreme southern end of the Army of the Potomac on
Little Round Top. Leading this understrength, battle-weary unit,
Chamberlain saved the entire Army of the Potomac from a crushing
defeat in that turning point battle. Three years later, now holding the
brevet rank of major general, Chamberlain was once again in the
right place at the right time—Appomattox, Virginia—on the morning of April 9, 1865. He was awaiting an attack order on a morning
still heavy with mist. He did his best to peer through it, watching to
detect any movement in the enemy line. Later he wrote about it. He
wrote of how, through the shimmering veil, there "rose to sight . . . a
soldierly young figure, a Confederate staff officer undoubtedly. Now
I see the white flag earnestly borne, and its possible purport sweeps
before my inner vision like a wraith of morning mist."

Tested in desperate combat, Chamberlain time and again proved
himself a man of uncommon valor, yet that "wraith" wrapped around
his very nerves, which now tightened to the extremity of suspense.
He saw the young man approach "steadily on, the mysterious form
in gray, my mood so whimsically sensitive that I could even smile
at the material of the flag—wondering where in either army was
found a towel, and one so white." At long last, the figure stopped,
dismounted, and, "with graceful salutation and hardly suppressed
emotion, delivered his message."

"Sir, I am from General Gordon."

Chamberlain knew John Brown Gordon to be a commander of
boundless gallantry. At Bloody Lane in the Battle of Antietam, a
Minié ball tore through his calf, another hit him higher up on the
same leg, and a third buried itself in his left arm. He nevertheless
continued to command his Confederates. When a fourth ball struck
his shoulder, a subordinate begged him to retire to the rear at last.
He refused—and continued to refuse, until a round struck his face,
piercing the left cheek through and through and exiting his jaw.
That fourth blow sent him down. He was carried off the field, and
a Confederate surgeon pronounced his case hopeless. But his wife,
a steadfast soldier's wife, saw to his recovery, and he returned to
combat months later. As the war approached its end, Gordon commanded II Corps of the Army of Northern Virginia and was among

Robert E. Lee's most trusted lieutenants, entrusted now with seeking terms from General Grant. To Chamberlain, the young messenger announced the subject of Gordon's note: "General Lee desires a cessation of hostilities until he can hear from General Grant as to the proposed surrender."

Struggling to contain himself, Chamberlain replied to the emissary, "Sir, that matter exceeds my authority. I will send to my superior," adding: "General Lee is right. He can do no more."

Actually, Lee believed there was one more thing he could do. Wrung out and heartbroken by four years of war and, more immediately, worn out by the twelve-day running fight called the Appomattox Campaign, the commanding general of the Army of Northern Virginia decided to make good use of the interval during which he awaited Grant's reply to his offer of surrender. Summoning his aide-de-camp, Colonel Charles Marshall, Lee asked him to seek a house where he could parley with the Union general-in-chief. Marshall rode off and soon encountered a farmer named Wilmer McLean. Marshall asked him if he knew the area well. McLean explained that he "used to live on the first battle field of Manassas"—Bull Run— "at a house about a mile from Manassas Junction." He hated the war, he said, and thought he should "get away where there wouldn't be any more fighting." So he moved to Appomattox Court House. Now the war had caught up with him again. In response to Marshall's request that he point out a house where the two generals could meet to bring that hated war to an end, McLean took Marshall to a structure ruined by battle, a shell, gutted, and without furniture. When Marshall shook his head no, McLean suggested: "Maybe my house will do!"

It was a plain brick farmhouse, not a grand plantation manor, but it was neat, intact, and fully furnished. Marshall chose it, and so the McLean house would enter history.

* * *

Almost from its very formation, in July 1861, the implicit mission of the Union's Army of the Potomac had been to decapitate the Confederacy by capturing Richmond, its capital. That objective eluded every commander from McClellan to Grant, whose Overland Campaign ended not at the gates of Richmond, but in the prolonged siege of Petersburg. Only after nine and a half months, from June 9, 1864, to March 25, 1865, were the Petersburg defenses breached, sending the Confederate government in flight from Richmond on April 2, 1865.

It was the downfall of the Confederate States of America. The night that followed the Union breakthrough (according to Edward Pollard, editor of the *Richmond Examiner*) "was an extraordinary night; disorder, pillage, shouts, mad revelry of confusion . . . . The gutters ran with a liquor freshet, and the fumes filled the air." Straggling Confederate troops drank themselves into blind, raging stupors, "sidewalks were encumbered with broken glass; stores were entered at pleasure and stripped from top to bottom; yells of drunken men, shouts of roving pillagers, wild cries of distress filled the air, and made night hideous." Morning, Pollard wrote, "broke on a scene never to be forgotten . . . . The smoke and glare of fire mingled with the golden beams of the rising sun . . . . The fire was reaching to whole blocks of buildings . . . . Pillagers were busy at their vocation, and in the hot breath of the fire were figures as of demons contending for prey."

Richmond fell, and Major General Godfrey Weitzel led the Army of the Potomac's XXV Corps into the shattered city on April 3. Seeking out the "Confederate White House," Weitzel found that the residence had been evacuated by President Jefferson Davis and his family. He seized it as his headquarters and ordered his chief of staff, Johnston de Peyster, to climb to the roof and raise over it the Stars and Stripes.

President Lincoln arrived the next day. "Thank God I have lived to see this," he said softly. "It seems to me that I have been dreaming a horrid dream for four years, and now the nightmare is gone."

For Robert E. Lee and the tattered, half-starved remains of the Army of Northern Virginia, the nightmare was still unfolding. Practically speaking, the fall of Petersburg was the end of the Confederacy. Nevertheless, Lee withdrew from Petersburg what was left of his army, not quite 50,000 men, and marched west. His forlorn hope was to link up with Joseph E. Johnston's Army of Tennessee in

North Carolina and continue to fight, presumably with the intention of coaxing the Lincoln government into a settlement more favorable to the South than unconditional surrender. Getting his army to North Carolina required marching to the town of Amelia Court House, in which, Lee believed, was a cache of provisions as well as access to transportation via the Danville and Richmond Railroad.

Even in defeat, Robert E. Lee commanded the respect and loyalty of his men. His motive was no longer victory. Lee just wanted to leave the Army of Northern Virginia with something more than abject defeat. This desire was about to run up against a military leader as vainglorious as Lee was selfless. Brevet Major General George Armstrong Custer graduated dead last in the West Point class of 1861 but distinguished himself in the Civil War with one display of reckless gallantry under fire after another. Now he found himself in position to play a high-profile role in the climactic campaign of the Civil War, the pursuit of the Army of Northern Virginia to Appomattox Court House.

After taking part in the Battle of Five Forks (April 1, 1865), Custer led a brigade of his division in pursuit of Confederate cavalry under Robert E. Lee's nephew Fitzhugh Lee. Custer fought him to a standstill at Willicomack Creek, but Fitzhugh Lee broke free until he and his command were run down again at Namozine Church (April 3). Instead of giving up or digging in, Fitzhugh Lee wheeled his men around in a fierce counterattack, which Custer skillfully parried. Fitzhugh Lee then divided his command, sending some of his cavalrymen riding off toward Bevill's Bridge over the Appomattox River. They followed behind yet another Lee, William Henry Fitzhugh ("Rooney") Lee, the second-eldest son of Robert E. Lee. Fitzhugh Lee personally led his remaining cavalry directly toward Amelia Court House, where, on April 5, eluding Custer, they linked up with the rest of the Army of Northern Virginia.

Amelia Court House was thirty miles west of Petersburg, and Custer and the other commanders under Major General Philip Sheridan resolved to allow Lee to withdraw no farther. Custer immediately deployed his division to block the Richmond and Danville Railroad and thus prevent the Army of Northern Virginia from achieving a breakout. For his part, Lee had intended to draw rations at Amelia Court House, but amid the chaos of Richmond's collapse, the Confederate army quartermaster had failed to send them. Now Lee and his army were bottled up in the small town, desperately hungry, awaiting Sheridan's inevitable attack.

The Union commander took his time, sending a brigade to reconnoiter Amelia Springs, in the rear of the Army of Northern Virginia. The Union brigade located a Confederate wagon train there and promptly put it to the torch, burning the very last of Lee's provisions as well as most of his papers. Lee was now completely without supplies and still unable to push past Amelia Court House. He therefore turned his army to the southwest and began a march toward Rice Station, still hopeful of finding provisions.

Unlike so many other Union generals before him, Ulysses Grant was dogged in pursuit of the enemy, regardless of cost. He now dogged the Army of Northern Virginia, whichever way Lee turned, attacking the army's rear. At Little Sayler's Creek on April 6, Confederate General Richard S. Ewell counterattacked the pursuers, who were stunned by the ferocity of the "beaten" men. How could a defeated army counterpunch so fast and so hard? Indeed, Ewell pushed back the Union's center—for a time. But then Union reinforcements began to arrive, and they kept coming. Soon overwhelmingly outnumbered, Ewell found himself caught in a double envelopment, yet refused to submit. There was no hope of victory, but Ewell was determined to save as much of the army as possible. He bought time for three of his subordinate commanders, Richard H. Anderson, Bushrod Johnson, and George Pickett, to escape with most of their commands intact. Ewell, in the meantime, fought a desperate rearguard action, much of it hand-to-hand. Many of his soldiers, shoeless, fought barefoot before they, along with Ewell and five other Confederate commanders, were taken prisoner. Among the latter was Lee's eldest son, George Washington Custis Lee. From a distance, the father watched it all, making the bland assessment that "half of our army is destroyed."

Lee, it turned out, overestimated his losses at Little Sayler's Creek. About a third, not a half, of the Army of Northern Virginia had evaporated. John Brown Gordon continued to lead his corps farther west, to High Bridge, an impressive railway span lofted atop sixty-foot piers across the Appomattox at Farmville. Detaching a portion of the corps under Fitzhugh Lee to fight a rearguard action, Gordon linked up with James A. Longstreet's corps and withdrew across High Bridge.

Any ordinary army would never have gotten this far. The partial breakout from Little Sayler's Creek was magnificent, but it was also marred by a fatal error. William "Little Billy" Mahone, commanding one of the divisions covering Gordon's withdrawal, had orders to blow up High Bridge after the Confederates had safely crossed it. This would have significantly slowed the Union pursuit. But in civilian life Mahone had been a railway engineer and president of the Southside Railroad, the builder of High Bridge. He could not bring himself to order its demolition, and so Lee's pursuers had a bridge across the river and closed in on Gordon and Longstreet.

The two Confederate commanders marched their men—hard— to Farmville, where the famished army at last found something to eat. But, while they ate, Lee received a note from Grant:

> April 7. General: The result of the last week must convince you of the hopelessness of further resistance on the part of the Army of Northern Virginia in this struggle. I feel that it is so, and regard it as my duty to shift from myself the responsibility of any further effusion of blood, by asking of you the surrender of that portion of the C. S. army known as the Army of Northern Virginia.

Without word, Lee passed the note to Longstreet, a valiant commander, yet one so perpetually gloomy he was known to his closest associates as "Old Pete," although he was not past his mid-forties. It was Longstreet who had advised Lee against invading Maryland and also against launching "Pickett's Charge" at Gettysburg. Lee must therefore have expected him to counsel immediate acceptance of the surrender demand. Instead, Old Pete handed the note back to Lee with just two words, "Not yet."

Lee nevertheless sent a reply not offering surrender but inquiring as to the terms Grant would offer. "Peace being my great desire," Grant wrote in return, "there is but one condition I would insist upon, namely, that the men and officers surrendered shall be disqualified for taking up arms again against the Government of the United States until properly exchanged."

Lee withheld his response to this, and (as Grant wrote in his *Personal Memoirs*), "Early on the morning of the 8th the pursuit was resumed."

The Confederate general deployed his army between Appomattox Station, along the railroad tracks, and Appomattox Court House, a few miles northeast of the station. Custer led his division in an attack against Appomattox Station, forcing two of Lee's divisions to retreat and abandon their supply train as well as about thirty cannon. The Confederates then marched toward Appomattox Court House, where they set up a defensive line southwest of town. Custer waited for the arrival of his commanding officer, Phil Sheridan, with the main body of the Union cavalry. Establishing themselves opposite the Confederate defenses, Sheridan and Custer prepared to attack on April 9.

What they expected of Lee was for him to hunker down and resist their onslaught. Instead, Lee launched a preemptive attack. At five o'clock on the morning of April 9, he sent John Brown Gordon and Fitzhugh Lee against the Union's field fortifications. A sharp and unexpected blow, it nevertheless succeeded only in triggering the Union assault that had been planned for later in the day.

The Army of the Potomac had been pursuing Lee westward in two columns, one to the north, the other to the south. The southern column now wheeled to the north against Appomattox Station southwest of Appomattox Court House while the northern column closed in directly on Appomattox Court House from the east. At this point, Lee had perhaps 30,000 men, of whom no more than half were armed. The two Union columns were set on either side of Lee as the opposing jaws of a vise. The Confederate had no way forward, back, or sideways. Turning to a staff officer, Lee said, "There is nothing left me but to go and see General Grant, and I had rather die a thousand deaths." With that, he sent one of one of General John Brown Gordon's young staff officers into the morning mist, bearing a white flag.

* * *

At the invitation of Samuel Langhorne Clemens—Mark Twain—
who was majority owner of Charles L. Webster and Company, pub-
lishers, Ulysses S. Grant, terminally ill with cancer of the throat,
wrote his *Personal Memoirs* in 1885. Grant turned out a plain-spo-
ken historical and literary masterpiece, completing the manuscript
just five days before he died. The work includes our fullest first-per-
son account of Lee's surrender of the Army of Northern Virginia in
the parlor of Wilmer McLean's farmhouse, April 9, 1865.

It was an event, Grant wrote, that he had hardly expected to take
place when he left camp that morning. For this reason, he "was in
rough garb" without time to don a dress uniform.

> I was without a sword, as I usually was when on horseback on
> the field, and wore a soldier's blouse for a coat, with the shoul-
> der straps of my rank to indicate to the army who I was. When I
> went into the house I found General Lee. We greeted each other,
> and after shaking hands took our seats. I had my staff with me, a
> good portion of whom were in the room during the whole of the
> interview.
>
> What General Lee's feelings were I do not know. As he was a
> man of much dignity, with an impassable face, it was impossible
> to say whether he felt inwardly glad that the end had finally come,
> or felt sad over the result, and was too manly to show it. Whatever
> his feelings, they were entirely concealed from my observation;
> but my own feelings, which had been quite jubilant on the receipt
> of his letter [offering surrender], were sad and depressed. I felt
> like anything rather than rejoicing at the downfall of a foe who
> had fought so long and valiantly, and had suffered so much for a
> cause, though that cause was, I believe, one of the worst for which
> a people ever fought.

Between the lines of Grant's memoir, we can feel the painful
self-consciousness of the victorious general in the presence of the
iconic figure he had defeated. Lee was "in a full uniform which was
entirely new, and . . . wearing a sword of considerable value, very
likely the sword which had been presented by the State of Virginia."
As for Grant, in a "rough traveling suit, the uniform of a private

with the straps of a lieutenant-general, I must have contrasted very strangely with a man so handsomely dressed, six feet high and of faultless form." Yet the two men, who, like so many other highly placed officers in the armies of the Union and the Confederacy, had served in the pre-Civil War army together and had even fought as comrades in the US-Mexican War, readily "fell into a conversation about old army times." It was talk that "grew so pleasant that I almost forgot the object of our meeting," Grant, almost incredibly, confessed. He admitted that it was Lee who "called my attention to the object of our meeting, and said that he had asked for this interview for the purpose of getting from me the terms I proposed to give his army."

Some say character is best measured in defeat. Surely, Lee was never more impressive than at this moment. Yet character may be gauged perhaps even more accurately in victory. Grant could have exulted, scolded, damned, threatened, and demanded. Instead, he elaborated on what he had earlier proposed in writing. "I said that I meant merely that his army should lay down their arms, not to take them up again during the continuance of the war unless duly and properly exchanged." Lee responded by suggesting that "the terms I proposed to give his army ought to be written out." With that, Grant sat down and did just that.

Grant had made himself infamous throughout the Confederacy by abolishing the practice of prisoner parole and exchange, which had been policy on both sides early in the war. Grant correctly believed that the parole and exchange benefitted the chronically undermanned Confederate military far more than it did the Union army, which had access to a larger population of recruits and conscripts. The abolition of exchange and parole brought into being such POW hellholes as Andersonville in Georgia and Elmira (called "Hellmira") in New York State. In the McLean parlor, Grant now announced that he would take no prisoners. Instead, he would accept the word of officers and men to lay down arms "until properly exchanged."

Lee's surrender did not formally end the Civil War, but it ended the existence of its primary military force. Although the war continued, Grant not only foreswore the taking of prisoners, he also gave permission for Confederate officers to retain their sidearms and allowed all personnel to keep their horses and personal property. Everyone, Grant stipulated, would be "allowed to return to their homes, not to be disturbed by United States authority so long as they observe their paroles."

The simple letter of surrender duly signed and witnessed, Lee lingered to inform Grant that the Army of Northern Virginia "was in a very bad condition for want of food, and . . . had been living for some days on parched corn exclusively." To Lee's request "for rations and forage," Grant responded with a single word: "Certainly." He asked for how many men were rations required. Lee's answer revealed just how diminished his great army was—"about twenty-five thousand." Grant authorized Lee "to send his own commissary and quartermaster to Appomattox Station . . . where he could have, out of the trains we had stopped, all the provisions wanted."

It now fell to the Confederate general to take up the pen. On April 10, 1865, he distributed General Order No. 9, his last command to the Army of Northern Virginia:

> After four years of arduous service, marked by unsurpassed courage and fortitude, the Army of Northern Virginia has been compelled to yield to overwhelming numbers and resources.
>
> I need not tell the brave survivors of so many hard fought battles who have remained steadfast to the last, that I have consented to this result from no distrust of them. But feeling that valor and devotion could accomplish nothing that could compensate for the loss that must have attended the continuance of the contest, I determined to avoid the useless sacrifice of those whose past services have endeared them to their countrymen.
>
> By the terms of the agreement, officers and men can return to their homes and remain there until exchanged. You will take with you the satisfaction that proceeds from the consciousness of duty faithfully performed and I earnestly pray that a Merciful God will extend to you his blessing and protection.
>
> With an unceasing admiration of your constancy and devotion to your Country, and a grateful remembrance of your kind and generous consideration for myself, I bid you all an affectionate farewell.

As he and his headquarters staff bade Lee farewell, Grant ordered no ceremony, no lowering of one flag and hoisting of another. The surrender of Lee to Grant began with the conversation of former brothers in arms who had become enemies but were enemies no longer. After this, it turned to practical matters, matters of survival, decency, and the return home.

The surrender of the Army of Northern Virginia did not end the Civil War. There were about seven more weeks of fighting, much of it desultory, but some of it fierce. The Army of Tennessee, the last major Confederate army still in the field, surrendered to William Tecumseh Sherman on April 18. Andrew Johnson, who had become president of the United States following the death of Abraham Lincoln on April 15, 1865, repudiated the terms Sherman offered, but Johnson accepted, on April 26, terms identical to those Grant had offered Lee. On May 8, Confederate Lieutenant General Richard Taylor—the son of Zachary Taylor, hero of the US-Mexican War and twelfth president of the United States—surrendered the Department of East Louisiana, Mississippi, and Alabama, the very last remaining Confederate military formation of significant size. Despite this, a skirmish developed between Confederate troops under John Salmon "Rip" Ford and Union forces at Palmito Ranch, near Brownsville, Texas on May 13. The final armed exchange of the war, it ended in a Confederate victory. Nevertheless, Ford's commanding officer, General Edmund Kirby Smith, surrendered to Union Major General Edward R. S. Canby on May 26.

These battles and skirmishes prove that the surrender at the McLean house did not officially end the war. In a far more meaningful sense, that surrender, which embodied the character, honor, and goodwill of both Grant and Lee, truly did end the war. Without the simplicity, honor, and humanity of the meeting at Appomattox, the War between the States might well have continued for who knows how long in the chronic spasms of guerrilla conflict that have marked so many other of history's civil wars. Grant's generosity and Lee's frank and wholehearted acceptance of his adversary's terms set the example for all the former soldiers of both the Confederate and Union forces. The guns fell silent and remained so.

6

November 19, 1863

Two Minutes at Gettysburg

Why it's significant. The Battle of Megiddo in 1469 BC brought Egypt to the pinnacle of its power. The Battle of Hastings in 1066 made William of Normandy William the Conqueror. The Battle of Yorktown in 1781 transformed a doubtful "American Revolution" into a victorious "American War of Independence." And the Battle of Gettysburg—July 1–3, 1863—was the beginning of the end of the Civil War, the Confederacy, and a nation divided half-slave and half-free. Abraham Lincoln understood this, and in two minutes of sublime eloquence delivered at the dedication of a military cemetery on the battlefield, the American president lifted the bloodiest three days in American history to their rightful place among the most significant battles in the history of civilization. In just 272 words, he explained to his fellow Americans why Gettysburg was "a new birth of freedom" that rescued and redeemed the imperiled ideal of "government of the people, by the people, for the people" and ensured that it would "not perish from the earth."

CLOSE TO THE Maryland state line in Adams County, southern Pennsylvania, Gettysburg was known, prior to July 1863, for no more than two things. It was the place at which the wagon roads between Shippensburg and Baltimore and between Philadelphia and Pittsburgh crossed and it was home to the nation's first Lutheran Theological Seminary. The town had some 2,400 residents and about 450 commercial buildings, mostly tanneries, cobblers, and carriage makers.

As these facts suggest, there was nothing of strategic military value in Gettysburg; however, Confederate general Henry Heth might have thought the town's shoemakers had created a supply of footwear sufficient for his division. In 1877, he wrote, "Hearing that a supply of shoes was to be obtained in Gettysburg . . . and greatly needing shoes for my men, I directed General Pettigrew to go to Gettysburg and get these supplies." The fact is, while Gettysburg had a handful of cobblers, it had no shoe factory. So, the idea that the momentous Battle of Gettysburg, the costliest battle of the Civil War and the turning point of that war, was fought over shoes is mistaken. South-central Pennsylvania had few roads in the 1860s, and two of the largest ran through Gettysburg. If you happened to be traveling in Adams or York counties in 1863, it was almost impossible *not* to pass through Gettysburg sooner or later.

And that was unfortunate for the residents of the town. Having defeated the Union's Army of the Potomac in two titanic Virginia battles, Fredericksburg (December 11–15, 1862) and Chancellorsville (April 30-May 6, 1863), Robert E. Lee made the decision to take the war into the North for a second time. In September 1862, he had invaded Maryland and was forced to withdraw back to Virginia after the Battle of Antietam (September 17, 1862). Now he decided to invade Pennsylvania. While some of his top commanders, most notably James Longstreet, tried to talk him out of the plan, Lee argued that the Confederacy, especially war-ravaged Virginia, could endure the attrition of a defensive war no longer. Moreover, an invasion now would take some pressure off besieged Vicksburg, Mississippi, the fall of which would tear the Confederacy in two along its east-west axis and deprive it of Mississippi River navigation. But, more important, invading the North would give the Army of Northern Virginia a position from which it could menace Baltimore, Philadelphia, and Washington and, in the process, bolster the peace movement developing in many parts of the Union.

So, Lee dismissed all objections and marched northward, with Ewell's Corps crossing the Potomac on June 15 and the corps of Generals Hill and Longstreet on the 24th and 25th. A portion of Major General Jubal Early's division of Ewell's Corps readily brushed aside a unit of Pennsylvania militia and briefly occupied Gettysburg on June 26 before moving on to neighboring York County.

The presence of a Confederate corps was unnerving for the 2,400 people of Gettysburg, but they lost remarkably little by it, General Lee having admonished his commanders to see to it that hardships on civilians were minimized. Lee was, in fact, little concerned with Gettysburg. He was intent on the major cities. As part of his bigger-picture plans, he permitted J. E. B. Stuart to take part of his army's cavalry on a ride around the left flank of the Army of the Potomac, which had positioned itself between Lee's main columns and Washington. The problem was that, as Lee's principal cavalryman, Stuart was supposed to be the eyes of the Army of Northern Virginia. But his long ride put him out of communication with Lee at precisely a time when information was of greatest importance to the invading army. So when, on June 29, Lee heard that the Army of the Potomac had crossed the Potomac River, he could only assume that he was being pursued, and he could only guess where to concentrate his troops for maximum advantage. He decided to concentrate part of Hill's Corps near Cashtown east of South Mountain and eight miles west of Gettysburg. It was from Cashtown that Heth, one of Hill's division commanders, sent a brigade of North Carolina soldiers under Brigadier General J. Johnston Pettigrew toward Gettysburg, perhaps to get shoes. On June 30, Pettigrew's advance party saw Union cavalry under Brigadier General John Buford riding into the southern outskirts of Gettysburg. Pettigrew returned to Cashtown to report to Hill and Heth what his men had seen. They could not estimate the size of the force, but it did not look very large, and they certainly did not believe it indicated the proximity of anything as grand as the Army of the Potomac. Although Lee had ordered his subordinates to avoid a major engagement until all of the Army of Northern Virginia was concentrated, Hill sent two full brigades of Heth's division back to Gettysburg to make a reconnaissance in force. At the very least, he wanted to clear those enemy cavalrymen out of Gettysburg. More than that, he wanted to know just how small—or large—that cavalry detachment was.

Neither Hill nor Lee was looking to fight a major battle at Gettysburg. In the end, what they got was a three-day battle, the deadliest and, arguably, the most consequential of the entire war.

As for the residents of Gettysburg, they were left after those three days with the massive burden of helping to treat the wounded and bury the dead. More than 104,000 Army of the Potomac soldiers were ready for duty during the battle (about 90,000 were actively engaged). They faced as many as 75,000 Confederates. Of a combined total of some 179,000 men, between 46,000 and 51,000 became casualties. Of these, about 8,000 were corpses bloating in the July sun. Added to the human remains were the carcasses of perhaps 3,000 horses. The Confederates having withdrawn, Union troops and townspeople hurriedly buried the dead in shallow graves. After days of sunshine, the heavens opened up with torrential rains, which washed a great many of the bodies out of their inadequately prepared burial places. The flies swarmed, and pigs, loosed from their damaged enclosures, rooted around the bodies. It was a vision of obscenity permeated by the stench of mass decomposition. Putrefaction and pestilence could not be allowed to stand as the only monument of a great battle. A combination of nausea, propriety, religious belief, patriotism, and fear of epidemic disease moved the people of the town to take matters into their own hands.

They appealed to Pennsylvania Governor Andrew Gregg Curtin, who appointed a Gettysburg attorney, David Wills, to preside over an interstate commission for the creation of a great military memorial cemetery. Under Wills's leadership, the commission raised funds from private and individual sources, and seventeen acres were purchased, the federal government agreeing to contribute all necessary coffins. Wills invited the most celebrated orator of the day, Edward Everett, former member of Congress, Massachusetts governor, ambassador to the United Kingdom, senator from Massachusetts, and secretary of state, to appear as the featured speaker at the dedication of the cemetery. Only as the day (November 19, 1863) of that dedication approached did it occur to Wills to invite President Abraham Lincoln to attend. He issued the invitation on November 2, assuming that the heavily burdened chief executive would be unable to accept. Given the last-minute nature of the invitation, surely Lincoln must have been aware that he was an afterthought, but he eagerly accepted nonetheless.

The president actually harbored some disappointment about the victory at Gettysburg. Having defeated Lee decisively, George Meade, commanding general of the Army of the Potomac, chose not pursue the Army of Northern Virginia as it limped away from the three-day battle. Lincoln felt about this much as he had felt about General McClellan's failure to pursue Lee after eking out a narrow victory at Antietam, the bloodiest single-day battle in American history. But just as Lincoln made the most he could out of McClellan's imperfect triumph, using it as a platform from which to launch the Emancipation Proclamation, so he now seized on an opportunity to make the most of Gettysburg. True, Meade had allowed the Army of Northern Virginia to get away, but he had driven it and its legendary commanding general out of the North. Robert E. Lee had done his worst to intimidate the Union, its army, and its people. In this he failed because his invasion failed. Now Lincoln wanted to make certain that all Americans—in the Union and in the Confederacy—understood this, understood the meaning of Gettysburg. In modern parlance, Lincoln saw it as an eminently teachable moment.

The sudden illness of his youngest son, Tad, almost persuaded Lincoln to remain at home in the White House. His wife, Mary Todd, begged him not to leave her and the boy. Her anxiety, bordering on hysteria, was understandable. The couple's second son, Edward (Eddie), had died in 1850 at the age of four, most likely the victim of tuberculosis, and their third son, William (Willie), succumbed to the measles as recently as 1862. Tad contracted that disease at the same time, but pulled through, and now he was very ill again. As hard as it must have been for him, Lincoln tore himself away and arrived by train in Gettysburg the night before the dedication. He stayed with the Wills family in their home.

Legend has it that Lincoln hastily scribbled his speech on an envelope. In fact, he labored over it as a great poet might labor over a poem written for the ages. While he clearly had an acute sense of what was at stake in his message, he never succumbed to a sense of his own self-importance. In 1931, eighty-seven-year-old Sarah A. Myers (called Sallie Cook as a young woman) recalled how she, nineteen in 1863, was living with her widowed mother and her siblings in "our beloved old family homestead," Cook's Mill on Possum Creek in the foothills of South Mountain. With her older sister, Elmira, she traveled the eleven miles to Gettysburg to see the dedication and hear the speeches, and, early on the morning of November 19, she was invited into the parlor of the Wills home to meet President Lincoln.

"I shook [his] hand . . . He was so tall that he stooped to take my hand, which seemed so small in his. Silently, he smiled down upon me. I then [walked] up to the Cemetery before the President's procession started and sat upon the rough wooden platform."

Lincoln must have been heartened by the size of the throng that had gathered for the dedication, an audience estimated at between 15,000 and 20,000, but he also knew that he was neither the first nor the featured speaker that day. That, of course, was Edward Everett, who delivered a nearly two-hour address of more than 13,000 words, of which the opening sentence alone totaled fifty-two. It was greeted with much applause, which must have been intimidating to the president—especially because he knew his speech was nowhere nearly so long.

"I was close to the President and heard all of the Address," Sarah Myers recalled, "but it seemed short."

It was short, very short—just 272 words—which took all of two minutes to deliver:

> Four score and seven years ago our fathers brought forth on this continent, a new nation, conceived in Liberty, and dedicated to the proposition that all men are created equal.
>
> Now we are engaged in a great civil war, testing whether that nation, or any nation so conceived and so dedicated, can long endure. We are met on a great battle-field of that war. We have come to dedicate a portion of that field, as a final resting place for those who here gave their lives that that nation might live. It is altogether fitting and proper that we should do this.

But, in a larger sense, we can not dedicate—we can not consecrate—we can not hallow—this ground. The brave men, living
and dead, who struggled here, have consecrated it, far above our
poor power to add or detract. The world will little note, nor long
remember what we say here, but it can never forget what they
did here. It is for us the living, rather, to be dedicated here to
the unfinished work which they who fought here have thus far so
nobly advanced. It is rather for us to be here dedicated to the great
task remaining before us—that from these honored dead we take
increased devotion to that cause for which they gave the last full
measure of devotion—that we here highly resolve that these dead
shall not have died in vain—that this nation, under God, shall
have a new birth of freedom—and that government of the people,
by the people, for the people, shall not perish from the earth.

Myers, who described herself as a "birthright Quaker," remembered
that an "impressive silence" followed the speech, "like our Menallen
Friends Meeting. There was no applause when he stopped speaking." In fact, Lincoln turned to a companion and remarked, "It is a
flat failure and the people are disappointed." The next day, some of
the nation's newspapers agreed, judging two minutes far too slim a
sentimental investment for such a solemn occasion. Others, however,
praised the speech, and Everett himself congratulated the president
on its "eloquent simplicity & appropriateness," adding "I should be
glad, if I could flatter myself that I came as near to the central idea
of the occasion, in two hours, as you did in two minutes." Indeed,
within days of the ceremony, the national press seems to have wak-
ened to the importance as well as the eloquence of Lincoln's "Gettysburg Address." It was published in full or quoted in newspapers
across the country.

* * *

For Lincoln, the fullest meaning of the victory at Gettysburg was
expressed to the living by the dead. Their "last full measure of
devotion" was meant to inspire "us the living" to dedicate ourselves
to ensuring "that this nation, under God, shall have a new birth of

freedom—and that government of the people, by the people, for the people, shall not perish from the earth." Yet the Battle of Gettysburg is also rich with lessons from both the living and the dead. Here are the three most significant.

Buford Holds the High Ground

When Henry Heth reported to General Hill the presence of enemy cavalry in Gettysburg on June 31, it occurred to neither man that these horse soldiers were the advance guard of the entire Army of the Potomac. Robert E. Lee did have an inkling, however. General Longstreet had hired Henry Thomas Harrison, a Mississippian by birth and an actor by vocation, to find and spy on any Union military activity nearby. He now reported to Longstreet and Lincoln that the Army of the Potomac was closing in. He could not, however, give Lee an estimate as to numbers.

Rural Pennsylvania is not where Lee wanted to fight. Nor was his objective to seek out and defeat a major Union Army in a great battle. His aim was merely to raid and to menace, to target Baltimore and perhaps Philadelphia, but, most of all, Washington. His ultimate purpose was to attack and undermine the confidence of the people of the United States. Nevertheless, if a battle was being forced upon him, he was determined to make the very most of it. He meant to win a big victory.

Lee's own track record gave him reason for confidence. He had, after all, decisively defeated the Army of the Potomac twice before, at Fredericksburg and at Chancellorsville. Besides, this time he even had the element of surprise on his side. It was a magnificent opportunity, with the stakes of the contest higher than ever. The earlier victories had been won while defending Confederate soil. If Lee could triumph at Gettysburg, in the United States, against an army he had twice bested, he might well bring about the turning point in the war.

Not everyone agreed with him. Longstreet, his favorite among his subordinates, had counseled against the Northern invasion in the first place, and he now tried to talk him out of seeking a showdown battle at Gettysburg. Not only would the Army of Northern Virginia be outnumbered, it would be put at risk for an objective, Gettysburg, of no special strategic value. Lee countered that Meade's army was spread out and therefore vulnerable. Gettysburg wasn't the point. The opportunity to defeat the flagship military force of the Union was. At best, such a victory could bring about peace talks favorable to the Confederacy. At the very least, it would likely cause Lincoln's defeat when he ran for reelection in 1864. That would bring a Democrat into office, and the Democrats would run on a platform pledge to bring the war to an immediate end. Finally—and this may have been the most critical factor in his decision—Lee believed that General Meade saw the same opportunity he saw, namely an army strung out over a considerable distance and therefore vulnerable. If the Army of Northern Virginia failed to concentrate at Gettysburg, there was every possibility that Meade would attack and defeat the Confederate flagship force in detail.

Major General John Buford, at the head of a detachment of his Union cavalry brigade in Gettysburg, did not know exactly where the Army of Northern Virginia was, but he knew it was nearby. He was a tough, savvy commander. His prewar experience fighting Native Americans in Texas and the Southwest developed in him *coup d'oeil*, the power to look at a landscape and see in it all the advantages and disadvantages of a coming battle. What Buford saw at Gettysburg was the high ground—McPherson Ridge, it was called—on the western edge of town. He had detected Heth probing close by, and he assumed that a larger force was on its way. There were just two choices. Buford could hightail it back to the rest of his brigade, or he could stay where he was, in harm's way, to occupy McPherson Ridge and hold it until more of the Army of the Potomac could get to Gettysburg. Having survived the carnage of Fredericksburg, a place at which the Confederates held the heights, he knew the murderous consequences of giving up high ground to the enemy.

Buford dismounted his troopers and deployed them along the ridge. Their mission was to hold it until more of the army arrived. That could be hours—even longer. He didn't know how long it would be, but he knew for certain that his men would be badly outnumbered for however long it was. Nevertheless, he resolved to make the most of his advantages: possession of the high ground and the fact that, as cavalrymen, his troopers carried breech-loading repeating carbines whereas the infantry was armed with muzzle-loading rifle-muskets. His men should be able to fire and reload much faster than the Confederates—at least as long as their limited supply of ammunition held out. It might just buy time enough for reinforcements to arrive.

Buford deployed his troopers on the morning of July 1. By nine, the fighting had begun. His dismounted cavalry repulsed the first Confederate waves, and McPherson Ridge was still in Union hands when the first elements of Major General John Reynolds's I Corps, Army of the Potomac, arrived at about 10:30. Better yet, Reynolds conveyed the news that General O. O. Howard was also on the way, with XI Corps.

But the Confederates were rapidly building superior strength *right now*. Like John Buford, John Reynolds was a soldier of great courage, gallantry, and energy. No corps commander was more beloved in the entire Union Army. As was his custom, he assumed personal command of the first of his units that got into position. They were the 1,800 "Black Hats" of the already legendary "Iron Brigade." Leading from the front, Reynolds intended to prevent a Confederate breakthrough, and he formed up the brigade in McPherson's Woods, just west of the ridge. Before he could lead them out of the woods and against the enemy, however, a Confederate bullet tore into his neck. He fell from his saddle, dead.

There is no substitute for personal leadership, but there is a downside to dependence on any one commander. The men of the mighty Iron Brigade were stricken by the decapitating blow, and their confusion spread throughout I Corps. By the time Major General Howard appeared with much of his XI Corps, the Gettysburg battlefield was in chaos. He quickly assumed command of both I Corps and XI Corps and scrambled to consolidate the still-outnumbered Union forces, but he was unable to deploy fast enough on the hotly contested McPherson Ridge Buford had fought so hard to hold. At last, Confederate units under generals Robert Rodes, Jubal Early, and A. P. Hill pushed the Federals off the ridge and routed them from every position they held west and the north of town. The Union line of retreat snaked down McPherson Ridge and spilled into the town of Gettysburg, its few lanes soon jammed with troops. Fighting house to house and hand to hand, the Confederates drove the

Federals through the town and onto the Baltimore Pike, principal route to the southeast.

Hearing of Reynold's death, General Meade sent another beloved commander, Winfield Scott Hancock, to rally and regroup the defense. There was no way that Hancock could snatch victory from the jaws of defeat that first day of the Battle of Gettysburg, but he did restore order to the Army of the Potomac there and, building on the precious time Buford's stand had bought at the start of the battle, he prevented defeat from becoming complete destruction. True, McPherson Ridge had been lost, but the Union still clung to East Cemetery Hill, Cemetery Ridge, and Culp's Hill, together forming a high-ground position that ran south then southeast of the town, so that, by nightfall on July 1, the opposing armies occupied ridges and hills southwest and south of town. The Confederate infantry division under Major General William Dorsey Pender, a fierce warrior, was dug in on Seminary Ridge, the southwestern high ground, while Jubal Early's understrength infantry division was at the southeastern edge of town, menacingly near the northernmost flank of the Union position, Howard's XI Corps and Abner Doubleday's I Corps, spread out from northeast to southwest along Cemetery Ridge just below town. About a mile and a half south of these corps were two more Union divisions, holding positions north of two hills, Round Top and Little Round Top. Between Pender's Confederates and the Union troops under Howard and Doubleday was a mile-wide expanse of open fields and patches of woodland. By any measure, Lee had won the day. But thanks to Buford and then to Howard, he had not yet won the battle.

Chamberlain holds Little Round Top

No one understood better than Robert E. Lee that though the day was won, the battle still hung in the balance. He instructed Major General Richard Stoddart Ewell to exploit what he termed the initial rout of the Union army, adding to his instructions the phrase "if he found it practicable." No Civil War general was—or is—more universally revered than Lee, and not just for his military genius, but also for his character. It was the character of a gentleman, and Lee led his officers in the manner of a gentleman speaking to other gentlemen. Ewell needed to be told that he had to fight as if the entire war depended on it. Instead, he was given directions without any particular urgency. Lee's subdued leadership style unwittingly gave the edge, on Day 2, to the Army of the Potomac.

The position of the Union army at Gettysburg on the morning of July 2, 1863, is often described as an inverted fishhook. The curve of the hook was at the northeastern end, around the top of Cemetery Hill (defended by I Corps). East and slightly south of this was the barb, consisting of most of XI Corps, on Culp's Hill. The shaft ran southwest along Cemetery Ridge, occupied by II Corps, which had been joined by III Corps on its flank. The shaft's "tie end" stopped just short of the two hills south of town known as Little Round Top and Round Top. Lee directed Longstreet to attack the shaft all along Cemetery Ridge, ending at the Round Tops. This position was the left flank of the Army of the Potomac at Gettysburg. Lee's intention was to position his own corps northwest of the fishhook to attack where the curve joined the shaft at Cemetery Hill. He instructed Ewell, whose corps was due north of Cemetery Hill, above the curve of the hook, to swing down swiftly and hit the Union's right.

But just how hard he would hit it depended on how he might interpret that phrase "if practicable." Lee had failed to make absolutely clear the need for all of his commanders to hit the Union line in rapid succession or, even better, simultaneously. Lee needed to break the line, without giving it any time to heal. Break it, and the Army of the Potomac would be unable to maintain possession of Cemetery Ridge and all the other high ground adjacent. Since rapid, orderly withdrawal from high, rugged ground is virtually impossible, the Union army would be set up for a cataclysmic rout.

Confederate forces encircled the Union fishhook on three sides: along the length of the shaft, above the curve of the hook, and to the east of the barb. Nevertheless, the Union's I and XI Corps, surrounded though they were, occupied the highest ground at every point. This meant that any Confederate attack would not only have to be made uphill, it would require an initial advance over open fields exposed to fire from above. Moreover, thanks to the time Brigadier General Buford had bought, nearly 90,000 soldiers of the Army of the Potomac were now in position at Gettysburg, whereas

Lee commanded at most seventy-five thousand—deployed not in concentration, but strung out along a wide encirclement on high ground and low.

At the southwest "tie-end" of the upside-down fishhook was the freshly arrived III Corps commanded by Major General Daniel Sickles. He occupied *the* critical position that morning. It was the left flank of the Army of the Potomac, the very end of the Union line. Head-to-head fighting is brutal, but if an enemy can hit you at the *end* of your line, bringing *his* front against *your* flank, he gains a virtually overwhelming advantage. He can bring a whole line of fire to bear upon a point from which you can offer but little resistance. It is like a classic battle at sea in which the skillful captain "crosses the T," bringing the many guns of his broadside to bear upon the less-skilled captain's bow or stern, two places nearly undefended.

The Union could not afford for Dant Sickles to falter. But he was not a career military man. Far from it, he had been a congressman who earned a sensationally seedy reputation for having left his pregnant wife in New York City to tour England with a prostitute. Later, when he discovered that the very wife he had humiliated was having an affair with Philip Barton Key, district attorney of the District of Columbia *and* the son of "Star-Spangled Banner" lyricist Francis Scott Key, Sickles shot him dead in broad daylight, in Lafayette Park, across the street from the White House. (His attorney, future secretary of war Edwin M. Stanton, pleaded Sickles not guilty by reason of temporary insanity—the first time in US legal history that such a plea had ever been entered. He won.) With the outbreak of the Civil War, Sickles became one of Lincoln's most unsavory "political generals," as those appointed by reason of their political influence rather than for military expertise were called. Unlike most officers in this category, however, Sickles managed to compile a decent record of command in several major battles. Unfortunately, Gettysburg would not be among them.

For reasons that have never been made clear and without being ordered to do so by General Meade, Sickles made the perverse decision to lead III Corps out of its assigned anchor position at the end of the Union line by advancing over a half-mile west. This move not only isolated the corps, it laid bare the flank of just about the entire Union force assembled at Gettysburg on July 2, 1863.

For the Union, a tragedy was in the making—or should have been. But James Longstreet, commanding the Confederate force opposite Sickles, was so baffled by his movement out of line that, instead of seeing it as the blunder it was, he worried that it was a ruse meant to draw him into an enveloping attack. Instead of seizing the battle-winning, maybe war-winning, opportunity presented to him, Longstreet pondered and delayed, waiting until four in the afternoon before he finally decided to attack. He ordered his most aggressive division commander, Major General John Bell Hood, to hit III Corps in the "Peach Orchard," where it was now positioned, northwest of the Round Tops. Sickles's soldiers were forced to fall back toward Little Round Top, traversing a boulder-strewn patch of ground Hood's soldiers came to call Devil's Den because of the fierce fight that ensued there.

The Union line seemed destined to break at this place, but, shortly before Hood commenced his attack, the eye of Brigadier General Gouverneur K. Warren, chief engineer of the Army of the Potomac, took in something no one else seems to have noticed. Little Round Top, the rise of ground below the tie end of the Union fishhook, was vacant, unoccupied except for a few signalmen. To Warren, the sight signified only one thing: utter disaster. In a moment, he pictured the enemy charging up the undefended slope of the hill, concentrating forces on the high ground, and then charging down from it to crush the Union's flank. If Hood could maintain the momentum of such a thrust, there would be nothing to stop him from rolling up the fishhook shaft. With that, Gettysburg would join Fredericksburg and Chancellorsville in the list of Lee's victories over the Army of the Potomac.

Wasting no time, Warren sent a staff officer to Colonel Strong Vincent with orders that he lead a brigade to Little Round Top—*now*. Vincent did just that and was killed in resisting Hood's advance, but his brigade bought just enough time for another brigade, under Brigadier General Stephen Weed, to get into position. At the extreme southern end of this brigade—and thus at the very end of the Army of the Potomac—was the 20th Maine Regiment, a battered unit wasted to half its original strength by continuous combat. Its remaining five hundred men—which included a number of captured deserters the regiment had been assigned to guard—were commanded by Colonel Joshua Lawrence Chamberlain, the Bowdoin College professor of rhetoric we briefly met in chapter 5. The severely depleted 20th Maine fell under attack by one of Longstreet's Alabama regiments, fresh and at full strength. They charged Chamberlain's men, who fought fiercely, refusing to yield an inch of Little Round Top.

But then word reached Chamberlain that his regiment's ammunition was exhausted. In this circumstance, surrender loomed as the only option. Instead, Chamberlain gave the order to fix bayonets and counterattack. Charging downhill, his men so intimidated the Alabamans that the Southerners threw down *their* weapons and surrendered. Absent Chamberlain, the Battle of Gettysburg might have ended on July 2, 1863, with the collapse of the Army of the Potomac. His order to fight without ammunition was a bluff backed by extraordinary courage, and while it did not win the Battle of Gettysburg, it surely kept the Union from losing it. Combat would resume for a third day.

Pickett's Charge

By afternoon of Day 3, it became clear that the momentum had shifted to the Union. Culp's Hill, which had been contested on Day 2, was secured by the Union in the course of a bitter seven-hour fight. But Lee was convinced the battle as a whole could still be won. The first day had been his, and while he had failed to win the battle on Day 2, Lee had surely wearied and worn down the Union defenders. Their hold on the high ground, the Confederate commander believed, was tenuous. The Union position would fall to an overwhelming final assault.

Unsurprisingly, Longstreet disagreed. He warned Lee that Union forces now enjoyed superior numbers and, more importantly, they were fighting like men who had no intention of losing. The only counterargument Lee could summon was that far too much blood had been spilled to give up now. He therefore ordered—not, this time, merely requested—a massive infantry charge, essentially head on, across a wide-open field of fire, followed by an uphill assault.

"My heart was heavy," Longstreet later wrote. "I could see the desperate and hopeless nature of the charge and the hopeless slaughter it would cause."

The operation would later be immortalized as "Pickett's Charge," even though Major General George Pickett led but three of the nine brigades Lee committed to it. Generals James Johnston Pettigrew and Isaac Ridgeway Trimble led the other six, with three each. Against the ceaseless explosion of cannon and roar of musketry, the three generals and their subordinate commanders formed up their grand ranks—some 12,500 men in all, arrayed as if for a parade. They advanced from all along Seminary Ridge onto the mile of open field separating that ridge from the Union line on Cemetery Ridge to the east.

From Seminary Ridge, 150 Confederate Napoleons (field cannon) opened fire against Cemetery Ridge. Intended to soften Union resistance, the bombardment did nothing but elicit an intense return of artillery fire from Union gunners. Never before in the Civil War had there been such a cannon duel. It ended abruptly, however, at 1:45 when the Confederate guns fell silent, and nine brigades, 12,500 men, rank on gray rank, marched forward. The pace began at a steady walk, even after the Union gunners trained their cannon onto the field. The impact of cannonballs and canister shot—not solid balls, but fragmentation shells intended to explode, sending shot and shrapnel in all directions—thinned the oncoming ranks, but did not change their direction or their pace. Those who survived to reach the foot of Cemetery Ridge raised, in unison, of the fabled "rebel yell" and broke into a trot.

More antipersonnel canister rounds poured down from Federal cannon lined up wheel to wheel. The plain below was transformed into a killing field, raked by jagged iron shards.

That night, after it was over and done, Pickett would write about it all to his fiancée: "Over on Cemetery Ridge the Federals beheld a scene which has never previously been enacted, an army forming in line of battle in full view," he began.

Indeed, the Army of the Potomac men watched it form and then watched it advance, wave upon gray wave, which, like ocean waves in a storm, seemed to break in jagged lines as men fell first to the detonation of canister shot and then, as the waves became individual soldiers at closer approach, to the impact of Minié balls from thousands of Union rifle-muskets.

Yet no matter how many fell, the soldiers kept coming. It was, one Union man later recalled, "an overwhelming relentless tide of an ocean of armed men sweeping upon us! On the move, as with one soul in perfect order . . . magnificent, grim, irresistible." Pickett himself wrote to his beloved: "My brave boys were so full of hope and confident of victory as I led them forth!" He wrote of how they charged "across a space nearly a mile in length, pride and glory soon to be crushed by an overwhelming heartbreak" and then abruptly broke off with, "Well, it is all over now. The awful rain of shot and shell was a sob—a gasp."

Thanks to his letter, we know how Pickett felt. We can imagine his sleepless night, as he continued to hear in his fevered imagination his men "cheering as I gave the order, 'Forward!' the thrill of their joyous voices as they called out, 'We'll follow you, Marse George, we'll follow you!' On, how faithfully they followed me on—on—to their death, and I led them on—on—on—Oh God!"

We know all this because, of the three generals who led the charge, only Pickett was able to write about it that night. Armistead had been killed, and Pettigrew grievously wounded. The fifteen regimental commanders in the charge were all killed or wounded, and of the 12,500 soldiers who set out from Seminary Ridge, only five thousand returned from the assault on Cemetery Ridge. Perhaps 150 men, with Brigadier General Lewis Armistead at their head, actually managed to ascend Cemetery Ridge. They even planted the Confederate battle flag, which waved briefly amid the Federal soldiers until Armistead was cut down and the men with him killed or captured.

* * *

By destroying the brigades sent against them, the Union defenders of Cemetery Hill won the Battle of Gettysburg, the meaning of which President Abraham Lincoln did his best in the course of two incredible minutes to explain. A turning point, the battle pointed the war down a path by which the Union cause would ascend and the

Confederate cause decline. Yet the blood sacrifice of so many in the attack on Cemetery Hill revealed that the soldiers of Robert E. Lee's Army of Northern Virginia intended to make that downward path a very long and costly journey. The war was but half over.

7

November 4, 1864

Lincoln Wins Reelection

Why it's significant. Abraham Lincoln ran for reelection in 1864 on a platform that included fighting the Civil War to absolute victory, which meant the unconditional surrender of the Confederacy and an end to slavery forever. Lincoln's opponent, George B. McClellan, promised a negotiated peace that included abolition. The president feared that Northern war weariness would cost him reelection and preserve slavery forever. In the end, Union military triumphs in the run-up to the election returned Lincoln to office by a wide margin, and the war was fought to total victory.

IF MAJOR GENERAL George Brinton McClellan had something of a messiah complex—"The people call upon me to save the country," he once wrote in a letter to his adoring wife, Ellen Mary Marcy—the Northern public and the press helped to plant it in him. They hailed him as the "Young Napoleon," and even President Abraham Lincoln put his full confidence in him, challenging McClellan to build a war-winning Union army after the humiliating defeat of Irvin McDowell at the First Battle of Bull Run (July 21, 1861). At first, the adulation and faith seemed amply justified. McClellan transformed the undisciplined band of Sunday soldiers defeated at Bull Run into the Army of the Potomac, the largest, best-equipped, and best-trained military formation the United States had ever fielded.

Lincoln was grateful to McClellan, but the general did not reciprocate. On the contrary, he was among the many Americans at this time who had doubts about Lincoln. In a November 17, 1861 letter to Ellen, McClellan wrote of going "to the White House shortly after tea where I found 'the original gorilla,' about as intelligent as ever. What a specimen to be at the head of our affairs now!" It was a phrase he had picked up from Edwin Stanton, Lincoln's contentious secretary of war. Little wonder that it did not sit well with McClellan when President Lincoln began to goad and criticize him for his protracted delay in leading into battle the magnificent weapon he had forged. To a meeting of generals that did not include McClellan, an exasperated Lincoln remarked on January 10, 1862, "If General McClellan does not want to use the army, I would like to borrow it for a time." In March, the Young Napoleon finally embarked on his Peninsula Campaign, the objective of which was the capture of Richmond. By July, however, the campaign had ended, without the Army of the Potomac having gotten anywhere near the Confederate capital.

The bad blood between the general and the president became more toxic when Lincoln detached and moved a large portion of McClellan's Army of the Potomac north—*minus* McClellan—to join John Pope's Army of Virginia. Unfortunately, what Pope did with the combined forces (about 51,000 men of the Army of Virginia and 26,000 from the Army of the Potomac) was even worse than what McClellan did (and failed to do) with the Army of the Potomac alone. Pope suffered a humiliating defeat at the hands of Robert E. Lee in the Second Battle of Bull Run (August 28–30, 1862). This gave Lee an opening to invade Maryland and prompted Lincoln, fresh out of options, to once more tap McClellan to lead the Army of the Potomac against Lee. To his wife, on September 5, the general wrote: "Again I have been called to save my country."

McClellan did battle with Lee at Antietam, Maryland, on September 17, 1862—the single bloodiest day in US history. Although his army suffered horrific casualties there, McClellan did narrowly gain a strategic victory by forcing Lee to withdraw to Virginia (Chapter 4). Having achieved this, however, McClellan failed to pursue the retreating Army of Northern Virginia to its destruction. Lincoln traveled to Antietam to personally confront McClellan and urge him forward. To a friend who accompanied him on the journey, Lincoln pointed to the vast encampment of the Army of the Potomac and asked his companion if he knew what lay before them. "It is the Army of the Potomac," the man answered. "So it is called," President Lincoln replied, "but that is a mistake; it is only McClellan's bodyguard."

The meeting between the president and his general produced no action. On October 6, 1862, Lincoln wrote McClellan a letter ordering him to "cross the Potomac and give battle to the enemy." By way of reply, McClellan did nothing. A week later, the president wrote another letter, demanding to know why he had failed to carry out his mission. This time, McClellan wrote a reply, explaining that his horses were worn out. Lincoln shot back: "I have just read your dispatch about sore-tongued and fatigued horses. Will you pardon me for asking what the horses of your army have done since the Battle of Antietam that fatigues anything?" It was not merely that President Lincoln had lost faith in McClellan, he had lost respect for him. On November 5, 1862, Lincoln relieved the Young Napoleon of command of the Army of the Potomac. Secretary of War Stanton ordered McClellan to Trenton, New Jersey, to await further orders. The general waited. The orders never arrived, and, while waiting, George B. McClellan accepted the Democratic nomination for president, resigning his commission on Election Day, November 8, 1864.

McClellan doubtless relished the prospect of dashing the reelection hopes of his nemesis in the White House. His contempt for Lincoln was personal—but his political opposition to Lincoln was also a matter of policy. McClellan was an outspoken and sincere advocate of an expeditiously negotiated end to the war and restoration of the Union. He saw the demand for the abolition of slavery as the chief obstacle to such a negotiation, and he therefore proposed to take abolition off the table. So compelling was McClellan's desire for reconciliation between North and South that some historians attribute it to a deficiency of aggression in his martial make-up. When he actually ran for president, however, McClellan felt compelled to repudiate the platform of his own Democratic Party, which called for an immediate end to the war to be *followed* by a negotiated settlement with "the Confederacy." *End now, negotiate later?* This implied, first and foremost, the legitimacy of the Confederacy and, second, the very real possibility that the war would end without restoring the Union. McClellan could not step this far into conciliation. While he wanted to negotiate and was quite willing to take abolition off the table, he insisted on restoring the Union *before* declaring the war to be at an end. At odds with his own party, McClellan conducted a political campaign marked by an inconsistency that failed to win votes.

Yet Abraham Lincoln was far from confident that the people would reelect him. After all, he had so far failed to win the war, a war that was claiming hundreds of thousands of lives. Without question, war weariness spread throughout the North, and many of Lincoln's fellow Republicans shared the president's doubts. Senator Samuel C. Pomeroy, a Kansas Republican, wrote an open letter, widely published in newspapers in the North and South, arguing that Lincoln could not win reelection and that Salmon P. Chase, Lincoln's secretary of the treasury at the time, would make a more viable Republican nominee. In August of 1864, Thurlow Weed, a newspaper publisher who was a political advisor to Secretary of State William H. Seward, told Seward that Lincoln's "re-election was an impossibility" because "the People are wild for Peace" and yet "are told that the President will only listen to terms of Peace on condition Slavery be 'abandoned.'" Others in the Republican fold urged President Lincoln to offer the South peace on the sole condition that the Constitution be acknowledged as final and supreme. This would provide a basis for ending the war and restoring the Union—while also protecting slavery.

For his part, while Lincoln greatly feared the pessimism he shared with his own party was justified, he refused to now divorce from the war the issues of abolition and emancipation. He believed the peace McClellan intended to negotiate with the Confederacy would perpetuate slavery. He therefore took, on August 23, the

unprecedented step of writing a sealed memorandum and present-
ing it to his Cabinet with the request that they endorse it without
knowing its contents. It is a testament to the Cabinet's loyalty and
confidence that they complied. Only after the election was won did
Lincoln unseal the document, revealing it as a solemn pledge of the
Cabinet's full cooperation with the president-elect for the sake of
the nation.

Lincoln went further. He was so convinced of the probability of
McClellan's election that he summoned the dean of African American abolitionists, Frederick Douglass, to the White House and asked
him to draw up a covert plan for facilitating the exodus of as many
slaves as possible from the slave states—*before* the election.

Douglass did as he was asked, and on August 29, 1864, delivered to President Lincoln his plan. Five days later, however, Atlanta
fell to the combined Union armies of the Cumberland, Ohio, and the
Tennessee, which were collectively under the command of William
Tecumseh Sherman. The loss of its industrial and transportation hub
seemed to set the seal on the fate of the Confederacy. Throughout
the North, enthusiasm revived for fighting the war through to nothing less than total victory, which meant the unconditional surrender
of the Confederacy. Moreover, former US Army general and ardent
abolitionist John C. Frémont, the nominee of a short-lived Republican splinter party called the Radical Democracy Party, dropped
out of the presidential race and endorsed Lincoln. This removed the
threat that the abolitionist vote would be split between anti-Lincoln
Radical Republicans and pro-Lincoln Republicans. The president
therefore tucked the Douglass plan into a drawer. It was no longer necessary to implement it, he believed, since his prospects for
reelection were looking much brighter.

In May 1864, the Republican Party temporarily renamed itself
the National Union Party, mainly as a way to invite non-Republican
voters in the Border States and so-called War Democrats—Democrats who wanted total victory, not an immediate negotiated end to
the war—to vote the Republican ticket. In the spirit of the party's
new name, Lincoln chose as his running mate a Democrat, Andrew
Johnson, who had never wavered in his loyalty to the Union and
was the only senator from a seceded state to remain in the United

States Senate during the Civil War. In March 1862, President Lincoln appointed Johnson to serve as military governor of Tennessee, whose central and western sections had been brought under the control of the Union army. By now offering voters Johnson as vice-president, Lincoln intended to demonstrate his commitment to the full restoration of the Union with, to borrow a phrase from his own Second Inaugural Address, "malice toward none."

By Election Day, November 8, 1864, the luster of the Democratic peace platform had dulled and the value of a negotiated peace had plummeted. Even the most pessimistic of Northerners glimpsed light at the end of the tunnel. To the majority of the Northern electorate, offering the South anything more than the opportunity to give up and dissolve their Confederacy began to seem like a sucker's bargain. Too many of the Union's sons, brothers, and fathers had given their lives or their limbs for the war to mean anything less than total victory—and total victory included an end to slavery. The proof of this came in the election returns. Abraham Lincoln earned 2,218,288 votes to McClellan's 1,812,807. Lincoln won 212 electoral votes to his opponent's 21. Lincoln carried twenty-two states plus the districts of Confederate Louisiana and Tennessee that were now under Federal military control. McClellan carried just three states: Kentucky, New Jersey (his home state), and Delaware. The greatest blow to the former general was the army vote. Of the officers and men who cast their ballots in 1864, 70 percent chose Lincoln.

The total voter turnout, 73.8 percent, dwarfs the anemic numbers in recent election history and speaks of how seriously Americans took this election. They understood that it was a referendum on whether or not to fight the Civil War to total victory. By returning Abraham Lincoln to office, the American majority voted for Union, liberty, and social justice and, what is more, affirmed that they were willing to pay the full price to secure these.

Those voters who also looked forward to visiting vengeance upon the South were bound for disappointment. Abraham Lincoln did not crow over the coming victory against the Confederacy, much less threaten the defeated "rebels" with some stern retribution. Rather, in his Second Inaugural Address, delivered on March 4, 1865, the president asked his listeners to "strive on to finish the work we are in," but to do so "with malice toward none" and "with charity for all." He asked that, together, they "bind up the nation's wounds," that they "care for him who shall have borne the battle and for his widow and his orphan" and "do all which may achieve and cherish a just and lasting peace among ourselves and with all nations." Having won the war, Abraham Lincoln did not want to lose the peace, peace he would live long enough barely to glimpse.

Contrary to his own expectations, President Lincoln won reelection to a second term—a powerful affirmation of his countrymen's desire to see the terrible war through to a total victory that would restore the Union and end slavery. One of the most immediate reasons for the nation's vote of confidence was General Sherman's victory in the Atlanta Campaign (May 7-September 2, 1864). This was followed by his March to the Sea (November 15-December 21), culminating in the capture of Savannah, Georgia (December 21). These triumphs doomed the Confederacy—while also revealing Sherman's cold genius for waging "total war," war directed against civilian populations, not just the opposing military. Atlanta and the March to the Sea foreshadowed war as it would be fought globally in the first half of the twentieth century.

8

July 13, 1863

New York Draft Rioters Set Fire
to the Orphan Asylum for Colored Children

Why it's significant. A bloody three-day race riot in New York City, pitting recent white immigrants against free black residents of the city, exposed a deep Northern divide over the "new" abolitionist element in Abraham Lincoln's war aims, as well as the resolve to fight the war to absolute victory and the unconditional defeat of the Confederacy.

T HE UNION VICTORY at Gettysburg came on July 3, 1863. Just one day later, on the Fourth of July no less, Vicksburg, Mississippi, the fortress-town known as the "Gibraltar of the Confederacy," fell to the Union's Army of the Tennessee, led by Ulysses S. Grant. Little wonder that history books treat these tandem events as the unmistakable "turning points" of the Civil War. Certainly there were those in the North—and even in the South—who saw things precisely this way, but an oppressive war weariness bore down on much of the North, and it was not easily lifted by all the hopeful news from Pennsylvania and Mississippi. Without a doubt, what many Northerners wanted was an end to the war.

At the outbreak of the conflict in 1861, volunteers rallied around both the Stars and Bars in the South and the Stars and Stripes in the

North. Calls for troops from Confederate President Jefferson Davis and from United States President Abraham Lincoln were answered in such overabundance that some comers had to be turned back, at least temporarily, for lack of sufficient supplies, shelter, and experienced commissioned and noncommissioned officers to train, lead, and manage them. By the second year of the war, however, both sides began to experience a drought of recruits even as both faced a flood of casualties and an urgent need to replace them, let alone enlarge the armies. The shortfall hit the Confederacy first and hardest. Having seceded from the Union in response to what it claimed was the tyranny of Washington, Richmond enacted a conscription law on April 16, 1862, that many Southerners believed was the very height of tyranny.

The 1862 Confederate law required all white males between eighteen and thirty-five years of age to render three years of military service. Before the end of the year, the upper age limit was pushed to forty-five, and in February 1864, to fifty, at which time the lower limit was set at seventeen. Moreover, the Confederate draft law was inherently unjust and inequitable. It provided two alternatives to compulsory military service—but they were alternatives available only to those with the means to pay for them. A man could avoid service by either paying a "commutation fee" or by hiring an acceptable substitute to serve in his stead. Those men who owned (or oversaw) twenty slaves or more were also exempt. Few Southerners could afford to pay the commutation fee or pay for a substitute, and even fewer owned or oversaw twenty slaves. In effect, the draft applied unconditionally to the poor and even the middling majority while exempting the wealthy minority.

It took the North nearly a year longer than the South to enact conscription, but come it did, on March 3, 1863. Like the Confederate law, the Northern law gave the well-heeled an out, either by hiring a substitute or by paying a $300 commutation fee. A manual laborer in the Northern states earned about a dollar a day in 1860 currency, so that the price of avoiding conscription was a year's wages.

Now, it must be noted that of the total number of enlisted men who served in the Union army during the war—2,778,304—the great majority enlisted voluntarily. After March 1863, many of these voluntary enlistments were doubtless motivated by the prospect of being involuntarily drafted. A mere 52,068 Union conscripts were held to service during the entire war. A total of 86,724 men subject to conscripted service paid the $300 commutation fee to receive exemption, and 42,581 hired substitutes. The Confederacy kept poor records, and many records were destroyed in the course of the war; however, it is clear that, throughout the war, the Confederate forces consisted, like those of the Union, mostly of volunteers. Still, on both sides, enactment of conscription caused unrest and outrage over the perceived exploitation of hard-working, hard-pressed men. In both the South and the North, there were anti-draft demonstrations, which sometimes turned violent. In the North, towns and cities in Iowa, Illinois, Indiana, and Ohio saw rioting, but it was in New York City that the explosion assumed a scale and duration greater than anywhere else.

In this, the first quarter of the twenty-first century, we Americans often regard our nation as seriously divided, but, as alienated as it seems, we still think of the United States as a divided *America.* In the mid-nineteenth century, most Americans did not even think of themselves first and foremost as *Americans.* While the states were putatively "united," most Americans identified themselves primarily as citizens of their home state. They were Virginians, Ohioans, Alabamans, New Yorkers, and so on. It was largely for this reason that the likes of Robert E. Lee, a distinguished career US Army officer, resigned his commission to join the Confederate army because he could not bring himself to "lift his sword" against *Virginia*, whereas he had no problem lifting it against the *United States.* This was the feeling of many throughout the nation in 1861.

Along this spectrum of nationalist/non-nationalist sentiment, New York City had long been a very special case, and, in 1860–1861, as civil war appeared increasingly inevitable, relatively few New Yorkers eagerly rallied 'round the flag. Mayor Fernando Wood even proposed that the city secede from the Union—albeit without joining the Confederacy. His argument was that the wealth of New York was bound by trade to both the South and the North, and he envisioned declaring it a kind of "free city," in the European sense, a city-state doing business equally with Union and Confederacy. Of course, New York City never chose so radical a path, but, throughout the war, it harnessed the force of commerce more than it embraced fierce loyalty to the Union. The city was a stronghold of "peace Democrats," who believed the war should be ended quickly with a negotiated settlement.

New York at mid-century was also a magnet for immigrants, who came mostly from Europe. The first generation struggled to make a living at whatever low-wage labor they could find. Living in a town driven more by commercial pragmatism than be patriotic idealism, the immigrants in New York (and some other Northern cities) feared and resented three things by the summer of 1863. First, they feared the consequences of the Emancipation Proclamation that became final on January 1. They believed it would open a great flood of freedmen bubbling up in a torrent from the South, offering to work for slave wages and thereby usurping the low-wage jobs that barely served to keep many immigrants alive. Second, they were outraged by the draft, which required them to give up their meager but much-needed jobs to fight—and quite possibly die—for the express purpose of liberating people who, once free, would take from them their livelihood. Third, they felt betrayed by a draft law that, ultimately, applied only to men like themselves, who could not afford to buy their way out of conscription. Most of this generation of immigrants had fled such injustice in Europe. Some tens of thousands of Irish immigrants had fled their homeland to escape a great potato famine that was exacerbated by the greed of rich English landlords. America promised equality, but now offered only more of the treatment to which they had been subject and subjugated in the old country.

In 1863, the first- and second-generation Irish immigrants and their sons and daughters living in New York City numbered more than 200,000. The powder was thus packed in the keg. The match that lit the fuse was the commencement of the draft lottery in New York City on Saturday, July 11, 1863. Within two days, on Monday, journalist Joel T. Headley described "a ragged, coatless, heterogeneously weaponed army [that] heaved tumultuously along toward Third Avenue. Tearing down the telegraph poles as it crossed the Harlem & New Haven Railroad track, it surged angrily up around the building where the drafting was going on . . . . The mob seized the [draft-lottery] wheel in which were the names, and what books, papers, and lists were left, and tore them up." Seeking more of the records without which the draft could not proceed, some of the mob attempted to break open a safe inside the draft office. Unable to tear the iron box open, they put the building to the torch. Against the backdrop of that blaze, the rioters advanced toward the Second Avenue armory, intent on seizing more lethal weapons than the clubs, brickbats, fists, and torches they currently possessed. Along the way, however, they were frequently distracted by such inviting targets as jewelry and liquor shops.

At some point, a far more vulnerable target loomed—African Americans. When rioters began running down whatever persons of color were unfortunate enough to cross their paths, the so-called draft riot became a race riot—and the rage that had been directed against the draft was now concentrated on black New Yorkers.

Mobs roamed the streets where the city's working-class blacks lived. They chased down their victims. Some they beat, and some they lynched, hanging them from lampposts. The race riot intensified on Tuesday, and, this time, the rioters focused on the Colored Orphan Asylum at 43rd Street and Fifth Avenue. The institution had been established in 1836, down on 12th Street between Fifth and Sixth Avenues, by a trio of white Quaker women, Anna and Hanna Shotwell and Mary Murray. It moved uptown to 43rd Street in 1843. By 1863, the large four-story structure sheltered (according to *Harper's Weekly*) an average of "600 or 800 homeless colored orphans." *Harper's* reported that when "it became evident that the crowd designed to destroy it, a flag of truce appeared on the walk opposite, and the principals of the establishment made an appeal to the excited populace, but in vain."

Fortunately, the first objective of the rioters was to loot the building of "every article deemed worth carrying away." This gave orphanage caretakers sufficient time to evacuate the children by a back exit. Moreover, the first attempt to burn the building down failed, as the facility's "Chief-Engineer," a man named Decker, was able to extinguish the first fires. Aided by a "half-dozen of his men," Decker was even able to defeat a second attempt at arson, but, outnumbered 2,000:1 (if the *Harper's* report is accurate), he and his helpers gave up, and a third attempt succeeded in burning the building to the ground. Members of a city fire brigade saved Decker from the wrath of the mob, but they could not save the building. Some persons were injured by falling debris, but the children had all escaped to safety.

Wednesday, the third day of the New York riot, began with mobs tearing down the houses of black residents by hand. The frenzy of devastation continued though the afternoon until, at the approach of evening, a detachment of Army of the Potomac troops, diverted from their march out of Gettysburg—that bloody "turning point" of the Civil War—advanced into the greatest city of the North with a new mission: *to restore order.*

These were soldiers who had been part of the deadliest battle ever fought on American soil. Victorious though they had been, they had seen many of their brothers-in-arms fall, and they were now inclined to treat the rioters as just another set of enemy combatants. As one eyewitness recalled, the fighting was "terrific . . . Streets were swept again and again by grape"—a type of artillery ammunition in which lead balls, tightly packed into a canvas container, are driven out in a wide dispersal pattern when the projectile is fired. Grapeshot and the similar canister shot (in which a tin or brass container replaces the canvas bag) were the primary, and very deadly, antipersonnel ammunition types during the Civil War. In addition, infantrymen stormed houses "at the point of the bayonet," while sharpshooters, firing from housetops, "picked off" individual troublemakers. The same eyewitness who spoke of "terrific" fighting reported that, in the aftermath, "men were hurled, dying or dead, into the streets." And so the Civil War came to Broadway.

Indeed, civil war had become universal war—at least for a time. For it did not take long for Meade's soldiers to quench the New York City Draft Riot—although outbreaks continued to flare both nearby, in Brooklyn, Jamaica, Staten Island, Jersey City, and Newark, as well farther afield, in Albany and Troy, New York, in Boston, Massachusetts, and Portsmouth, New Hampshire, in the Pennsylvania counties of Columbia and Bucks, and in parts of Kentucky, as well as Milwaukee and Ozaukee County, Wisconsin.

None of these outbreaks approached the casualty levels reached in New York City, where estimates of loss of life ranged from 300 to more than a thousand.

There were some Americans, of course, who welcomed it all. J. B. Jones, a clerk in the Confederate War Department at Richmond, Virginia, recorded in his diary on July 17 the *"awfully* good news from New York: an INSURRECTION, the loss of many lives, extensive pillage and burning." And there were loyal Northerners who did not see the riots as racially motivated protests over unjust draft laws, but, rather, the result of a conspiracy of Confederate *agents provocateurs.* While it is true that Confederate agents were active throughout the North, the riots were homegrown and did not require the handiwork of outsiders. Nevertheless, the violence exposed the fragility, in some areas and among some groups, of the North's will to continue to fight the Civil War to total victory. Among Northern Democrats, there was a faction known as "Peace Democrats." They did not exactly want a Confederate triumph, but they did unquestionably want an immediate end to the war, which meant negotiating peace on terms favorable to the South.

As it turns out, "Peace Democrats" was the polite name for this faction. The more commonly heard appellation was *Copperheads.* A term first used in print by the *New York Tribune* on July 20, 1861, it equated Peace Democrats with a deadly snake in the grass liable to attack without warning. As for the Peace Democrats themselves, many embraced the ugly label by taking copper pennies, cutting out the head of the Liberty goddess who adorned them, and using these as improvised "copperhead" lapel badges.

Copperheads were often derided as "Confederate sympathizers." Almost certainly, some among them actively worked toward a Confederate victory. The great majority, however, simply opposed both the Emancipation Proclamation and the Conscription Act, arguing that fighting to preserve the Union was constitutional, but fighting a war to free black slaves was not. Most believed that Radical Republicans had not only transformed the conflict into a "war for the Negro," but were also using it as a war against the Democratic Party, which would be purged (they believed) on the heels of a Northern victory and occupation of the Confederate states.

Motivated by a mixture of racial prejudice and a will to political survival—plus a sincere desire to end the slaughter of the most cataclysmic war ever fought in North America—the most dedicated Copperheads organized secret societies, especially in Kentucky, Missouri, Iowa, Illinois, Indiana, and Ohio, where the Democratic Party's appetite for compromise with the South far outweighed Republican zeal for total victory at any cost. The aim of these covert organizations was ending the war, letting the seceded states go their own way, and preventing African Americans from becoming integrated into white American society. Some of these groups were not content with fomenting mere civil disturbance. Some were bent on outright rebellion. Many Copperheads inclined in this direction rallied behind one Clement Vallandigham, a member of the US House of Representatives from Ohio's 3rd District who served from 1858 to 1863, and who was the editor of the *Western Empire*, a radical Democratic newspaper. His Copperhead sentiments were too strong for a majority of his Ohio constituents, who voted him out of office in the 1862 elections. His final speech in the House, made just after that body passed the Conscription Act, was to urge all Union men inducted to simply stop fighting. Once out of Congress, Vallandigham made another speech, on May 1, 1863, this time claiming that the Civil War was being fought not to save the Union but to free the slaves at the expense of the liberty of all Americans, who henceforward would be subjects of "King Lincoln."

The May speech prompted Vallandigham's arrest for violating General Order Number 38, issued by Major General Ambrose Burnside (commanding officer of the Union army's Department of the Ohio), which ordered those who declared "sympathies with the enemy" to be either executed as traitors or "sent beyond our lines into the lines of their friends." Found guilty by a military tribunal, Vallandigham was sentenced to imprisonment for the duration of the war. Fearing that this would make him a martyr to the Copperhead cause, President Lincoln ordered him expelled to the Confederacy. Out of sight, out of mind.

Vallandigham presented himself in Richmond, which he soon covertly left, traveling by blockade runner via Bermuda. From here, he traveled to Windsor, Ontario, from which he conducted a campaign (in absentia) for Ohio governor. It was, of course, a long shot, and, after he lost, he conspired with one Jacob Thompson, a Confederate agent posted in Canada, to create a Northwestern Confederacy. His idea was to overthrow the existing governments of Ohio, Illinois, Kentucky, and Indiana, proclaim these as the Northwestern Confederacy, and secede. Unsurprisingly, the scheme came to nothing, but Vallandigham was able to sneak back into the United States and attend the 1864 Democratic National Convention in Chicago as a delegate from Ohio. He introduced a peace plank into the party's platform, unilaterally declaring the war "a failure" and demanding an immediate cessation of hostilities. George B. McClellan, in accepting the party's nomination to oppose Lincoln for reelection, did so on the understanding that peace would be wholly conditional on the Confederacy's rejoining the Union. This outraged Vallandigham, who was conciliated by being included on the Democratic ticket as secretary of war. McClellan raised no objection to this, but if he had had any real chance of defeating Lincoln, putting such an extremist on the ticket surely ended it.

Propelled by major Union victories at Mobile Bay (August 23, 1864) and Atlanta (September 2, 1864), Lincoln's successful reelection (Chapter 7) came as the death blow to the Copperhead movement and any possibility that a Northwestern Confederacy would be created in the Midwest. Moreover, the performance of African American troops in the Union army, especially the heroism of the 54th Regiment Massachusetts Volunteer Infantry at the Second Battle of Fort Wagner (July 18, 1863) broadened Northern enthusiasm for the abolitionist dimension of the Civil War. Thus the New York Draft Riot and the burning of the Orphan Asylum for Colored Children on July 13, 1863, became the high-water mark of major Northern resistance to embracing the absolute defeat and unconditional surrender of the Confederacy as the only acceptable ends of the Civil War.

9

April 14, 1865

John Wilkes Booth Assassinates Abraham Lincoln

Why it's significant. In his second inaugural address, delivered when Union victory in the Civil War was near at hand, President Lincoln proclaimed a policy of "malice toward none" and "charity for all" as Americans prepared to "bind up the nation's wounds." Clearly, Lincoln was prepared to institute and preside over a regime of reconciliation with the South. His death on April 15, 1865, from a gunshot wound suffered the night before, left a leadership vacuum that poisoned reconciliation, made a harsh and punitive program of Reconstruction all but inevitable, retarded the economic recovery of the South, and left fertile ground for a reign of terror and repression against African Americans in the former Confederacy.

T HE WHITE HOUSE, Good Friday, April 14, 1865, 8 a.m. Abraham Lincoln was at breakfast with his wife, Mary, and their sons, twelve-year-old Tad and Robert, twenty-two. The president picked at his meal, one egg, and sipped at his single cup of coffee. The six-foot-four Lincoln had weighed 180 pounds at his first inauguration in 1861. After four years of war, he was a gaunt 145. Still, he was eager to hear Robert's account of Lee's surrender at Appomattox Court House just five days earlier. As a captain on General Grant's staff, Robert had witnessed the two generals negotiate in the parlor of Wilmer McLean's farmhouse the terms by which the Army of Northern Virginia, beaten but unbowed, laid down its arms.

Robert began his narrative, only to be cut off by his mother, who had, she insisted, an *important* matter to discuss. She announced that although she already had tickets to a great gala at Grover's Theatre for tonight, she *really* wanted to see Laura Keene—the nation's most popular comic actress—in *Our American Cousin,* the hit comedy of the day. She insisted that her husband get tickets to Ford's Theatre.

He would get the tickets, he assured her. And when Mary asked if she might invite the General and Mrs. Grant to join them, Lincoln agreed to that, too. Then he turned back to his son. Before the young man resumed his account of the surrender, he presented his father with a little gift. It was a tintype of Robert E. Lee, which he gave to the president as something of a lighthearted joke. But Lincoln, fixing his glasses on his nose, studied the image intently and without smiling.

"It is a good face," he said. "I am glad the war is over at last."

* * *

At Appomattox Court House on April 9, 1865, Lee had surrendered the Army of Northern Virginia, chief military instrument of the Confederacy. The generals leading some 175,000 other Confederate soldiers had yet to raise the white flag, but, as Lincoln was aware, that very morning, April 14, 1865, Major Robert Anderson, Union commandant of Fort Sumter in 1861, would return to the site of his surrender to hoist once more the Stars and Stripes over the ruined fort. He would do this at 11:12 a.m., four years to the minute after those colors had been lowered. Later that afternoon, Mrs. Lincoln would remark on her husband's "great cheerfulness," and he replied: "Mary, I consider *this day*, the war has come to a close."

No American president had ever borne so great a burden as he. The war—in many ways, *his* war—produced more than 1.1 million casualties on both sides, more than a fifth of the nation's men of military age.

* * *

After breakfast on April 14, the president worked through his always voluminous stack of correspondence and had numerous meetings, one after another, including one with former senator John P. Hale of New Hampshire, whom he had just appointed minister (ambassador) to Spain. Lincoln advised Hale to work closely with Frederick Seward, assistant secretary of state under his father, William H. Seward, who was bedridden, undergoing a painful convalescence from severe injuries suffered in a carriage accident. No one knows if Hale mentioned to Lincoln what he had already confided to a few friends: that he was greatly relieved to be taking himself and his family to Spain because his daughter, Lucy Lambert Hale, was becoming seriously involved in a romance with an actor. Hale did not like the man—partly because he was an actor, but mostly because he was an outspoken pro-slavery white supremacist. His name was John Wilkes Booth.

After Hale left, Lincoln met with his Cabinet and his top general, Ulysses S. Grant, mainly to discuss policy for the postwar "Reconstruction" of the Union. During the meeting, Edwin Stanton, Lincoln's imperious secretary of war, raised a document in the air. "I will see that each of you gets a copy of this." It was his comprehensive, dictatorial, and, above all, punitive Reconstruction plan. Thanking him for it, the president cautioned, "We can't take to running state governments in all of these southern states. Their people must do that, although I reckon at first, they may do it badly."

Stanton pressed his punitive agenda, pointing out that the House and Senate would surely demand punishment of the leaders of the rebellion. Lincoln pronounced it "providential that this great rebellion is crushed just as Congress has adjourned . . . If we are wise and discreet we shall reanimate the states and get their governments in successful operation . . . before Congress comes together in December. I hope that there will be no persecution, no bloody work after the war is over. No one need expect me to take any part in hanging or killing these men, even the worst of them. Frighten them out of the country, open the gates, let down the bars, scare them off, enough lives have been sacrificed."

For Lincoln, Reconstruction was about healing; but for many others, it was about vengeance.

* * *

At two in the afternoon, the cabinet meeting ended, but General Grant lingered to explain why his wife, Julia, had declined Mrs. Lincoln's invitation to Ford's Theatre. They were leaving that very evening to visit their children at school in Burlington, New Jersey, and he had a great deal of paperwork to attend to beforehand. The president replied that he understood perfectly. (He likely also understood that Julia Grant had little affection for Mary Todd Lincoln.) There is a story—perhaps true—that Secretary Stanton overheard this exchange between Lincoln and Grant and warned both that "Neither . . . should go to the theater tonight."

Following the cabinet meeting, Lincoln granted six pardons: one was for an ailing Confederate prisoner, one for a Confederate seeking amnesty, and another for a youthful Confederate soldier about to be executed. "I think this boy can do more good above ground than under ground," Lincoln remarked to his secretary, John Hay. He also pardoned an underage Union soldier, writing to Major General George Meade, commanding the Army of the Potomac: "I am appealed to in behalf of August Bittersdorf, at Mitchells Station, Va. to be shot to-morrow as a deserter. I am unwilling for any boy under eighteen to be shot; and his father affirms that he is under sixteen." Two more individuals received presidential pardons on April 14, a man accused of intimidating loyal citizens into joining the Confederate army and another accused of deserting from one regiment only to enlist in another. Both had been condemned to death by firing squad.

The Cabinet meeting finished and the pardons issued, the president joined Mrs. Lincoln for a carriage ride he had earlier promised her. As Lincoln was washing his hands before leaving for the excursion, Assistant Secretary of War Charles A. Dana presented an urgent dispatch from the provost marshal at Portland, Maine. It concerned Jacob Thompson, a Confederate agent about to board a Canadian steamer bound for Liverpool, England.

What did Stanton want to do? the President asked.

Arrest him, Dana replied.

Drying his hands, Lincoln turned to the young man: "I rather guess not. When you have an elephant in hand, and he wants to run away, you better let him run." (In the wee hours of the morning of April 15, even as Abraham Lincoln lay in coma, Stanton would order the arrest not only of Thompson, but every other agent associated with his Canadian-based operation.)

The President and Mrs. Lincoln rode out to the Navy Yard in the southeast quadrant of the capital. "I never saw him so supremely cheerful" as he was during the drive, Mary Lincoln later recalled.

* * *

Dinner that evening lasted only from 7 to 7:30, presumably abbreviated to permit the Lincolns to make an eight o'clock curtain at Ford's. Mary announced that she had replaced the Grants with Major Henry Rathbone and his fiancée, Clara Harris, as their theater companions for the evening. The Lincolns would pick them up on the way to the theater.

With a stop to pick up their guests, the carriage rolled up at the theater door at 8:25. Metropolitan Police officer John F. Parker, Lincoln's regular evening-shift bodyguard, had arrived in advance to inspect the theater and the "State Box," which was actually Boxes 7 and 8 with the thin pine partition normally separating them removed. Finding all in order, he went out to the front door to await the arrival of the presidential party. Parker neither reported nor, apparently, worried that the lock on the inner door to Box 7 was broken.

With Parker taking the lead, the party made its way into the theater, up the stairs to the balcony, and across the rear of the balcony toward the State Box. Seeing Lincoln's arrival, patrons in the first balcony rose and applauded. On stage, Laura Keene (as Florence Trenchard) was trading puns with the resolutely clueless Lord

Dundreary. They bantered about a window *draft*, a *draught* of medicine, and a bank *draft*.

"Good gracious!" Keene's character exclaimed. "You have almost a game of *draughts*."

This sent Dundreary into a convulsion of stage laughter.

"What is the matter?" asked Keene.

"That wath a joke," Dundreary sputtered, "that wath."

Now seeing the president, Laura Keene stepped out of character, stopped the action, looked to the guests of honor, and joined the swelling applause. At this, the entire theater, 1,675 patrons, rose to its feet in applause.

With quick wit, Laura Keene ad libbed yet another pun, in reference to the end of military conscription. "The draft has been suspended," she said, and the orchestra struck up "Hail to the Chief."

After acknowledging the greeting, Lincoln settled into the high-backed rocker the management reserved for him. Officer Parker withdrew to a cane chair positioned outside the outer door of the State Box. Major Rathbone took the hand of Clara Harris, and President Lincoln took Mary's.

"What will Miss Harris think of my hanging onto you so?"

"Why, she will think nothing about it," Abraham Lincoln replied.

* * *

Madman, drunkard, failed actor—John Wilkes Booth has been called all of these. Twenty-six years old, he was in fact a matinee idol earning $20,000 a year in an age when a common working man eked out about a dollar a day. Maryland, the state of his birth and upbringing, was a border state, a slave state that remained loyal to the Union, but Booth, like many other Marylanders, identified more closely with the South than the North. As an actor, his greatest popularity was south of the Mason-Dixon Line. Perhaps this is why he was so passionate a supporter of the Confederacy, so vocal an advocate of slavery, and so vehement a hater of "Black Lincoln."

On December 2, 1859, as a volunteer with the Richmond militia, Booth attended the hanging of radical abolitionist John Brown. Although Booth never formally took up arms on behalf of the Confederacy, some historians believe the Confederacy covertly employed him as a "courier" (for which, read *spy*). Whether a Confederate agent or not, during the fall of 1864, Booth hatched the first of several bizarre plots to kidnap Lincoln and exchange him for Confederate prisoners of war. He wrote a letter justifying the planned kidnapping and entrusted it, sealed, to his sister's husband, the actor John Sleeper Clarke. The document was signed, "A Confederate doing duty upon his own responsibility. J. Wilkes Booth." Some scholars take this as proof that Booth was a lone wolf. Others believe the signature was a ploy to save the Confederate government from implication in an unseemly plot. In either case, after the abduction plots fizzled during the winter of 1864–65, Booth was left with just three active conspirators. George A. Atzerodt was a dipsomaniac Maryland carriage maker. David Herold, a twenty-three-year-old drugstore clerk, had an infantile intellect and a puppy-like desire to please Booth. Added to this pair was a large, square, powerfully built former Confederate soldier who called himself Lewis Paine, but whose real name was Louis Thornton Powell. Abandoning the kidnapping plot, Booth proposed to use the trio in the assassination of Abraham Lincoln.

As a prominent actor, Booth was well known at both Grover's Theatre and at Ford's. In conversation, he learned that Lincoln and Grant would be Ford's. He decided to kill both of them while Atzerodt would do in Vice President Andrew Johnson and Paine and Herold would murder Secretary of State Seward. Intimately acquainted with the layout of Ford's Theatre, Booth inspected the State Box during the afternoon of April 14. He noted the broken lock on the inner door to Box 7 and also a bore hole drilled into that door. (For years after the assassination, it was assumed that Booth himself had drilled the hole, but in 1962, Frank Ford, son of Harry Clay Ford, one of the theater's owners, revealed that it had been drilled on his father's orders, so that Lincoln's guard could look into the box without disturbing the occupants.) Finally, Booth also obtained a piece of wood from a music stand backstage. He would use it to wedge shut the outer door of the State Box.

Booth armed himself lightly, with a bowie knife and a diminutive single-shot derringer. He planned to use the knife on Lincoln's guard and on the president, reserving the derringer to dispatch

Grant. With the outer door wedged shut behind him, he would then leap over the railing of the box, onto the stage, cross it to the north wing, and make his way to a backstage exit onto a driveway called Baptist Alley, where a horse would be waiting for him.

Before evening, Booth learned that Grant would not be with Lincoln. Now he could use the derringer on the president. He knew exactly when to fire his single shot. Well versed in the script of *Our American Cousin*, he knew when the play's biggest, loudest laugh could come. The pretentious English mother, Mrs. Mountchessington, declares to Harry Hawk's character, Asa Trenchard, "I am aware, Mr. Trenchard, that you are not used to the manners of good society, and that alone will excuse the impertinence of which you have been guilty." Trenchard, the backwoods American, drawls in reply, "Wal, I guess I know enough to turn you inside out, you sockdologizing old mantrap." With the audience erupting, no one would hear the fatal shot—until he had made his escape. Booth calculated the line would be delivered at about 10:15 p.m.

* * *

But things went wrong from the start. Atzerodt got cold feet and never even attempted to kill Vice President Johnson. Herold held Paine's horse while the latter proceeded to make a bloody mess of the Seward assassination. In the course of the attempt on the secretary's life, Paine fractured the skull of Seward's son, Frederick, slashed the forehead of a male army nurse, knocked unconscious Seward's young daughter, then repeatedly stabbed Seward himself—an old man recovering from a carriage accident—tearing a gaping hole in his cheek before the secretary saved himself by rolling off and under the bed. In the meantime, the nurse revived sufficiently to attack Paine, who stabbed him just as another of Seward's sons, Major Augustus Seward, entered the bedroom. Paine slashed his forehead and hand before running down the stairs, where he encountered a State Department messenger, whom he also slashed. Bounding out the front door of the Seward house, Paine screamed "I am mad! I am mad!" (The mayhem notwithstanding, all survived and recovered from the assassination attempt.)

Just as Paine was beginning his bloody work, Booth made his way to the State Box. He approached the outer door, prepared to dispatch the president's bodyguard with his bowie knife. But Officer John F. Parker was not there. Tradition has it that, bored with sitting outside of the president's box, he nipped off to Taltavull's Saloon, next door to the theater. All that is known for certain, however, is that Parker was not at his post when Booth approached, entered the little blind corridor leading to the box, wedged closed the outer door, and peered through the bore hole in the inner door to Box 7.

He saw the rocker, Lincoln's head resting against its high back. At about 10:15, as Harry Hawk's anticipated line produced the anticipated laughter, Booth eased the inner door open, entered the box, leveled his derringer between Lincoln's left ear and spine, squeezed the trigger, and discharged from a distance of two feet the weapon's half-inch diameter ball.

Propelled by the derringer's small charge, the projectile entered Lincoln's skull at its base, traveled through the brain diagonally from left to right, and lodged behind the right eye, fracturing the orbital socket. In timing his shot, Booth had planned well indeed. No one in the audience heard the report of the diminutive weapon. Even Mrs. Lincoln (seated next to her husband), Rathbone, and Clara Harris were barely startled by the dull pop. But soon a blue cloud of smoke drifted above the balcony and over the stage. A shriek shrilled from the State Box, then the sounds of a scuffle as Major Rathbone tangled with Booth, who, stabbing him in the arm and tearing a deep gash that ran from shoulder to elbow, broke free. The assassin swung his legs over the balustrade, which was festooned with a pair of flags, the Stars and Stripes below Box 8 and the banner of the Treasury Regiment below Box 7. Dressed in a stylish black suit, his tightly tailored trousers tucked into highly polished tan calf-length boots, the actor caught his right spur in the Treasury Regiment flag. As he leapt to the stage below, this caused his left foot to take the full weight of his fall. The small bone in that leg snapped on impact a few inches above the ankle.

As a dazed Harry Hawk stood, frozen, center stage, Booth raised himself from a crouch, theatrically thrust his arms into the air, and declaimed "Sic semper tyrannis!" The state motto of Virginia, it translates as, *Thus ever to tyrants.*

The shouting began. "Stop that man!" "It's Booth!" "Stop that man!" But no one did. Booth lurched, limping across the stage, and made his way to the stage door opening onto Baptist Alley. His horse was held by a dim-witted peanut vendor and Ford's Theatre factotum named Joseph "Johnny Peanuts" Burroughs, who dozed on a carpenter's bench as he held the reins. Booth struck him hard on the head with the handle of his bowie knife, snatched the reins, mounted, and rode off.

Twenty-three-year-old army surgeon Charles Augustus Leale had been seated in the first balcony, not far from the State Box. Plowing his way through a gathering crowd, he reached the wedged outer door. He was unable to force it, but the wounded Rathbone managed to remove the wedge from the other side. Leale identified himself as a surgeon and was quickly joined by a civilian physician, Dr. Albert F. A. King, and a government employee, William Kent.

Badly bleeding, Rathbone asked Leale to attend to his torn arm. The physician turned first to the president. Rathbone's blood soaked his fiancée's clothing, but Lincoln hardly bled. Leale had trouble finding the wound. He and the others gently laid the president on the floor, Leale supporting the head. When his hand came away slightly bloody, his first thought was that he had been stabbed in the back or the neck. At this point, audience member Thomas Bradford Sanders boosted Dr. Charles Sabin Taft, another army surgeon, from the orchestra level up over the balustrade and into the president's box. Behind him was Lieutenant James Bolton of the DC provost marshal's guard. Although senior in rank to Leale, Taft offered to assist *him* in locating the wound. Leale borrowed a penknife to cut away Lincoln's collar and split open his shirt and coat. Both doctors now frantically peered and felt. They found nothing.

Leale lifted Lincoln's eyelids. Noting that the pupil of the left eye was fixed and dilated, he quickly diagnosed brain injury. Running his fingers through Lincoln's hair, he at last encountered the entry wound at the back of the head. It was clotted. The surgeon removed the clot, and the comatose president, who had been struggling for breath, began to breathe more easily. But Leale turned to

Taft: "I can't save him. His wound is mortal. It is impossible for him to recover."

By now Miss Laura Keene herself appeared in the box. She had responded to a call for water, and, grabbing a pitcher from the backstage green room, she made her way up a set of back stairs. She appealed to Dr. Leale for permission to hold the president's head. "I granted the request," Leale later wrote, "and she sat on the floor of the box and held his head in her lap." (She would preserve, lifelong, the dress stained with Lincoln's blood.)

Should Lincoln be taken to the White House? No, the doctors agreed. The seven-block trip would kill him. Leale proposed instead taking his patient to the nearest available house. Assigning Dr. Taft to carry his right shoulder, Dr. King his left, and commandeering four soldiers from Thompson's Battery C, Independent Pennsylvania Artillery to assist in carrying the body, Leale cradled the head. Emerging onto Tenth Street, the desperate cortège scanned for an available house. Suddenly, one Henry S. Safford appeared, candle in hand, at the front door of number 453 (now 516) Tenth Street, the house of William Petersen, tailor.

"Bring him in here! Bring him in here!" he shouted, lifting the candle.

Safford, one of nine paying boarders who lived with the nine members of the Petersen family, led the way to a bedroom nine and a half feet wide by seventeen feet long, furnished with a dresser and two chairs in addition to the bed. It was much too short for the six-foot-four Lincoln, who was laid diagonally across it.

The doctors set about doing what little they could. Noting that the president's hands and feet were like ice, Leale ordered hot water bottles, hot blankets, and, for placement on the chest, a mustard plaster. He then summoned Mrs. Lincoln, who sat by her husband's head, kissing him, imploring him to say just one word to her. A messenger was sent to son Robert, who brought back with him Elizabeth Dixon, wife of Senator James Dixon of Connecticut. She stayed by Mary Lincoln's side throughout the long night.

The president was doomed, but when he at last appeared more comfortable, Dr. Leale wrote a note summoning Lincoln's pastor, the Reverend Phineas T. Gurley of the New York Avenue

Presbyterian Church. He also wrote to US Army Surgeon General Joseph K. Barnes, Dr. Willard Bliss (Leale's commanding officer at the Armory Square Hospital), and Dr. Robert K. Stone (the Lincoln family physician). Then he sent word to every member of the cabinet, beginning with Edwin Stanton.

Just before Leale's messenger reached Stanton, the secretary of war was preparing for bed. He was startled by a scream from his wife downstairs: "My God! Mr. Seward has been murdered!" The news had come from another messenger, who then led the secretary of war to a waiting carriage. Arriving at Seward's house, Stanton met Navy secretary Gideon Welles, who had already heard about the events at Ford's Theatre and informed Stanton that Lincoln had been shot. Stanton and Welles entered the Seward house, gasped at the carnage, but decided that Seward could recover without them and drove off to the Petersen house. There, Stanton set up the government of the United States in the rear parlor, effectively appointing himself acting president—without a thought to summoning Vice President Andrew Johnson. His first order of business was to take testimony from witnesses and to dispatch police officers and soldiers to hunt down the guilty. In fifteen minutes, he "had testimony enough down to hang John Wilkes Booth."

As Stanton coordinated the manhunt, the doctors waited and watched through the long night. Shortly before seven in the morning, Leale told Mrs. Lincoln that the end was near. She fainted at the news. Leale revived her, and recorded the words she spoke to her husband: "Love, live but one moment to speak to me once—to speak to our children."

With that, she was led back to the front parlor as Leale, Surgeon General Barnes, Dr. Stone, and Robert Lincoln—around whose shoulders Senator Charles Sumner put his arm—looked on. Leale held the president's hand, his forefinger over the pulse. When he could no longer feel a beat or detect signs of respiration, he looked toward Barnes. Barnes rose, peeled back one of Lincoln's eyelids, then put his ear to the president's chest.

"He is gone."

It was twenty-two minutes and ten seconds after seven o'clock in the morning of April 15, 1865.

Secretary of War Edwin Stanton turned to Reverend Gurley: "Doctor, will you say anything?"

Nodding his assent, Gurley knelt. In silence, all placed their hands on the bed. The reverend began to pray aloud, asking God to accept Abraham Lincoln, His humble servant, into His glorious Kingdom.

Having with Lincoln directed the cruelest, costliest war the nation ever fought, Edwin Stanton sobbed. Through tears, he spoke the words history has accepted as the epitaph of the sixteenth president: "Now he belongs to the ages."

* * *

For eleven days after Abraham Lincoln's death, John Wilkes Booth eluded the thousands of soldiers, policemen, and detectives sent in pursuit of him—the biggest manhunt in American history to that point. After midnight on April 26, a detachment of Union cavalry ran the assassin to the ground at a tobacco farm near Port Royal, Virginia. He and David Herold huddled in a barn. Herold quickly surrendered, but Booth refused. Meaning to drive him out, the troopers set the barn ablaze. Through a window, the assassin appeared, a broken-legged man leaning on a crutch, silhouetted against the flames, and cradling a carbine in his free arm. Without orders ("Providence directed me," he later said), Sergeant Boston Corbett, 16th New York Cavalry, fired his Colt .45 revolver once at the silhouette. The bullet passed through the actor's neck.

The troopers dragged Booth out of the blazing barn. The bullet having severed his spinal cord, the assassin was paralyzed. Lieutenant Colonel Everton J. Conger knelt down and put his ear close to Booth's lips. "Tell . . . my . . . Mother . . . I . . . die . . . for my country."

Booth's dying words were spoken at sunup on the day that General Kirby Smith, commanding the 50,000 men of the last Confederate army remaining in the field, surrendered to Union general Edward R. S. Canby.

Lewis Paine—who had made a bloody bungle of his attempt to stab and bludgeon Secretary Seward to death—David Herold, and

George Atzerodt were each rounded up, tried, convicted, and sentenced to hang, along with Mary Surratt, mother of another accused Booth conspirator, John Surratt, and owner of the Washington boarding house in which the Booth conspirators had hatched the plot. All except John Surratt (who was tried and acquitted in 1867) were hanged on July 7, 1865. Dr. Samuel Mudd, a Maryland physician who splinted Booth's broken leg early in his eleven-day flight from justice, was sentenced to life imprisonment, but was pardoned by President Andrew Johnson in 1868 after he saved many lives during a virulent prison yellow fever epidemic.

Secretary of State William H. Seward recovered from his grievous wounds. He continued to serve in the cabinet of President Andrew Johnson and is best remembered for purchasing Alaska from the czar of Russia in 1867, an act derided at the time as "Seward's folly."

Secretary Stanton clashed with Johnson, who tried to remove him from office. This action gave a hostile Radical Republican Congress an excuse to impeach Johnson. A single Senate vote in 1868 saved him from removal, but he served out the remainder of his term virtually without authority, chief executive in name only.

Officer John F. Parker, the Washington Metropolitan policeman who was absent from his post outside of the State Box at Ford's Theatre, was neither investigated nor reprimanded. He continued to serve the citizens of the District.

Major Henry Rathbone married his fiancée, Clara Harris. In 1894, he murdered her because (he testified) he was jealous of her love for their children. Found not guilty by reason of insanity, he was committed to an asylum, where he died in 1911. His last words were: "The man with the knife! I can't stop him! I can't stop him!"

The sanity of Mary Todd Lincoln was repeatedly questioned in the years following her husband's death, and in 1875 her only surviving son, Robert (her youngest, Tad, having died in 1871), persuaded a judge to commit her to a private sanatorium. Early the following year, another judge reversed the commitment. Released, the president's widow never lived down the public humiliation. She died in 1882 and was buried beside her husband at Oak Ridge Cemetery in Springfield, Illinois.

* * *

A few historians believe Booth had acted on secret Confederate orders. More likely, the assassination was a self-appointed mission to avenge the South. But it was the people of the South, white and black alike, who suffered most bitterly in consequence of the crime.

It was thanks to Lincoln that the North had fought the Civil War to its bloody, bitter end: the total surrender of the Confederacy and the abolition of slavery forever. Yet it was also Lincoln who, in his Second Inaugural Address, admonished his fellow citizens to act with "malice toward none, with charity for all . . . to finish the work we are in, to bind up the nation's wounds, to care for him who shall have borne the battle and for his widow and his orphan, to do all which may achieve and cherish a just and a lasting peace among ourselves and with all nations."

Had Lincoln lived, there is every indication that he would have moved heaven and earth to hasten the healing of a truly restored Union. But he was dead, and a vengeful Congress found within itself little charity and much malice. Reconstruction, the subject of Lincoln's final Cabinet meeting, became an instrument for the punishment, humiliation, and economic oppression of the former Confederacy. On account of it, the South, and in particular the black South, would suffer throughout the nineteenth century and well into the twentieth. The shooting ended, but a mutual regional resentment and mistrust smoldered on, long after Appomattox.

10

July 21, 1861

The Rebels Win at Bull Run

Why it's significant. The victory of Confederate forces at Bull Run (Manassas, Virginia) on July 21, 1861, against a numerically superior Union force revealed not only the depth of the South's resolve to win its independence from the United States but further suggested that its military, created from scratch, might well have the strategic and tactical skill to achieve this goal. The Union defeat at once shook the North out of its complacency, moved President Lincoln to lead the creation of a military machine unprecedented in North America, and began to convince both sides that the Civil War would be a long, costly, and bitter struggle.

WITH ULYSSES SIMPSON Grant, William Tecumseh Sherman would prove himself one of the fiercest and most efficient of the Union's warriors. No one, however, could have predicted this on Christmas Eve 1860, when he shared a collegial dinner with the professor of classics at the brand-new Louisiana State Seminary of Learning & Military Academy, of which Sherman was the first superintendent. He had taken the job in Pineville, Louisiana, because he had given up on the army as a dead-end career and had failed everything else he tried. Like many West Point alumni (he was Class of 1840), Sherman served in the US-Mexican War (1846–1848), but, unlike them, had seen no combat, being assigned instead to dull administrative duties in California. In the 1850s, he tried his hand at banking in San Francisco and failed, along with his bank. He turned next to the law among other enterprises and failed as well at these. In 1859, thanks to his military experience, he was hired by the academy.

His meal was interrupted by the news that South Carolina had just seceded from the Union, the first state of eleven to do so. Sherman stunned his dinner companion by declaring, "This country will be drenched in blood, and God only knows how it will end. It is all folly, madness, a crime against civilization!" Fixing his somewhat wild eyes on the classicist, Sherman warned: "You people"—meaning the people of the South—"speak so lightly of war; you don't know what you're talking about. War is a terrible thing!"

In truth, he could have said the same about the people of the North. For that matter, since he himself had yet to participate in major combat, much the same might have been said about him. Nobody in 1860 America had an inkling of the horror of all-out war on a mass scale. The United States had never experienced it, not against Mexico in 1846–1848 and not against the British in the War of 1812 or the Revolution in 1775–1783. But what he said next did apply more exclusively to the South, and it expressed the attitude of the North perfectly:

> Besides, where are your men and appliances of war . . . ? The North can make a steam engine, locomotive or railway car; hardly a yard of cloth or a pair of shoes can you make. You are rushing into war with one of the most powerful, ingeniously mechanical and determined people on earth—right at your doors. You are bound to fail. Only in your spirit and determination are you prepared for war. In all else you are totally unprepared, with a bad cause to start with. At first you will make headway, but as your limited resources begin to fail, shut out from the markets of Europe as you will be, your cause will begin to wane. If your people will but stop and think, they must see that in the end you will surely fail.

In 1860, most Northerners were confident that a Southern bid for independence was doomed to fail, to fail quickly, and to fail with little cost to the rest of the nation.

Sherman waited until January 18, 1861, to formally resign from the academy, though it took him another month to arrange his affairs and those of the institution before he actually departed. During this interval, he wrote to his brother John, a senator from Ohio, for advice on his next move. Senator Sherman advised him to call on Abraham Lincoln, inaugurated on March 4 as the sixteenth president, and offer him his services in the Union army.

What Sherman saw in Washington set him back on his heels. The capital, though adjacent to the section of the nation even then rapidly slipping away, appeared like anything but a city on the brink of war. No great armies were assembling, and people went about their business in the same sleepy way they always had. Virginia had not yet seceded when Sherman arrived in DC, but was expected to do so any day. That would instantly put a hostile Confederacy on Washington's doorstep, and yet the city's defenses consisted of just one hundred regular army troops, most of them accustomed to military life behind a desk rather than a musket. Another 300 or 400 marines were quartered in the old barracks at the corner of Eighth and I Streets. In addition, a handful of privately organized local militia companies were scattered throughout the town, but these were more in the nature of social clubs than practical military units.

Chagrined though he was, Sherman met with his brother, who took him to the White House. As Sherman recalled in his postwar *Memoirs,* the senator introduced him to Lincoln as a West Point officer who had just resigned from a post in the South.

"Ah," Lincoln acknowledged matter-of-factly, "how are they getting along down there?"

Taken aback by the president's bantering tone, Sherman replied acidly: "They think they are getting along swimmingly." Then he added a warning: "They are preparing for war."

"Oh, well, I guess we'll manage to keep house."

Sherman confessed in his *Memoirs* to being utterly "silenced" by this comeback. He said no more to the president and departed with his brother as abruptly as courtesy allowed. Once outside the

White House, he exploded to John Sherman: "You have got things in a hell of a fix and you may get them out as best you can." With that, William Tecumseh Sherman accepted an appointment as president—of a St. Louis streetcar company.

On April 17, the Virginia legislature finally voted to secede, and the Northern public, politicians, and press clamored loudly for President Lincoln to invade the South and give the rebels the come-uppance they so richly deserved. Like Sherman, most Northerners were aware of the economic and industrial weakness of the South. Unlike Sherman, however, they overwhelmingly believed that it would be no great task to crush the rebellion with a blow or two, once and for all. Two days earlier, on April 15, after the fall of Fort Sumter, Lincoln had called for 75,000 three-month volunteers. Lincoln was pressed from all quarters to make decisive use of them before their enlistment terms expired.

Winfield Scott, the aged and obese general-in-chief of the army, believed the raw recruits who had answered the president's call for volunteers would not be ready for a major battle for some time. His first war had been the War of 1812, and it had taught him a bitter lesson about the unreliability of militiamen—which, practically speaking, was what the current crop of volunteers were. While he understood the urge to invade the Confederacy and take Richmond, he counseled against it, arguing that even if the currently available troops managed to take Richmond, the Confederates would still hold all their most important military assets and would have plenty of room to maneuver and remain on the defensive. Taking Richmond, he said, would not mean a quick end to the war. On the contrary, a strategy that depended on capturing that city would require years to execute. Scott proposed instead to outflank the Confederate forces. The first step would be to impose a naval blockade of all Southern harbors. More troops would be needed. Simultaneously with the naval blockade, he proposed deploying a force of about 100,000, not against Richmond directly, and not even to fight elsewhere in the eastern portion of the Confederacy. While maintaining an army sufficient to defend Washington and the rest of the North against Confederate attack, Scott wanted to send the 100,000-man offensive force on an overland course paralleling the Mississippi River to fight along that river in concert with a great riverine naval flotilla (yet to be built). Scott believed the operation could begin by early November 1861 and would, in the space of a year, penetrate from Cairo, Illinois, in the North to the mouth of the Mississippi at New Orleans in the South, cutting the Confederacy in half, stopping most of its shipping, and bringing about the collapse of the rebellion within a year. It was a version of the strategy by which he had led the US Army to victory against Mexico some fifteen years earlier. It consisted of seizing control of the key strategic places on which the enemy, both civilian and military, depended.

When members of Lincoln's cabinet objected on the grounds that the American people would never stand for such an inglorious approach to rebellion—a delay in acting followed by the most roundabout action—Scott agreed that the strategy would be unpopular. He pointed out, however, that, throughout history, almost every plan that involved outflanking the enemy army and attacking it from the rear produced victory. He did not address the more serious problem with what the press would soon mock as "Scott's Anaconda," a great snake that was supposed to constrict the South. The US Navy had fewer than forty warships. Not only would it need several hundred to effectively blockade some 2,500 miles of Southern seacoast, a whole new class of shallow-draft ironclad gunboat would have to be innovated, designed, and built to operate on the shallow Mississippi for the riverine portion of the operation.

It was President Lincoln who had the final word and made the final decision. He authorized the blockade. Navy ships and revenue cutters would attempt to interdict Southern trade. But Lincoln would not authorize a major offensive in the Western and Trans-Mississippi Theaters at the expense of offensive action in the Eastern Theater. The "Western Theater" was somewhat misleadingly named, since it encompassed the area west of the Appalachians but east of the Mississippi River, which included all of the southeast except Virginia. The Trans-Mississippi Theater included Missouri, Arkansas, and Louisiana, as well as other areas west of these. The Eastern Theater, which consisted of Virginia (and, after 1863, West Virginia), Maryland, and Pennsylvania, was nearest to where most Americans lived, including those in loyal states. The president believed that the people would simply never stand for deferring action in the Eastern

Theater and that the war effort would suffer a blow to morale from which it could not recover.

Having made his decision to conduct an immediate offensive against Virginia, Lincoln had only to glance at a map to see that Manassas Junction on the banks of Bull Run, thirty miles southwest of Washington, was a likely objective to attack and seize. Two important Southern railroads, the Manassas Gap and the Orange & Alexandria, crossed here. Moreover, the Manassas Gap currently split the Confederate army in half, 11,000 troops under Joseph E. Johnston were in the Shenandoah Valley and 22,000, commanded by P. G. T. Beauregard, were concentrated west of them at Manassas, Centreville, and Fairfax Court House. Thus divided, the Confederates were vulnerable to defeat in detail—provided the Union forces made haste to attack and prevented their consolidation.

Major General Irvin McDowell, US Military Academy Class of 1838, had a reputation as a highly competent staff officer, and it was in this capacity that Scott had come to know and admire him. Even though he had no experience as a combat leader—he was aide-de-camp to Brigadier General John E. Wool during the US-Mexican War—Scott recommended him to lead the offensive Lincoln demanded. His force consisted of 35,000 troops, the vast majority the brand-new volunteers in whom Scott had such little faith. While McDowell led these men against Beauregard, another force, 18,000 men at the head of the Shenandoah Valley under Major General Robert Patterson, would deal with Johnston's 11,000 and prevent their linking up with Beauregard's command. Thus, on both fronts, Union forces outnumbered Confederate—an advantage that would hold as long as the two Southern armies were not allowed to join forces.

Per Lincoln's direct order, McDowell led his army south out of Washington on July 16. His plan was to move against Centreville and then advance to Manassas Junction. Here, he would attack and sever the rail line that connected the Shenandoah Valley—and Johnston's army—with Beauregard's. To take the two objectives, McDowell relied on Patterson to hold Johnston, to block him, and to pin him down.

At first, the Union forces made good progress—though McDowell's undisciplined troops often behaved as if the march were a summer outing rather than a deadly serious military expedition. Men would frequently fall out of line to pick blackberries along the way. Civilians from Washington trailed the march, hoping to get an entertaining glimpse of combat. Some even brought picnic supplies. On July 17, Beauregard telegraphed President Jefferson Davis that "the enemy have assailed my outposts in heavy force" and that he had been compelled to fall back from Centreville toward Bull Run. Beauregard also sent another telegram, this one to Joe Johnston, telling him that McDowell was advancing and fighting had begun. Johnston saw that Patterson was making no advance toward him. The Union commander's evident absence of initiative was an opportunity Johnston jumped at. He replied to Beauregard's message, telling him that he would transport his troops by train to Manassas. He was convinced that Patterson presented no threat.

On July 18, Union Brigadier General Daniel Tyler marched through Centreville, from which Beauregard had withdrawn. McDowell had ordered him to do no more than this, but Tyler took it upon himself to engage Confederate forces at Blackburn's Ford, due south of Centreville. Here, troops under Confederate Major General James Longstreet lay in ambush. The resulting skirmish stopped Tyler cold, though it did not produce heavy casualties. What the attack did do, however, is persuade McDowell to avoid engaging Longstreet's large force at Blackburn's Ford. He changed course, making a sharp turn to the west, and advanced toward Sudley Ford, where he intended to cross Bull Run well beyond the Confederate left flank. If he could make a crossing here, he could then wheel around to attack Beauregard from behind. On paper, it was a very reasonable plan; in reality, however, it required a great deal of marching, maneuvering, and speed, which his ill-disciplined troops were not entirely up to.

While the main portion of his army was concentrated in what was now a flanking column, McDowell tasked other detachments to make diversionary "demonstrations"—shows of force intended to misdirect the enemy—at Blackburn's Ford and Stone Bridge. Unknown to McDowell, however, Johnston had given Patterson the slip and telegraphed Beauregard that he was en route by rail. This maneuver made military history as the first time—anywhere in the world—troops were transported by train directly into battle. The Civil War would emerge as a war of an industrial age.

At this point, the Confederate strategy called for Beauregard to pin down McDowell's demonstration at Blackburn's Ford while Johnston's forces arrived and began maneuvering around the Union right flank. In effect, the Confederates would turn McDowell's demonstration against his own forces, distracting them from the all-important movement of Johnston's 11,000 reinforcements.

Johnston's men began arriving at Manassas Junction on July 19, with the commanding officer himself joining them on July 20. Now that the Confederate forces had consolidated, it became imperative for Johnston and Beauregard to counterattack McDowell quickly. The two Confederates agreed that, sooner or later, Patterson would realize that Johnston's army had evaded him. Once that epiphany struck, he would link up with McDowell, and the numerical superiority the Confederates currently enjoyed would evaporate in the blink of an eye. Accordingly, Beauregard and Johnston thought better of the original plan, by which Johnston was going to march around the Union flank. This would take far too much time, they decided. The imperative was to strike *now*, before Patterson arrived. Instead of attacking, therefore, the combined Confederate force would concentrate at Blackburn's Ford and wait for McDowell to attack, knowing that he was not expecting the presence of Johnston. When the attack came, Johnston and Beauregard would overwhelm and destroy it. Then Johnston would send his troops across Bull Run and advance to Centreville. This would block McDowell's line of retreat. Having destroyed McDowell's *attack*, the combined Confederate forces would aim to destroy McDowell's *army*. This sequence would constitute the First Battle of Bull Run proper.

Early on the morning of July 21, Johnston moved two brigades toward his left to shore up that position. One brigade was commanded by South Carolina's Barnard Bee, the other by Virginia's Thomas J. Jackson. While this was taking place on the Confederate side, McDowell's troops began to move into their positions for battle. At 6 a.m., Tyler's soldiers descended from the east to attack Stone Bridge. It was a demonstration designed to draw and hold Confederate attention while McDowell's main flanking column continued its advance on Sudley Ford, where they planned to cross Bull Run in order to flank the Confederates and, ultimately, attack from the rear.

At Stone Bridge, Confederate Colonel Nathan Evans—nick-named "Shanks" by his West Point classmates on account of his long, spindly legs—hid most of his command, openly deploying only pickets to fire on the first arrivals from Tyler's contingent. From either bank, the two sides traded shots across Bull Run. In the meantime, at nine o'clock, a Confederate signal officer, E. Porter Alexander, spotted McDowell's flanking column crossing Sudley Ford. Using "wigwag" signals (handheld flag signaling that employed a Morse-like code), he warned Shanks Evans that he was being "turned" on his left—in other words, that he was about to be attacked on his vulnerable flank. This was the battle's second military first; while Johnson's arrival by train was the first-ever instance of troops being transported directly into battle via rail, Alexander's warning was the first use of wigwag signaling in combat. It would eventually become a mainstay of the Civil War and would be used in future combat prior to the development of field telephones and portable radio communication.

Alexander's signal did not come a moment too soon. Evans immediately grasped that he was in danger of being rolled up, and he immediately ordered most of his men to block the advance of McDowell's flanking column. This left very few of his troops to hold Tyler at bay, but the danger from McDowell's column was both imminent and great. Evans commanded but a single brigade. The advancing flanking column consisted of two entire divisions. Deter-mined to make the best of a precarious situation, Evans deployed his men on the high ground, the slopes of Matthews Hill.

In the tradition of classic commanders, Brigadier General Barnard Bee followed the sound of the guns into the heart of the battle. Hearing firing early in the day, he led his brigade, in con-cert with Francis Bartow's brigade, toward the Confederate left. The two brigades marched up Henry House Hill, high ground east of Matthews Hill, and there encountered the head end of the Union flanking column, led by Ambrose E. Burnside. It was engaged in an armed exchange with Evans's line. Bee and Bartow arrived just as that line was beginning to break under pressure from Burnside. Bee and Bartow now advanced from Henry House Hill to Matthews Hill in an effort to take the pressure off Evans's beleaguered line. This transformed the exchange into a slugging match, and the arrival of a fresh Union brigade under Colonel William T. Sherman tipped the balance toward the Union. The Confederates began to retreat from Matthews Hill.

Suddenly, it looked as if the battle and the day would go to McDowell. Survivors from three Confederate brigades poured down Matthews Hill and retreated eastward. Responding rapidly to this development, Johnston and Beauregard bolstered the Confederate defensive position by sending more troops to the left to resist the Union onslaught. McDowell's correct move would have been to pursue the retreating brigades. Any military formation is most vulnerable in retreat. For unknown reasons, however, McDowell held his men back, declining to give chase. This gave Colonel Thomas J. Jackson the opening he needed to form up a new defensive line along Henry House Hill. Seeing this, Barnard Bee sought to rally his faltering brigade on Jackson. He called out to his men, "There's Jackson, standing like a stone wall. Rally to the Virginians!" Bee would not survive the battle that day, but Jackson would enter history as "Stonewall."

Henry House Hill became the focal point of an increasingly intense battle. Onto this prominence, each side sent more troops. The combat became chaotic, and since neither side had yet standardized the familiar Union blue uniforms versus Confederate gray, friendly fire was a major killer on both sides. It was in just such friendly fire exchanges that both generals Bee and Bartow were killed. Nevertheless, thanks to the timely arrival of Stonewall Jackson, the Confederates reached the verge of triumph at Henry House Hill. McDowell responded by advancing against Chinn Ridge, a high-ground position southwest of Henry House Hill. His hope was to flank the Confederate position, but since this was the obvious thing to do, the Confederates anticipated the move and preempted it. Arnold Elzey and Jubal A. Early took up blocking positions that arrested the Union advance on Chinn Ridge.

Checked in his attempt to flank Henry House Hill, McDowell decided he was out of options and ordered a withdrawal. He summoned his Regulars—his most disciplined soldiers—to cover the general retreat of the Union army.

All began as well as could be expected until some soldiers started yelling that they were about to be attacked by Confederate cavalry. Exhausted and dispirited, McDowell's troops panicked, and what had begun as an orderly withdrawal dissolved into a rout. In reality, Beauregard and Johnston had little available in the way of cavalry. They used what they had to harass the stricken Union troops, but they could do little material damage. Nevertheless, the emotional toll was heavy. By the time the Union troops reached Centreville, they constituted a broken army. McDowell had planned to regroup, but, recognizing that his command had crumbled, he decided to continue the withdrawal—all the way to Washington, DC. Popular myth portrays this second phase of the retreat as another rout. It was, in fact, orderly. But the sight of Union soldiers returning in something very like shame was shocking to onlookers who had expected to cheer a triumph. Suddenly, the reality of the Civil War made itself known in the capital.

The people who had so imperiously demanded that Lincoln crush the rebellion in its own homeland now began to understand that the Civil War would be far longer and bloodier than they had imagined. The Bull Run casualty reports confirmed this impression. The Union lost 2,708 killed, wounded, or missing. On the Confederate side, casualties were lighter—but still shocking in a nation that had never fought so massively destructive a battle: 1,982 Confederates were killed, wounded, or missing. The First Battle of Bull Run was the first major battle of the Civil War, the first major Union defeat, and, up to that time, the deadliest battle in US history. As a result, President Lincoln replaced Irvin McDowell with a general who had just won victories in western Virginia (today the state of West Virginia). They were relatively minor triumphs, to be sure, but they were wins nonetheless, and their author was a dashing figure named George Brinton McClellan. He took command of the veterans of Bull Run on July 26 and, in obedience to the president's orders, began to build a new army, larger than any that had ever marched and fought in North America. It would be called the Army of the Potomac.

11

June 1, 1862

Lee Rises to Top Command in the Confederacy

Why it's significant: In the title to his 1974 biography of George Washington, historian James Thomas Flexner bestowed on his subject the epithet that most adequately describes his significance to the birth of the United States: *The Indispensable Man.* When it comes to the military history of the Confederacy, this very tag best suits Robert E. Lee. By installing Lee as the principal commander of Confederate forces, Jefferson Davis gave the Southern cause a general who remains among the most universally admired of history's "great captains." During the war, the people of the South came to idolize him, while those of the North—especially in the Union army—paid him ungrudging respect. A master of battlefield topography and a bold tactical innovator, he created the only strategy that had any chance of producing victory: break the Northern people's support for the war with a relentless series of quick offensive blows that would force Union leaders to negotiate a peace favorable to the Confederacy. In this purpose, Lee ultimately failed, but when he judged that the time for surrender had finally come, Lee revealed another dimension of the qualities that made him the indispensable man. The force of his character helped ensure that the Confederates, having laid down their arms, did not take them up again for the kind of endless guerrilla struggle into which so many of history's civil wars inexorably degenerate.

HENRY LEE III left the practice of law at the outbreak of the American Revolution, was elected captain of a unit of Virginia dragoons, promoted to major in Washington's Continental Army, and earned renown as commander of Lee's Legion, a mixed cavalry-infantry unit, made up of highly mobile light troops, capable of guerrilla warfare as well as the most disciplined mobile warfare. "Light-Horse Harry" Lee—as he came to be called—emerged from the American Revolution as one of its most universally admired military figures, a hero given a gold medal by the Continental Congress, who went on to serve as governor of Virginia and US representative from the state's 19th district. This was the glorious and gloried father of Robert Edward Lee.

By the time Robert came into the world in 1807, the Lees' corner of that world was in steep decline. Light-Horse Harry's plantation house, Stratford Hall, in Westmoreland, was no longer a magnificent showplace, and the house, the surrounding plantation, and the Lee slaves were in hock to myriad creditors. Nothing, it seemed, could stem the outflow of cash. In 1810, the hero of the Revolution was bundled off to debtors' prison for a full year, and the rest of the family left Stratford for humbler quarters in Alexandria. When it looked as if circumstances could not possibly get worse, they did. On July 27, 1812, Baltimore newspaper editor Alexander Contee Hanson, a vigorous opponent of the War of 1812, was set upon by an angry mob. His friend Light-Horse Harry sprang to the rescue, waded into the melee, and was gravely injured. He tried to recover in the bosom of his family, but could not, and so, in 1813, set sail for the West Indies, where he lived apart from his wife and children until 1818. In that year, he embarked for home, but died, aged sixty-two, on Cumberland Island, Georgia, before he could reach Virginia.

The absence of husband and father had left the family even worse off financially than it had been, and Light-Horse Harry's death meant that they were quite frankly poor. It fell to Robert to look after his ailing, aging mother. But if he was at all resentful, he never let on. With his bankrupt father gone, first to the West Indies and then to the grave, young Robert filled the void with the legend. Light-Horse Harry became in his imagination the ideal Virginian, and Virginia became Robert's nation.

Robert E. Lee grew determined both to live up to his father's legend and to redeem the man's living memory. He secured nomination to the US Military Academy at West Point in 1825 and, over the next four years, made himself an academy legend. By the end of his plebe year, he was a cadet sergeant, an achievement literally unheard of at the time. By graduation, he stood second in his class but—and of this he was proudest—he had managed to earn not a single demerit in four years. He was an officer without blemish.

The best cadets were always routed into the Corps of Engineers, not only the most demanding army branch but, in an era when the mission of the United States Army was mainly to defend against invasion by sea, arguably the most important. The engineers designed and built seacoast forts, and Lee was assigned to oversee the laying of the foundation of Fort Pulaski on Cockspur Island, Georgia, and to work on Fort Calhoun and Fort Monroe— the "Gibraltar of the Chesapeake." While assigned to Fort Monroe, he began his courtship of Mary Anna Randolph Custis, daughter of George Washington Parke Custis, Martha Custis Washington's son, whom George Washington had adopted. They wed in 1831, a marriage of Virginia royalty.

Lee was a truly promising young officer. But there were any number of promising young officers in the American military, who generally struggled financially when there were no wars to fight. West Point graduates of Lee's vintage typically served for a time before resigning their commissions in order to pursue some more profitable civilian enterprise. For the army at peace could offer very little. Lee was an exception. As an engineer in a time of national expansion, he had much to do. He directed the survey of the Ohio-Michigan state line, and he drew up a successful plan to arrest the Mississippi River's movement away from the St. Louis levees. By this, he saved the river economy on which the city depended. He went on to other major civil engineering projects, which earned him acclaim and revealed a genius for strategic thinking. It was in 1842, while serving as post engineer at Fort Hamilton, in the Bay Ridge section of Brooklyn, that Captain Lee met Lieutenant Thomas J. Jackson, who, as Stonewall Jackson, was destined to become Lee's

Senator Charles Sumner, as photographed by Mathew Brady. *Library of Congress*

Abraham Lincoln's first inauguration, March 4, 1861. Lincoln is barely visible under the wooden canopy. *Library of Congress*

The Sylvester Rawding family's house was typical of the sod houses erected by homesteaders on the treeless Great Plains. This photograph was made by Solomon D. Butcher in 1886. *Wikimedia*

An ornamental print of the Emancipation Proclamation, published by R. A. Dimmock of New York City in 1864. *Wikimedia*

General Pierre Gustave Toutant-Beauregard, first general officer in the Confederate service and the commanding officer at the Battle of Fort Sumter. *National Archives and Records Administration*

The Wilmer McLean House, Appomattox Court House, Virginia, site of Lee's surrender on April 9, 1865. *Library of Congress*

President Abraham Lincoln at the dedication to the Soldiers' National Cemetery, Gettysburg, Pennsylvania, November 19, 1863. The president is visible slightly left of center, behind the blurred mass of people, facing the camera, head slightly down and tilted to his right. *Library of Congress*

Abraham Lincoln delivers his second inaugural address, March 4, 1865. He stands, bare-headed, before a small white table, speech in hand. *Architect of the United States Capitol*

The New York Draft Riot. Illustration from *Harper's Weekly* titled "The Rioters Burning and Sacking the Colored Orphan Asylum." *Wikimedia*

John Wilkes Booth, assassin of Abraham Lincoln. *Library of Congress*

Major General Irvin McDowell, defeated at the First Battle of Bull Run. *Library of Congress*

Robert E. Lee, commanding general of the Army of Northern Virginia. *Library of Congress*

"Whistling Dick," a Confederate eighteen-pounder, formed part of the defenses of Vicksburg, Mississippi. A projectile from this gun set USS *Cincinnati* aflame on May 28, 1863, sinking it. *Wikimedia*

Lieutenant General Ulysses S. Grant at Cold Harbor during the brutal Overland Campaign. Photograph by Edgar Guy Fawx. *Library of Congress*

Battle of Shiloh, American Civil War, a chromolithograph published by Louis Prang and Company, New York City, 1888, from a painting by Thure de Thulstrup (1848-1930). *Wikimedia*

A Mathew Brady photograph of the battlefield at Bull Run following the Second Battle of Bull Run, August 28-30, 1862. *National Archives and Records Administration*

Ambrose Burnside as photographed by Mathew Brady. *National Archives and Records Administration*

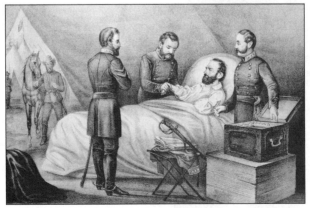

The *Death of Stonewall Jackson* as depicted in a Currier & Ives print. *Library of Congress*

John Brown, photographed in Kansas, about 1856. *Wikimedia*

Union infantryman in a Hardee hat. *Library of Congress.*

John L. Worden, commanding officer of USS *Monitor. Library of Congress*

"right arm" in the victory that has been called his military master-piece, the Battle of Chancellorsville (April 30-May 6, 1863).

Lee could justifiably take great satisfaction in his achievements as an engineer, but, with a heart and mind always dedicated to his father, he longed for glorious combat. Opportunity approached in the spring of 1846 when Major General Winfield Scott named him to his staff during the US-Mexican War (1846–1848). As part of the most ambitious military campaign the US Army had ever attempted up to this point in its history, Lee's staff service was no cushy rear-echelon job. As an engineer officer, he led topographical reconnaissance in advance of Scott's army as it invaded Mexico, bound for Mexico City following an amphibious assault (the first in US Army history) on Veracruz. Lee's mission was to determine the most advantageous routes of inland march and attack, as well as the best schemes for positioning artillery and field fortifications. There were no accurate maps to work from; therefore, there was no substitute for endless riding far in advance of the main columns. The hazard was extreme. Lee embraced it, and throughout the long march from Veracruz to the Mexican capital, it was Robert E. Lee who essentially commanded—and often personally carried out—the most important reconnaissance missions. At Cerro Gordo (April 18, 1847) and Chapultepec (September 12–13, 1847), his battle intel-ligence enabled Scott to plot overwhelmingly effective flanking attacks executed through terrain so rugged that the Mexican com-manders had left them undefended on the assumption that no army could negotiate such ground.

For gallantry, Lee was breveted to the rank of major after Cerro Gordo. He fought at Contreras (August 19–20, 1847) and Churu-busco (August 20, 1847) after this and received a brevet to lieutenant colonel. Wounded—though not seriously—at Chapultepec (Sep-tember 12–13, 1847) in the assault on Mexico City, Lee was brevet-ted to colonel. It brought as well high praise from fellow Virginian Winfield Scott, who called Lee the "very best soldier I ever saw in the field." When the Civil War erupted, Scott, as general-in-chief-of the US Army, tapped Lee to assume field command of Union forces. Lee not only turned him down, but resigned his commission, writing to General Scott on April 20, 1861, of his indebtedness to him for "uniform kindness & consideration" and promising to "carry with me to the grave the most grateful recollections of your kind consideration, & your name & fame," but expressing his own desire "never . . . again to draw my sword . . . [s]ave in the defence of my native State."

The US-Mexican War gave Lee and a generation of American military officers their first experience of battle against a large opposing army. Lee took more away from the experience than most. He honed an already acute sense of how "the ground"—landscape, topography—shapes battle. This was essential to his tactical genius. He also repeatedly saw that frontal attacks, when victoriously executed, could be overwhelmingly effective. Perhaps he called upon the memory of such attacks when he proposed a frontal infantry assault over nearly a mile of open fields against well-defended Union positions on Cemetery Ridge on the third day of the Battle of Gettysburg (July 3, 1863). "Pickett's Charge" would prove catastrophic for the Army of Northern Virginia and, ultimately, the Confederacy.

It is also likely that an extended experience of war during 1846–1848 made the peacetime army unappealing to Lee. He accepted appointment as superintendent of West Point in 1852 and performed brilliantly in the job, but jumped at the opportunity that President Franklin Pierce's secretary of war, future Confederate president Jefferson Davis, gave him in 1855 to serve as second in command of the 2nd US Cavalry Regiment in Apache and Comanche territory in Texas. His commanding officer was regimental Colonel Albert Sidney Johnston, who would become one of the early generals of the Provisional Confederate army.

At between 8,000 and 16,000 officers and men, the pre-Civil War US Army was an intimate band of brothers, and when Lee experienced a family emergency—the death in 1857 of his father-in-law, George Washington Parke Custis—he was readily granted leave to sort out a complex will and an estate encumbered by massive debts. At this time, Lee contemplated resigning his commission to try to save the estate, Arlington, and care for his wife, who was suffering from severe arthritis. But he could never quite bring himself to leave the army. Then, on October 16, 1859, radical abolitionist John Brown raided the federal arsenal and armory at Harpers Ferry,

Virginia (today West Virginia), taking about sixty townspeople hostage, among them the great-grandnephew of George Washington. Lee was assigned to lead an ad hoc assemblage of Maryland and Virginia militiamen and a Washington-based detachment of US Marines to recover the armory and arsenal and to rescue the hostages. Lee carried out his mission successfully (see Chapter 19) and thus played a role in an incident often seen as a prelude to the Civil War. He himself saw it only as the "attempt of a fanatic or madman" to set off a slave rebellion. But the nation rolled on toward dissolution. On February 1, 1861, shortly after Texas seceded from the Union, Brevet Major General David E. Twiggs, commanding officer of the Department of Texas, summarily surrendered his entire US Army command to Confederate authorities, resigned his commission, and accepted a commission as a general officer in the Confederate army. Now Lee paid attention. He immediately left Arlington for Washington. There he was promoted to full colonel in the regular army and assigned to command the 1st Cavalry on March 28, 1861.

That promotion had come at the urging of Winfield Scott, who also advised President Lincoln of his intention to give Lee the top field command of US Army forces. When Lee turned him down, Scott was both appalled and astonished. He had heard from others that Lee scorned the very idea of secession and thought the notion of a "Confederacy" ludicrous. It is unclear whether Scott knew that Lee had declared that he would "never bear arms against the Union" while simultaneously speculating that it might become "necessary for me to carry a musket in the defense of my native state, Virginia, in which case I shall not prove recreant to my duty." Yet Scott subsequently learned that Lee, after turning down his offer of command of Union forces in the field, had also deliberately ignored the offer of a commission in the Confederate army. Accordingly, Scott made a final, desperate attempt to give Lee command in the North. That offer prompted Lee's resignation, to which Scott responded that it was the "greatest mistake of [Lee's] life."

Three days after resigning his US Army commission, Lee accepted, on April 23, command of Virginia state militia forces. A short time later, he was transferred to the Provisional Army of the Confederate States as one of its first five full generals. But his maiden battle, in western Virginia (West Virginia today) was hardly impressive. His subordinates, who were state militia officers, were resistant to his authority, and the people of Virginia's western counties, who never wanted secession in the first place, were openly hostile. Nevertheless, on September 11, 1861, Lee decided to attack the Union position at Cheat Mountain, which looked down on an important turnpike as well as several mountain passes. Intelligence gathered from Union prisoners revealed that four thousand Union soldiers held the mountain, substantially outnumbering Lee's own force. The Confederate commander hesitated to attack, quite unaware that the mountain top was actually occupied by no more than 300 Union troops. His delay having lost him the advantage of surprise, Lee skirmished indecisively and then withdrew. He was denounced by the *Southern* press as "Evacuating Lee" and, even worse, "Granny Lee." Bumped from field command, he was assigned to organize the coastal defenses in the Carolinas and Georgia before President Jefferson Davis named him his personal military advisor. Davis acknowledged that Lee was unpopular with the press, but he shared the opinion of Lee's fellow officers that Lee had the makings of a great commander. Accordingly, when Joseph E. Johnston was badly wounded at the Battle of Seven Pines on June 1, 1862, Davis replaced Johnston with Lee as commanding officer of the Army of Northern Virginia.

Johnston, who enthusiastically supported Davis's choice, was widely admired, but he was committed to the defensive tactic of the strategic retreat. He met Major General George B. McClellan's Peninsula Campaign—the Union's first major offensive in southeastern Virginia—by yielding ground while claiming Union casualties. Lee believed this approach was fatal to Confederate morale, and as soon as he took command, he shocked McClellan by offering the fiercest of attacks in each of the so-called Seven Days Battles, which spanned June 25 to July 1, 1862. Lee transformed what McClellan had intended as a war-winning offensive targeting Richmond into a succession of Confederate attacks on the Army of the Potomac.

Contrary to both contemporary popular opinion and enduring myth, Lee was hardly at his tactical best in the Seven Days, but he did reveal himself as an inspiring commander with an ability to extract the utmost aggression from his men. The Battle of Oak Grove (June 25) ended inconclusively and with relatively light casualties on both sides, but it put Lee in position to seize the initiative on the following day at the Battle of Beaver Dam Creek (Battle of Mechanicsville, June 26). While Lee suffered a tactical defeat—1,484 casualties versus 361 for the Union—he set up a major strategic triumph by forcing McClellan to withdraw from the Richmond area.

The Battle of Gaines Mill (June 27) on the next day again resulted in heavier losses for Lee (7,993 killed, wounded, missing, or captured) than McClellan (6,837 killed, wounded, missing, or captured), but so unnerved the Union general that he began the retreat of the entire Army of the Potomac all the way back to his supply base on the James River. For his part, Lee was not about to let him go. He engaged portions of the withdrawing Union forces at Garnett's & Golding's Farms (June 27–28) before mounting a major attack at the Battle of Savage's Station (June 29), exacting more than a thousand casualties. By noon on June 30, most of the battered Army of the Potomac had retreated across White Oak Swamp Creek. Lee hit the main body of the army at Glendale (June 30) while his subordinate Stonewall Jackson attacked McClellan's rearguard (under Major General William B. Franklin) at White Oak Swamp (June 30). By the numbers, both engagements were inconclusive, but the humiliating "optics" were incredibly damaging to the Union and just as incredibly inspiring to the Confederacy. Lee was driving McClellan away, whipping him as a man might whip a dog.

The final battle of the Seven Days, at Malvern Hill (July 1), was evenly matched, pitting 54,000 men of the Army of the Potomac against 55,000 of the Army of Northern Virginia. Lee suffered 5,355 casualties to McClellan's 3,214, but persisted in pursuing McClellan. Concluding that McClellan was unwilling to use his army effectively against Lee, Lincoln ordered him to link up with John Pope's Army of Virginia to reinforce him at the Second Battle of Bull Run (August 28–30, 1862).

It was at this battle that Lee revealed the tactical daring absent from his action at the Seven Days. He attacked the Army of Virginia before the slow-moving McClellan arrived in to consolidate with it his Army of the Potomac. In this attack, Lee purposefully broke one of the supposedly inviolable military commandments by dividing his forces in the presence of the enemy. He sent one wing under Stonewall Jackson to attack on August 28. This deceived Pope into believing that he had Jackson exactly where *he* (Pope) wanted him. The Union general could taste victory. But, in fact, it was Jackson who was holding Pope, so that Longstreet, leading Lee's other wing, could launch a surprise counterattack on August 30. This attack, 25,000 men brought to bear all at once, was the single greatest mass attack of the Civil War, and it brought about a second Union defeat at Bull Run that was far costlier than the first. Pope lost 14,642 killed, wounded, captured, or missing. Lee lost half that number.

The Second Battle of Bull Run made Robert E. Lee the general to beat. Pope had been fired, and McClellan was recalled to lead the Army of the Potomac against the ever-aggressive Lee, who had decided to take the war to the North by invading Maryland. McClellan fought him at Antietam in that state on September 17, 1862.

At the beginning of the Seven Days, the battle line had been some six miles outside of Richmond. Three months later and thanks to Lee, it was at Antietam, just twenty miles outside of Washington. At the end of the day, McClellan had suffered heavier losses than Lee (12,410 to 10,316 killed, wounded, missing, or captured) but he had forced Lee to withdraw back into Virginia. President Lincoln used this narrow Union victory to launch his Emancipation Proclamation (Chapter 4), but, privately, he was bitterly disappointed—heartbroken, really—that McClellan had failed to pursue the retreating Lee in the way that Lee had earlier pursued the retreating McClellan.

Abraham Lincoln removed George McClellan from command of the Army of the Potomac and replaced him with Ambrose Burnside—despite Burnside's own protests that he was not up to commanding a full army. At Fredericksburg (December 11–15, 1862), Burnside proved his self-appraisal to be correct. Although substantially outnumbered (78,513 to 122,009), Lee dealt Burnside and the Army of the Potomac a catastrophic defeat, inflicting 12,653 casualties for his own losses of 4,201 killed, wounded, or missing.

Lincoln replaced Burnside with Joseph "Fighting Joe" Hooker, who proclaimed, "May God have mercy on General Lee, for I will have none." Hooker commanded an Army of the Potomac that now mustered nearly 134,000 men, whereas Lee's Army of Northern Virginia amounted to no more than 60,298. Lopsided though the numbers were, the Battle of Chancellorsville (April 30–May 6, 1863) was Lee's tactical masterpiece—arguably the tactical masterpiece of the Civil War itself. Once again, Lee divided his forces in the presence of the enemy, dispatching his cavalry to control the roads and bottle up Union reinforcements at Fredericksburg while 26,000 men under Stonewall Jackson surprised Hooker's flank even as he, Lee, personally commanded a force of 17,000 against Hooker's front. The result stunned the Union general into utter confusion. Jackson's surprise attack routed an entire corps and drove the principal portion of Hooker's army out of its well-prepared defensive positions. By May 2, the Army of the Potomac, though it outnumbered the Army of Northern Virginia two to one, had been sent into headlong retreat.

Yet Lee understood that he was in no position to bask in his triumph, great as it was. Hooker had suffered 17,287 casualties, but he himself had lost 13,303 killed, wounded, captured, or missing—all out of a much smaller force. Hooker's casualty rate was roughly 13 percent, whereas his own was a staggering 22 percent. Despite the victories he delivered, Lee was convinced that the Confederacy could not endure such attrition much longer. He therefore resolved to once again invade the North. This time, his objective was Pennsylvania. Not only did he want to raid the countryside for much-needed provisions, Lee believed a successful invasion would utterly demoralize the North and erode its will to continue the war while also opening up an avenue for an assault on Washington itself. This, he believed, would cost Lincoln reelection and bring into office a Democrat willing to conclude a negotiated end to the Civil War.

The grim fate of Lee's aspirations for the Battle of Gettysburg is one of the subjects of Chapter 4. Defeated badly here, Lee was nevertheless able to withdraw back into Virginia, his army diminished but still very much intact. He would lead it next against his most formidable adversary, Ulysses S. Grant, in the Civil War's culminating Virginia battles. In many of these engagements, Lee would, in fact, beat Grant. But, unlike the other Union opponents Lee had confronted, Grant responded to defeat not with retreat, but with continued advance toward Richmond. Each advance forced Lee to pit his dwindling Army of Northern Virginia against Grant's continually reinforced army. The Union general understood and embraced the ultimate calculus of the Civil War, which was that the North could afford to spend more lives than the South and could replenish most of its losses.

Lee's objective in the final months of the war was to make his own increasingly inevitable defeat so costly to the Union that the people of the North might demand a negotiated settlement after all. Costly he did make it, but, in the end, Robert E. Lee felt compelled to admit defeat. In this admission was perhaps the most profound and enduring significance of his elevation to top command of Confederate forces. For as he had been uncompromising in his quest for victory, so he proved equally uncompromising in his manner of surrender. He secured from Grant the best terms possible, namely the right of his men to return to their homes unmolested and without loss of honor. In return for this, he exercised his character and influence to ensure that the war would in fact end rather than devolve into a long and lawless guerrilla struggle, which is the fate of so many civil conflicts throughout history.

12

July 4, 1863

Vicksburg falls to Grant

Why it's significant: The successful conclusion to Grant's epic siege of Vicksburg, Mississippi, on July 4, 1863, secured Union control of the Mississippi River and its vast valley, cutting the Confederacy in two and effectively ending any hope for a Southern victory. With the Union triumph at Gettysburg the day before, the fall of Vicksburg was a major turning point in the war.

B Y THE TIME of the Civil War, Winfield Scott, who had begun his military career before the War of 1812 and who, more than any other American military leader, brought victory in the US-Mexican War of 1846–1848, was too old and, at considerably more than 300 pounds, much too fat to sit on a horse, let alone ride one. His corpulence and relative immobility had not extinguished his affection for ornate uniforms. His raiment was resplendent in gold leaves, massive epaulettes, and a bicorne hat that put Napoleon's in the shade. The picture *was* laughable, but, forgetting the hero of earlier days, one of the nation's truly prodigious military figures, the press saw only the gilded brass and the aging flesh. He was widely dismissed as "Old Fuss and Feathers," and his plan for victory was denounced as inglorious, even cowardly. Rather than waste lives in a fruitless offensive against Richmond, Scott proposed a naval blockade of the Atlantic and Gulf coasts and simultaneous seizure of control over Mississippi River navigation. This accomplished, he wanted to conduct an offensive not from the front but from the western flank.

Scorned in 1861, "Scott's Anaconda" (so called because the naval blockade was supposed to strangle the South in the manner of some great constrictor) was looking pretty good by 1863. With the spectacular growth of the Union navy, the blockade was inexorably throttling the South, and, while the war raged hottest near the eastern seaboard, Major General Henry Wager Halleck, the army's general in chief from July 1862 to March 1864, observed, "the opening of the Mississippi River will be to us more advantage than the capture of forty Richmonds," in effect echoing Scott's original assertion. As Ulysses S. Grant explained long after the war in his *Personal Memoirs,* the Mississippi town of "Vicksburg was the only channel . . . connecting parts of the Confederacy divided by the Mississippi. So long as it was held by the enemy, the free navigation of the river was prevented. Hence its importance."

In 1862, while the attention of most of the nation, North and South, was focused on the bloody duel between the Army of Northern Virginia and the Army of the Potomac in the southeast, Grant was taking Fort Henry on the Tennessee River (February 6, 1862) and Fort Donelson on the Cumberland (February 11–16, 1862). Confederate Major General Edmund Kirby Smith, having pulled out of Knoxville, Tennessee, invaded Kentucky in August 1862, and Confederate General Braxton Bragg and Union General Don Carlos Buell contested ground in these states. Gradually, Buell's pressure pushed the fighting farther southwest, into Mississippi. On September 19, 1862, Confederate Sterling Price suffered a sharp defeat at the hands of William S. Rosecrans, one of Grant's subordinates, at Iuka, Mississippi. Driven even farther south, Price linked up with General Earl Van Dorn to attack Corinth, Mississippi, which Rosecrans occupied. It was a brutal battle (October 3–4, 1862) between almost evenly matched forces—23,000 Federals against 22,000 Confederates—but Rosecrans, who lost 2,520 killed, wounded, missing, and captured, achieved a decisive victory, forcing Price and Van Dorn into retreat (with 4,233 casualties between them) and leaving Braxton Bragg stranded in Kentucky, cut off without hope of reinforcement. Buell struck against Bragg at the Battle of Perryville (October 8, 1862) but, even with vast numerical superiority—55,000 versus 16,000—Buell achieved no more than a costly strategic victory. The Confederates were pushed out of Kentucky, but Buell was replaced by William S. Rosecrans as commander of the Department of the Ohio.

In truth, the Union's real problem in the Western Theater was not the generals in the field, but the general behind the desk. General-in-Chief Henry Halleck was known throughout the army as "Old Brains," and it was hardly an affectionate sobriquet. A bureaucrat more than a soldier, he was more interested in occupying territory than in killing the enemy. For this reason, he broadcast his forces widely and thinly over the vast theater. Grant, in contrast, understood—and his victories at Forts Henry and Donelson proved—that success required concentration of forces for battle, one battle at a time. It wasn't that Grant was competent and Halleck not. It was that Grant's experience in the war with Mexico taught him the value of rapid movement and violent offensive, whereas Halleck, a student of the Napoleonic Wars, measured victory not by body count, but by the acquisition of ground. Halleck had about 100,000 men at his disposal in the Western Theater. Had he used these to attack the smaller Confederate forces there, he might have destroyed the Confederate military presence west of the Appalachians and thereby positioned the Union army to do what Scott had originally proposed: attack the Confederacy west to east, on its vulnerable western flank. Instead, he continued to conduct the war mainly in the southeast, with Richmond as his ultimate objective.

Subordinate to Old Brains, Grant did what he could with what he was given. Once Kentucky was secured in October 1862, he returned to his advance down the Mississippi, and that brought him up against the problem of Vicksburg. It was a fortress town, the Confederacy's "Gibraltar of the West," located on a sheer bluff overlooking the Mississippi at a sharp river bend to the southwest. Any vessels, including gunboats and transports, navigating here would have to slow down to make the turn and would therefore be fully exposed to artillery fire from the bluff. In addition to its natural defenses, Vicksburg was ringed by a six-and-a-half-mile defensive line that was a veritable catalog of nineteenth-century fortification as taught at West Point. There were field fortifications such as firing holes and trenches. Most of them were linked to built-up redoubts, which were typically constructed as crescent-shaped fortifications ("lunettes"). At wider intervals along all the defensive lines were full-scale forts: Fort Hill, Square Fort, South Fort, Stockade Redan, 3rd Louisiana Redan, and the Great Redoubt. All of the Vicksburg fortifications, big and small, were skillfully etched into the natural terrain so as to stop or slow any attacker. The slower the progress of an attack, the heavier the toll the artillery would take.

In December 1862, when Grant initiated his campaign to take Vicksburg, he had 35,000 men on hand. Reinforcements were available on short notice as well. His adversary, Confederate Lieutenant General John C. Pemberton, commanded a garrison of just 18,500. Nevertheless, they were covered by the Vicksburg defenses, so that the disparity in numbers mattered little. Grant had proven himself aggressive, both in open battle and in assault on fortifications, but he was not foolishly wedded to the frontal assault. He was willing to take casualties, but he was not willing to suffer them without the realistic prospect of positive results. Grant therefore understood that he would need to devise an alternative to a futile frontal attack. And now he revealed himself as that rarest of commanders, one who is driven by an aggressive bias for the offense, yet with a judgment tempered by patience and method. His first step was to establish a well-defended forward base at Holly Springs, Mississippi. This would serve as the rallying point for what he planned as a siege force of 40,000 troops. They would be loaded onto rail cars for transportation on the Mississippi Central Railroad right-of-way to link up 32,000 soldiers commanded by William Tecumseh Sherman, who was transporting them via river steamers.

Earl Van Dorn was not about to let Grant's build-up proceed unopposed. On December 20, he hit the encampment of the 8th Wisconsin Regiment as the Federals slept. From here, Van Dorn's raiders dashed through Holly Springs, where they put to the torch a massive stockpile of Grant's supplies. Propelled by their triumphal momentum, the Confederates hit Union outpost after outpost. While this was happening, Nathan Bedford Forrest, the fiercest Confederate cavalry commander in the Western Theater, set out to destroy as much of the Mississippi Central Railway's track as possible. His troopers managed to rip up well over sixty miles of rail. Between them, the two Confederate generals had dealt Grant a harsh rebuff. He could not tie into Sherman for an attack on the Confederate position at Chickasaw Bluffs, to the north of Vicksburg. Sherman nevertheless attempted to take his objective with what he had. It was not enough. After engaging the enemy during December 27–29, he reported to Grant: "I reached Vicksburg at the time appointed, landed, assaulted, and failed."

Determined not to be thwarted, Grant emulated Major General John Pope's bold evasion of the Confederate guns of Island No. 10 in the Mississippi (February 28-April 8, 1862). Like Vicksburg, the guns defending Island No. 10 commanded a sharp bend in the river. Pope dug a canal that cut across the bend and thus bypassed the guns. To be sure, digging a canal to avoid the Vicksburg artillery was a job on a vastly greater scale, but, if it worked, Grant could bring gunboats to bear on the town without fear of artillery counter-fire. What was supposed to be a combat expedient, however, turned into an epic engineering and construction project. In January 1863, Grant authorized work to begin on the Williams Canal across DeSoto Point on an island opposite Vicksburg. On the face of it, the project was the completion and enlargement of something that had begun in July 1862 by order of Union General Benjamin Butler but was soon abandoned. It seemed to Grant that this canal could now be completed along a course that would bypass the Vicksburg guns. This required widening the canal from a mere six feet to sixty while also dredging a foot more of depth, from six feet to seven. The work fell to Major General Sherman, and while he obeyed Grant's orders, he cordially resented the project, which he dubbed Butler's Ditch. In the event, Sherman's men did not get far. Confederate harassing artillery fire combined with torrential rains made the work impossible, and, in February, Sherman, like Butler before him, abandoned the project.

Grant did not give up on the idea of transforming the landscape in order to accomplish his mission. He ordered Brigadier General James B. McPherson to dredge a brand-new canal from the Mississippi River to Lake Providence, northwest of Vicksburg. This would allow troop transports to unload at a point from which the soldiers could get into the city. If fully completed, the canal would provide passage to Bayou Baxter and Bayou Macon, which, in turn, would allow navigation to the Tensas and Black Rivers, both of which feed into the Red River. The Red River furnished a connection with troops from the Department of the Gulf under Brigadier General Nathaniel Banks.

This, at any rate, was the plan. Remarkably enough, McPherson completed the work assigned to him on March 18, but the resulting assemblage of waterways was not uniformly navigable. In the end, only small boats of very shallow draft could negotiate the entire passage. These craft could not possibly carry the volume of troops necessary to make even the slightest strategic dent in Vicksburg.

Grant had one more string left to his bow. Even before giving up on both Butler's Ditch and the McPherson project, he had ordered his engineers to blow up a Mississippi River levee near Moon Lake (not far from Helena, Arkansas). This was some 150 miles above Vicksburg—a long way—but Grant reasoned that demolishing the levee would flood the Yazoo Pass from Yazoo City, Mississippi, to Memphis, Tennessee. The flood waters would sufficiently swell both the Coldwater and Tallahatchie rivers, rendering them navigable by troop transports, which could get onto the Yazoo River at Greenwood, Mississippi. From Greenwood, disembarked troops could ascend the bluffs northeast of Vicksburg and thereby hold the city under artillery siege. The so-called Yazoo Pass Expedition commenced promisingly enough with the demolition of the levees on February 3, 1863. The Confederates, however, who could read a map as well as Grant could, began felling trees into the rivers, creating snags that blocked the Union gunboats. By early April, Grant had been thwarted and added the Yazoo Pass Expedition to the grim litany of aborted canal projects.

A month before Grant gave up on Yazoo, the Union's Admiral David Dixon Porter had already concluded that the Yazoo Pass

Expedition was doomed. On his own initiative, he decided to essay a gunboat traversal of the Yazoo Delta via Steele's Bayou north of Vicksburg. If he could get his gunboats and troop transports to Deer Creek, they would be positioned for a flanking attack on Fort Pemberton, one of the most formidable Confederate forts, which was located at Greenwood, Mississippi. Take this fort and troops could be landed between Vicksburg and Yazoo City. The problem was that Porter's maps did not accurately reveal the hazards to navigation in the Yazoo Delta. The existing natural obstacles were multiplied and amplified by more of the Confederates' handiwork. Porter found that even his shallow-draft gunboats snagged on trees felled by Confederate soldiers. As the vessels bogged down, Confederate troops began firing from shore. Sherman rushed reinforcements to the rescue, but both he and Grant saw the handwriting on the wall. Vicksburg would not be taken via the Yazoo Delta.

Grant started yet another canal, from Duckport Landing to Walnut Bayou. He recognized that only a light, shallow craft would be able to move past Vicksburg along this canal, but he persuaded himself that he could make do. What he had not contemplated, however, was that water levels would severely shallow out in April. No vessel capable of carrying more than a handful of men at a time could use the canal, which was soon abandoned.

Ulysses S. Grant was nothing if not brutally honest with himself—at least as a rule. But he had just devoted four months to fruitless digging. In his *Private Memoirs* he made the implausible claim that the entire affair had been nothing more or less than a makework exercise intended to maintain and enforce discipline among his troops during weeks of idleness in winter and early spring.

Loath to let up the pressure in the area, Grant ordered two corps, one under McPherson, the other commanded by Sherman, to take Jackson, Mississippi, a rallying point for Confederate reinforcements. The May 14, 1863, attack succeeded, and Grant therefore ordered an attack at Champion Hill on May 16. Stunningly, McPherson met with an unanticipated level of resistance here, and while he won, he did so at the cost of nearly 2,500 casualties (to the CSA's 3,840). Halleck could not see the point of it and questioned Grant's strategy, which appeared to him nothing more than attacking whatever concentration of enemy troops happened to present itself anywhere. If asked, Grant would have admitted precisely this. His objective was to kill the enemy, and he continually invited them to present themselves for the killing. Nevertheless, everything he did was also done to advance the objective of taking Vicksburg. Key to this task was a continuous offensive. To Grant, the Vicksburg Campaign was all about giving battle at every opportunity.

Indeed, three days after Champion Hill, Grant convinced himself that he was finally in position to make an assault on Vicksburg itself. On May 19, he launched what he had sworn he would never attempt: a frontal assault on Vicksburg. The result was all too tragically predictable—a costly repulse. Three days later, he tried again and suffered an even heavier defeat, with more than 3,200 killed and wounded.

At this point, Grant reconciled himself to conducting what he knew would be a protracted siege. This is not what he wanted. Siege warfare ties up valuable manpower, even as it destroys morale, erodes the physical conditioning of troops, and, like any prolonged encampment, invites outbreaks of epidemic disease. But all of his attempts to work around Vicksburg's guns had failed, as had two frontal assaults. Siege was the third and final alternative, and so Grant ordered trenches to be dug. From the end of May through the start of July, his artillery shelled Vicksburg day and night. More than two hundred cannon and siege mortars were kept continuously active.

Vicksburg was both fortress and city. It was not only garrisoned by soldiers, but also peopled by ordinary citizens—men, women, children, the old, the infirm, and the healthy alike. They now found themselves sharing a terrible misery. As the bombardment became unendurable, the people dug caves out of the malleable yellow clay of the bluff. They devolved from surface dwellers to cave dwellers, abandoning their exposed homes to share dark, dank quarters with snakes, worms, and insects. In an effort to provide a modicum of civilized comfort, some installed a few pieces of furniture in their new earth-fast abodes. But food supplies dwindled. Dogs and rats began to appear less as pets and pests and more like food. Then, even these creatures began to disappear. "I think all the dogs and rats must be killed or starved," one woman wrote in her diary on May 28. "We don't see any more pitiful animals prowling around."

A week after this anonymous resident recorded her observation, Confederate General Pemberton sent Grant a note indicating his possible inclination to negotiate terms of surrender. When he took Fort Donelson, Grant rejected a similar offer to negotiate by stating that the only terms of surrender he would accept was unconditional surrender. From that point on, "U. S. Grant" became Unconditional Surrender Grant, and he saw no reason to depart from that policy now. His first reply, therefore, was a demand for unconditional surrender. Then he thought the better of it. Without question, Grant wanted total surrender. But there was one thing he did not want, and that was prisoners of war—30,000 of them, hungry and his to feed and guard and transport. So he sent Pemberton a second reply, this time offering him a single concession: parole. Those who surrendered would be relieved of their weapons and then released upon giving their word ("parole") that they would not take up arms again unless officially exchanged for Union POWs.

Grant's offer tipped the balance, and Pemberton surrendered his army on July 4—Independence Day. Without soldiers to defend them, the people of Vicksburg likewise gave up.

Like most victories that result from siege, this one did not feel particularly glorious to the winners. Worse, it was overshadowed in the Northern press by the Union victory, the day before, at Gettysburg. As usual, what took place in the east trumped what happened in the west. Yet while the fall of Vicksburg lacked the profound symbolic importance of Gettysburg—the ejection of Confederate forces from loyal Union land, and the defeat of the Confederacy's best by the Union's best—it was arguably of greater consequence in bringing about the decline of the Confederacy, an end to the war, and the abolition of slavery. Grant gave the Union the Mississippi River. This not only provided a major avenue of transport, both of supplies and of troops, it also gave the North control of the Confederacy's northern and western borderlands. Texas was entirely cut off, virtually excluded from any further significant role in the war. At will, the Union army could make that flanking invasion Scott had called for. In any case, the Confederacy was now contained on both the north and the west. It could do nothing but try to defend the diminishing territory it held with a dwindling body of soldiery it could neither reinforce nor replace.

Independence Day? Not for the Confederacy—and not for the people of Vicksburg, who henceforth refused to join the rest of the nation in celebration of the Fourth of July until 1945, when, with World War II victory achieved in Europe and imminent in the Pacific, the descendants of the bombardment and siege and surrender finally set off fire crackers and bottle rockets like any other American on the Fourth of July.

13

May 7, 1864

Defeated, Grant Advances

Why it's significant. After taking command as the Union's general-in-chief, Grant launched his Overland Campaign with a new strategy that was both instantly brutal and ultimately effective: force the Confederacy to choose between two non-negotiable outcomes—give up or bleed to death.

BEGINNING WITH IRVIN McDowell, the Union general who lost the First Battle of Bull Run (July 21, 1861), and continuing with George B. McClellan ("The Young Napoleon"), John Pope, Ambrose Burnside, Joseph Hooker ("Fighting Joe"), and Henry Wager Halleck ("Old Brains"), the Union's top generals were all West Point graduates and as highly qualified as it was possible to be in the nineteenth-century American military. Yet, to a man, they produced disappointing, often heartbreaking results on the field of battle. Even George Meade, under whose command the Army of the Potomac won the turning-point Battle of Gettysburg (July 1–3, 1863), let Lincoln and the Union down by failing to pursue the defeated Army of Northern Virginia in its withdrawal back to Confederate ground.

In contrast to varying degrees of failure in the Eastern Theater of the war, one general in the Western Theater was producing some remarkable results. He was Ulysses S. Grant.

For too long, hardly anybody paid attention. Halleck, his commanding officer in the Western Theater, was uncomfortable with Grant's relentlessly aggressive spirit. Halleck favored a strategy of protecting territory over killing the enemy, disdained Grant's personal appearance as insufficiently military, and was quick to give credence to unsubstantiated rumors of drunkenness. For his part and in contrast to Halleck, Grant was resolutely apolitical, which meant that he lacked the connections that advanced many other less-deserving officers.

But the most formidable obstacle to Grant's advancement was the very theater in which he achieved his successes. All eyes were on the Eastern Theater, especially Virginia. What happened in the vicinity of the Mississippi typically elicited from public and politicians little more than a nod. The one exception was Shiloh (April 6–7, 1862). While that battle (Chapter 14) ended in an important strategic victory for the Union, opening up an advance into northern Mississippi, its cost in casualties was unprecedented: more than 13,000 Union soldiers killed, wounded, captured, or missing—about one in five of the men who fought. From among a horrified public came demands that the president fire Grant. To these Lincoln responded that he *needed* Grant, needed him because "he fights." While the Northern press pointed to a 20 percent casualty rate among Union forces at Shiloh, Lincoln noted a nearly 26 percent rate among the Confederates. While the likes of McClellan and Halleck viewed strategy in the Napoleonic terms of controlling territory, Grant was killing the enemy army. Grant understood that the Union North not only possessed a stronger economy and much greater industrial capacity than the Confederate South, it also had many more people: 23 million versus 9 million in the South, of which 3.5 million were slaves. The North could make good its manpower losses. The South could not.

Still, it was not until March 9, 1864 that President Lincoln promoted Grant to lieutenant general—making him the highest-ranking officer in the US Army—and then appointed him chief of all

Union land forces. Up to this time, Lincoln had been replacing one general after another, vainly searching for the right combination of fighting spirit and strategic skill. In Grant, he finally found a military leader not with a little more of this or that, but with an entirely new approach to the war. Under Grant, the Union armies would have a single aim: destroy the Confederate armies. Yes, Grant would still attack major Southern cities, but less to simply occupy them than to deprive the Confederate army of its ability to furnish transportation and supplies. And, yes, he would resume the advance against Richmond, but less for the purpose of claiming the Confederate capital than with the objective of continually forcing Robert E. Lee to defend it and, in the process, sacrifice men he could not afford to lose.

By the time Grant was given the North's top military job, only two major Confederate armies remained on the field: the Army of Northern Virginia, commanded by Robert E. Lee, and the Army of Tennessee, under the command of Joseph E. Johnston. Kill these two armies, and the war would end. Grant had on hand two major instruments of their destruction. The first was the Army of the Potomac, and the second the Military Division of the Mississippi.

Before becoming the Union's general in chief, Grant held command of the Military Division of the Mississippi, having stepped up to the post from command the Army of the Tennessee. (Like most Union armies, it was named after the nearest river and is not to be confused with the Confederate Army of Tennessee, which, like most Confederate armies, was named after a state or region.) When he left to take command of the Division, William Tecumseh Sherman succeeded him as commanding general of the Army of the Tennessee. With Grant's appointment to the top Union command, Sherman then ascended to command of the Military Division of the Mississippi, whose main field armies were the Army of the Tennessee, the Army of the Ohio, and the Army of the Cumberland.

Sherman was every bit as aggressive as Grant, and, like him, possessed a keen faculty for cutting to the very heart of a problem. While Grant would use the Army of the Potomac, nominally commanded by George Meade, for the march against Richmond—all the while forcing repeated combat on Lee—Sherman summed up his mission in a single sentence: "I was to go for Joe Johnston." While Grant ate away at the Army of Northern Virginia, Sherman was to destroy the Army of Tennessee. As Grant fought his way toward Richmond, Sherman would follow the tracks of the Western and Atlantic Railroad to take Atlanta. Seizing this would deprive the Confederacy of its chief transportation hub, and it would certainly force Johnston to fight.

On May 4, 1864, Grant and Meade, with roughly 120,000 men of the Army of the Potomac, crossed the Rapidan River. This script had been followed before, early in the war, by George Brinton McClellan. Unlike him, however, Grant was not plagued by a morbid fear of being outnumbered. He had accurate intelligence, which told him that Lee could no longer field more than 65,000 men. A warrior at heart, Grant was confident in his ability to defeat Lee, whom he outnumbered nearly two to one. His intention, moreover, was to choose the battle ground. He wanted to force Lee into the open, to expose the Army of Northern Virginia and to give the Army of the Potomac vast room for maneuver and its artillery clear fields of fire. The superiority of Union artillery was one of the North's great advantages over the military of the depleted Confederacy.

Grant, to be sure, was not McClellan. But Lee was still Lee—a superb tactician when he was at his best and, even more, a commander committed to ceding nothing. He immediately understood that Grant meant to manipulate him into a position that favored the Union. Lee refused to be pushed. With numerically inferior forces and confronted by an invading army, a conventional commander would have dug in to make a stand in a static defense. Lee instead went on the attack, hurling his outnumbered army against the approaching columns. He hit Grant not out in the open, where the Union commander wanted to fight and where his artillery could be brought to bear, but in the dense forest known locally as the "Wilderness." It was not a virgin battlespace. Almost a year to the day earlier, Lee had dealt Joseph Hooker and the Army of the Potomac a massive defeat here at the conclusion of the Battle of Chancellorsville (Aril 30-May 6, 1863).

The tangled woods and undergrowth were allies for the outnumbered, outgunned Lee. Grant could not use his cavalry on this

ground, and artillery was all but useless. The Confederate commander had enlisted nature itself to even the long odds against him
as the fighting began on May 5. Grant turned over the tactical management of the battle to Meade. It was behavior typical of a humble
and selfless commander. Noble—but, in this case, a mistake. The
conventionally competent Meade was thoroughly out-generaled by
Lee. Not that fighting in the Wilderness was easy for the Army of
Northern Virginia. Confusion, in fact, gripped both sides, and while
the combat on May 5 was horrific, it was also non-decisive, necessi-
tating another day of battle.

On May 6, Confederate Lieutenant General James Longstreet
led his corps in an envelopment of Meade's inadequately deployed
troops. In a brilliant move, Longstreet drove one flank of the Army
of the Potomac into the other, creating a potentially catastrophic situation that prompted Grant to belatedly usurp Meade's command
prerogative by ordering him to make a fighting retreat. Nothing, not
even the commencement of an attack, is more intense and desperate
than a fighting withdrawal. In this case, the musket fire was so fierce
that the surrounding woods and brush soon caught flame. Within a
short time, entire tracts of the Wilderness were engulfed, and it is
believed that as many as two hundred men, both Confederate and
Union, either perished in the flames or were asphyxiated by smoke
during the hellish night of May 7–8.

The butcher's bill for two days of battle was 17,666 killed,
wounded, captured, or missing out of an engaged force of 101,895
soldiers in the Army of the Potomac—a 17 percent casualty rate that
included the deaths of two generals, the wounding of two more, and
the capture of another two. Less accurately recorded were Confederate losses, but it is estimated that out of 61,025 troops engaged,
11,125 were killed, wounded, missing, or captured. It was an 18
percent casualty rate, and it included three generals killed and four
(among them Longstreet) wounded.

Grant, having lost more men than Lee, was forced to disengage
from the battle. In this sense, he suffered defeat. But, in proportion
to the number of men fielded, Lee fared even worse, yet he held his
ground. It was not the way Grant wanted to begin his grand offensive. But it was also true that he could afford to lose men whereas

Lee certainly could not. In any case, whether he should be judged defeated or marginally victorious, Grant behaved nothing like a beaten general. Instead of withdrawing, he advanced. Having disengaged from Lee, he side-stepped the position held by the Army of Northern Virginia and continued south to a courthouse at a Virginia crossroads town called Spotsylvania Court House. One of the roads crossing here led straight to Richmond. Far from avoiding further battle, Grant invited it—for all practical purposes demanded it. Win, lose, or draw, he intended to kill more of Lee's army.

For his part, Lee saw that his men were in high spirits. For all the blood they had shed, they felt that they had won—as, by the raw numbers, they had. Anticipating Grant's destination, Lee drove his army to beat him in Spotsylvania. Elements of Jeb Stuart's Confederate cavalry and I Corps commanded by Richard H. Anderson (substituting for Longstreet, who was recovering from his wounds) clashed with the Army of the Potomac's V Corps under Major General Gouverneur K. Warren on May 8. The Battle of Spotsylvania Court House began as a skirmish, but Lee intended to fight on this spot the showdown battle of the Civil War. His aim was to exact a toll on Grant so terrible that the Northern electorate would not return Lincoln to the White House in the General Election of November 1864. His Democratic opponent—most believed it would be none other than George B. McClellan—would favor an immediate negotiated end to the war. That was the best the Confederacy could hope for, and, as Lee saw it, it was worth spilling blood for now.

A determined Lee initiated some of the most desperate fighting in a war that had been far more desperate than anyone could have imagined. He saw this engagement as quite possibly the last chance for the Confederacy. As for Grant, he deliberately avoided the behavior of a conventional commander. Instead of taking a stand or withdrawing, he did what virtually no commander would do under heavy attack. He maneuvered, repeatedly shifting his main line to his own left while continually counterpunching Lee, continually probing for a weak spot in the enemy flank. Lee was having none of it. Observing the action closely, he was always able to cover any portion of his flank that became exposed. His troops worked furiously to dig out of the Virginia clay a hasty defense. In some places, this consisted of shallow but serviceable trenches. In others, it was no more than a collection of holes, each dug by an individual soldier for his own protection. Elsewhere, a few men scraped out rifle pits, larger "firing holes" capable of accommodating several men. From their cover, crude as it might be, the Confederates took a terrible toll—yet Grant continued to sidestep, each time threatening to come around on *Lee's* exposed flank. And, each time, Lee was forced to extend an already undermanned defensive line. This meant more digging and more exhausting labor, while also spreading the entire line thinner and thinner.

The old rules of warfare, the Napoleonic rules, the rules taught at West Point by men like Old Brains Halleck dictated that whichever side could concentrate the most fire on the enemy would prevail. These old rules called for taking a stand and firing on the enemy until the enemy gave up. Grant broke those rules by combining attack with maneuver. He refused to simply mass against some particular point in Lee's line. Instead, he attacked and then sidestepped, threatening Lee's flank and thereby forcing him to keep extending his line, which thereby became thinner. Who would lose? The general whose line was the first to snap.

Grant needed to find an edge in this blood-soaked contest of endurance. He had earlier pressured Meade into installing Philip Sheridan to command the Cavalry Corps of the Army of the Potomac; however, Meade and Sheridan immediately came into conflict over the proper role of the cavalry. Sheridan wanted to use it offensively, as a means of conducting hit-and-run raids, whereas the conservative Meade insisted on reserving the cavalry mainly for traditional reconnaissance missions. Now locked in desperate combat at Spotsylvania Court House, Grant threw his weight behind Sheridan's proposal to lead the 10,000-man Cavalry Corps in a breakout toward Richmond. When Meade objected, Grant simply overruled him. Stuart's cavalry consisted of 4,500 troopers versus Sheridan's 10,000. Grant believed that menacing Richmond would force the outnumbered Stuart to fight and to lose. When Stuart was beaten, a gap would open up in the lines around Richmond, and then Lee would have no choice but to break off the battle at Spotsylvania

Court House, withdraw closer to the capital, and thereby allow an additional Union advance.

Sheridan considered the size of the Army of the Potomac Cavalry Corps to be a great asset, but he soon discovered that it was also a liability, since it made it impossible for him to mask its movement from Jeb Stuart's prying eyes. Seeing the approach—riding four abreast, the Union cavalry column extended about thirteen miles— Stuart decided to ambush Sheridan at Yellow Tavern, an abandoned inn six miles north of Richmond. He deployed his troopers in strong defensive positions, and he motivated them by explaining that they—and they alone—were all that stood between Grant and the capital city of their Confederacy.

Sheridan's men rode into the trap—though it was sprung only on the leading edge of the Union column. The Battle of Yellow Tavern (May 11, 1864) raged for three hours before Sheridan pulled back, but not before one of his troopers shot Jeb Stuart, who died two days later. As with the loss of Stonewall Jackson to friendly fire at the Battle of Chancellorsville a year earlier (wounded on May 2, he died on May 10, 1863), the death of Stuart was a blow from which there could be no recovery. Like Jackson, Stuart was irreplaceable.

In the meantime, Grant repeatedly struck at Lee's flank, only to be repulsed each time. At last, however, he was convinced he had found a vulnerability. He ordered Major General Winfield Scott Hancock and 20,000 men to engage Ewell's Corps. The Confederate general had deployed his line in a salient—entrenchments bulging toward the Union lines in a pattern that gave the rebels a 180-degree field of fire. To Hancock's men, it resembled an upside-down "U," which they called Mule Shoe. By the end of May 12, Mule Shoe would acquire a new name: Bloody Angle.

Hancock was one of the most admired officers in the Union army. At Gettysburg, he was among the most aggressive commanders, and, as Grant expected him to do on May 12, he pushed everything he had against Mule Shoe. Beginning well before dawn, at 4:30 in the morning, Hancock began punching through Ewell's line, breaching several places by five. Ewell, however, was not one given to panic. He sent every man he could to plug the breaches and, before noon, had managed to halt Hancock's advance.

At this point, the manner of the fighting changed. It was no longer something out of the industrial mid-nineteenth century—massed musket fire. It was primitive, hand-to-hand, the men fighting with fists or, grasping their muskets by the barrel, using the butt as a club. Grant's own aide-de-camp, Horace Porter, reported seeing "opposing flags . . . thrust against each other, and muskets . . . fired with muzzle against muzzle." He spoke of men ramming their swords and their bayonets "between the logs in the parapet which separated the combatants" blindly stabbing at the enemy. By day's end, a torrential rain began, but the fighting continued. Even darkness, which usually brought an intermission in battle, did not stop what Porter called "the fierce contest, and the deadly strife did not cease till after midnight."

Lee saw the Bloody Angle as the battle's crisis and, ignoring the entreaties of his officers and men, rode down to it, intending to command its defense in person. The men at the front threatened to mutiny if Lee, so important to them, refused to withdraw. At length, he did. Inspired nevertheless, his soldiers finally managed to beat back Hancock's assault, and thus the action at the Bloody Angle came to an end.

The Battle of Spotsylvania Court House would not end until nine days later—and then inconclusively. As before, Grant refused to withdraw. As before, he would side-slip his men and edged them closer to Richmond. On May 11, he telegraphed the War Department in Washington that he had suffered heavy losses. Eventually, these would be tallied as 18,399 killed, wounded, captured, or missing—a casualty rate of nearly 18 percent. In raw numbers, Confederate losses were 12,687 killed, wounded, captured, or missing. But this was out of a strength half that of the Army of the Potomac and amounted to a casualty rate of 23 percent. Grant concluded his telegram by declaring, "I . . . propose to fight it out on this line, if it takes all summer."

His next major move came on May 31. Mindful of what it had cost when Lee beat him to the crossroads at Spotsylvania Court House, he was determined to reach the next crossroads, Cold Harbor, before him. Because it was a mere half-dozen miles northeast of Richmond, Grant was certain Lee would do battle here. Yet again, however, Lee outguessed his opponent. When Grant arrived at Cold Harbor, Lee was waiting for him. The battle commenced on May 31, reached its height on June 2, and then petered out through June 12. This time, it ended in a frank defeat for the Army of the Potomac, which suffered nearly 13,000 casualties (killed, wounded, captured, or missing) to about 5,300 for the Army of Northern Virginia. Grant responded to this truly terrible defeat by continuing his advance despite a renewed public outcry in the North for his removal. Under his command in the Overland Campaign, 50,000 Union soldiers had been killed, wounded, captured, or had simply gone missing. This was 41 percent of the force (continually replenished) with which he had begun the campaign. Lincoln agreed with the public, including those who called for Grant's dismissal. These losses were indeed unthinkable. But then he pointed out that the losses among the Army of Northern Virginia amounted to 46 percent. The Army of the Potomac could be restored to its full strength. The Army of Northern Virginia could not. Robert E. Lee was losing the war.

And so Grant once again slipped his army out of Cold Harbor, doing so this time by night, and crossing the Chickahominy. Lee watched. Lee knew what it meant. Grant was continuing on to Richmond. The Confederate commander realized that, short of surrender, he had no choice but to fight again. He did not believe Grant would ever quit. His only hope was that the people of the North would elect a new president, come November, who *would* quit—right out from under their general. But, right now, under Lincoln, Grant would not turn back. He would fight again. There was no question about that, Lee knew. The only question Lee must have asked himself was whether the Army of Northern Virginia could possibly last to November.

14

April 6–7, 1862

Shiloh Creates a New American Reality

Why it's significant. When it occurred Shiloh (April 6–7, 1862) was the biggest and bloodiest battle ever fought on the North American continent. It was an early tipping point of the Civil War, convincing generals, politicians, and people, both North and South, that only a total victory would end the conflict—a total victory that would take many more months, maybe years, and would consume who knew how many more lives. Before Shiloh, the conflict that began with the firing on Fort Sumter, on April 12, 1861, had been an insurrection. Shiloh transformed it into total war between two peoples of one divided nation.

IN AMERICA IN the middle of the nineteenth century, disunity was the dominant theme. Yet, even as the divided nation was fighting a civil war, the North and the South could agree on at least one thing—the greatness of William Shakespeare. By 1810, scores of permanent theater companies, all offering Shakespeare and some specializing in the Bard, were thriving from Boston to the Gulf of Mexico and from the eastern seaboard to the Ohio River. By mid-century, the permanent companies had reached the Pacific Coast,

and those communities in between New York and San Francisco—
farming towns, trading posts, mining camps—not yet served by their
own company, welcomed regular visits by traveling Shakespeare
companies, both domestic and British.

One of the most popular plays in Civil War-era America was
also the bloodiest—*Macbeth.* The title character begins as the most
loyal servant of his king, Duncan, but by Act 3, Scene 4, having
done the unimaginable, having killed his monarch and others, too,
Macbeth explains to his wife:

> I am in blood
> Stepped in so far that, should I wade no more,
> Returning were as tedious as go o'er.

Having killed and killed again, Macbeth discovers that he has become
a confirmed assassin and murderer, a self-identity he could never
before have imagined. The two sides in the Civil War experienced a
similar self-revelation on April 7, 1862, at the end of a battle fought on
a wooded patch of southwestern Tennessee adjacent to a tiny Method-
ist chapel named Shiloh. The lovely name came from the Hebrew of
the Old Testament's Book of Joshua, in which Shiloh appears as the
town in Samara that built a sanctuary to shelter the Ark of the Cove-
nant. Modern biblical scholars disagree on how to translate this name.
Some have suggested "Tranquility Town," others "Place of Peace." In
the course of twelve hours, of the roughly 100,000 men who fought
in the vicinity of Shiloh's Tennessee namesake, nearly one in four,
just under 24,000, were killed, wounded, went missing, or were made
prisoners of war. Place of Peace? This Battle of Shiloh was the bloodiest in all American history up to that day.

No one imagined such a thing would or even could ever happen in the United States. Even Union commander Ulysses S. Grant
wrote in his *Private Memoirs,* published days after his death in
1885, "Up to the battle of Shiloh, I, as well as thousands of other
citizens, believed the rebellion against the Government would collapse suddenly and soon, if a decisive victory could be gained over
any of its armies." Grant noted that, prior to Shiloh, he had captured
the key Confederate strongholds of Forts Donelson and Henry, and

that a Confederate "army of more than 21,000 men was captured or destroyed" as a result. "Bowling Green, Columbus and Hickman, Kentucky, fell in consequence, and Clarksville and Nashville, Tennessee, the last two with an immense amount of stores, also fell into our hands. The Tennessee and Cumberland rivers, from their mouths to the head of navigation, were secured." It seemed impossible that the South would or even could continue to prosecute the war, but because the soldiers of the Confederacy at Shiloh "made such a gallant effort to regain what had been lost," Grant wrote, he was forced to give "up all idea of saving the Union except by complete conquest."

Some historians identify the Battle of Shiloh as the first turning point of the Civil War. But it was less a turning point—the result of one side's victory and the other's defeat—than it was a tipping point. The murderous product of this battle fought in an obscure patch of woods did not chasten the two sides, did not compel them to heed what Abraham Lincoln had called, in his first inaugural address, "the better angels of our nature." No, it committed both sides to redouble their mutual blood sacrifice. It committed both to a fight to the death.

Shiloh would not long hold the record for American bloodshed. Americans on both sides now believed they were "in blood / Stepped in so far" that they could not turn back. Total, brutal, annihilating war became an article of national political and military policy. As Grant noted in his *Personal Memoirs,* before Shiloh, "it had been the policy of our army . . . to protect the property of the citizens whose territory was invaded, without regard to their sentiments, whether Union or Secession." After Shiloh, it became Grant's policy to "protect the persons of those found at their homes, but to consume everything that could be used to support or supply armies." Shiloh was the tipping point at which a military action to suppress a sectional insurrection became an all-consuming war.

* * *

Somewhat more than half of the Union army was manned by first-generation immigrants. In contrast, 91 percent of the Confederate army consisted of native-born white men. One of the immigrant minority was a Welsh orphan, who sailed to the United States in 1859 at the age of eighteen, landed in New Orleans, randomly encountered a trader named Stanley, and asked him for a job. He phrased the request as a Welshman of the era would—"Do you want a boy, sir?"—and instead of getting a job, he got informally adopted. Young John Rowlands took the name of his new "father" and, in the fullness of time, made himself famous as a globe-trotting *New York Herald* journalist-adventurer, Henry Morton Stanley—yes, the man who would in 1871 find, in Africa, David Livingstone, a long-lost Scots missionary, drily greeting him with the phrase, "Dr. Livingstone, I presume."

At the outbreak of the Civil War, Stanley sought his first adventure by joining the Confederate army. He found himself at Shiloh, and, in a posthumously published autobiography, wrote of how the two commanding generals, Albert Sidney Johnston and Pierre Gustave Toutant-Beauregard, responded to the catalog of Confederate defeats Grant outlined in his own memoir. They "proposed to hurl into the Tennessee River an army of nearly 50,000 [the true number was about 63,000] rested and well-fed [Union] troops, by means of 40,000 [Confederate] soldiers, who, for two days, had subsisted on sodden biscuit and raw bacon, who had been exposed for two nights to rain and dew, and had marched twenty-three miles!" The thing is, Johnston and Beauregard would very nearly succeed.

In the run-up to Shiloh, Grant's Army of the Tennessee consisted of 44,895 soldiers (one authority puts the number at 48,894) organized into six divisions. He encamped five of his divisions at Pittsburg Landing, Tennessee, on the west bank of the Tennessee River. The remaining division, under Major General Lew Wallace (who would achieve literary fame in 1880 as the author of the novel *Ben-Hur*), was positioned on the Tennessee five miles downstream, at a place called Crump's Landing. Grant planned to launch an attack on the Confederate forces concentrated at Corinth, Mississippi, a short distance to the southwest of Shiloh. Wallace's division was deployed to prevent the Confederates from positioning artillery along the Tennessee. Grant also wanted Wallace to capture and control the railroad at nearby Bethel Station to prevent transportation of reinforcements.

Grant was anxious to launch his attack. His encampment at Pittsburg Landing was hastily established as a mere bivouac, essentially a platform from which to launch the attack, not a fully prepared defensive position. He had not ordered trenches to be dug or artillery to be emplaced. The rationale behind these decisions was that he wanted his troops to attack, not to dig in and defend. That Grant also neglected to post pickets—guards—out in front of the bivouac cannot be readily justified, however. It was a mistake for which he and his men would pay dearly.

One more unit, about 18,000 men of the Army of the Ohio, operating independently under Don Carlos Buell, were in the vicinity, at Duck River, northeast of Pittsburg Landing and Shiloh.

In his posthumous autobiography, Stanley provided a rare eyewitness account of the opening of the battle from the Confederate perspective. After marching into position with his regiment, Stanley was awakened at 4:00 on the morning of April 6. He and his comrades ate a miserable cold breakfast before forming into line. Stanley's regiment—the "Dixie Greys"— was positioned at the center of the attack. They loaded their obsolete flintlock muskets and marched to battle, tramping "solemnly and silently through the thin forest, and over its grass, still in its withered and wintry hue."

Stanley noted "that the sun was not far from appearing, that our regiment was keeping its formation admirably, [and] that the woods would have been a grand place for a picnic." At about 5:15 a.m., he and his comrades heard "some desultory firing in front." They "drew nearer to the firing, and soon a sharper rattling of musketry was heard. 'That is the enemy waking up,' we said. Within a few minutes, there was another explosive burst of musketry, the air was pierced by many missiles, which hummed and pinged sharply by our ears, pattered through the tree-tops, and brought twigs and leaves down on us."

What had begun as "desultory" gunfire soon thickened into a murderous hailstorm, through which the Dixie Greys advanced, heads lowered as if against a driving icy rain. It was fearful—yet nothing compared to what the Union troops endured, caught by surprise and virtually defenseless. Awakened from their early morning sleep, Grant's soldiers saw four divisions arrayed against them from west to east, emerging from the woods with muskets blazing. Instead of returning fire, many of the Union troops broke, ran, and sought cover. Their unpreparedness and absence of discipline made them all the more vulnerable. As Stanley and his fellows overtook their own skirmishers, a call went up: "There they are!" With that, Stanley recalled that "we cracked into them with levelled muskets," their captain admonishing them, "Aim low, men!"

But there really was no aiming. Civil War soldiers rarely aimed, except in the most general way. The Confederates this day used "marching fire," shooting while advancing. To Stanley, "it appeared absurd to be blazing away at shadows," but, finally, he

> saw a row of little globes of pearly smoke streaked with crimson, breaking-out, with sportive quickness, from a long line of bluey figures in front; and, simultaneously, there broke upon our ears an appalling crash of sound, the series of fusillades following one another with startling suddenness, which suggested to my somewhat moidered sense a mountain upheaved, with huge rocks tumbling and thundering down a slope, and the echoes rumbling and receding through space. Again and again, these loud and quick explosions were repeated, seemingly with increased violence, until they rose to the highest pitch of fury, and in unbroken continuity. All the world seemed involved in one tremendous ruin!

The Civil War was fought before the invention of so-called smokeless gunpowder. This meant that, in a pitched battle, the air quickly became so thick with smoke that it was impossible to see the enemy. Confusion reigned. All an advancing soldier could do was load, fire, reload, and fire—fire into the smoke. "My nerves tingled, my pulses beat double-quick, my heart throbbed loudly, and almost painfully; but, amid all the excitement, my thoughts, swift as the flash of lightning, took all sound, and sight, and self, into their purview. I listened to the battle raging far away on the flanks, to the thunder in front, to the various sounds made by the leaden storm."

By the sound far more than anything conveyed through sight, Stanley concluded that the Federals were pulling back. To the attackers' "every forward step, they took a backward move, loading and firing as they slowly withdrew. Twenty thousand muskets were being fired at this stage, but, though accuracy of aim was impossible, owing to our labouring hearts, and the jarring and excitement, many bullets found their destined billets on both sides."

In the end, marching fire could accomplish only so much. The muskets and rifle muskets of the era were muzzle loaders, which made reloading clumsy, time-consuming work. The officers accompanying their men had to judge when the attack had reached a critical point at which there was no time for all this. At that moment, they shouted, *Fix bayonets!*

When this order was given to the Dixie Greys, there "was a simultaneous bound forward, each soul doing his best for the emergency. The Federals appeared inclined to await us; but, at this juncture, our men raised a yell, thousands responded to it, and burst out into the wildest yelling it has ever been my lot to hear." This was the celebrated "rebel yell." Its purpose was to terrorize the enemy, but Stanley felt that its most immediate effect was on him and his fellows. The keening cry "drove all sanity and order from among us. It served the double purpose of relieving pent-up feelings, and transmitting encouragement along the attacking line. I rejoiced in the shouting like the rest. It reminded me that there were about four hundred companies like the Dixie Greys, who shared our feelings."

"'They fly!' was echoed from lip to lip," Stanley wrote. The exclamation spurred on the advance. "It deluged us with rapture, and transfigured each Southerner into an exulting victor. At such a moment, nothing could have halted us. Those savage yells, and the sight of thousands of racing figures coming towards them, discomfited the blue-coats; and when we arrived upon the place where they had stood, they had vanished."

In their flight, the Yankees left behind a "beautiful array of tents, before which they had made their stand, after being roused from their Sunday-morning sleep" as well as their "half-dressed dead and wounded . . . . Military equipments, uniform-coats, half-packed knapsacks, bedding, of a new and superior quality, littered the company streets."

Stanley's exultation was tempered by the sight of "a series of other camps" in the near distance, and he realized that the fight this first camp put up, though brief, "enabled the brigades in rear of the advance camp to recover from the shock of the surprise." Nevertheless, the initial attack had punched holes between the Union divisions. Through these, the rebels now advanced—but soon the Federal lines coalesced as order and discipline were restored. The rout ended by the afternoon, and Grant's men re-formed in a new line of battle through a dense thicket lying between the Tennessee River to the east and Owl Creek to the west. The Confederates would soon have reason to give this space a painful name: the Hornet's Nest.

Union troops under William Tecumseh Sherman had suffered the brunt of the initial attack. Formed up on either side of Shiloh Chapel, on the Union's west flank, they panicked and ran under the rebel onslaught. Steadfast, Sherman personally rode out to rally his badly shaken men, thereby stemming the entire Union rout and earning Grant's profound admiration. Of irascible temperament, Sherman had been unpopular in the army ever since he criticized, early on, the military and political leadership for failing to appreciate, as he did, that the war would be long and bloody. He tried in vain to make the case that the nation was experiencing no mere insurrection, but instead all-out warfare on a scale unprecedented in North America. The press, politicians, public, and many of his fellow officers called him unhinged. But Shiloh, bloody Shiloh, would be his vindication.

As Sherman emerged as one of the battle's fiercest heroes, so the humbler figure of Brigadier General Benjamin M. Prentiss proved the grit of both himself and his command in their defense of the Union's center as the "Hornet's Nest" coalesced. His division of the Army of the Tennessee was mauled in the opening hours of the battle, but he restored discipline and was able to buy time for the arrival of Lew Wallace's division of the Army of the Tennessee, as well as elements of the Army of the Ohio under Major General Buell. Prentiss's stout resistance cost him dearly. With 2,200 of his troops, he was captured at the Hornet's Nest and then suffered the indignity of blame by the Northern press, which reported—falsely—that he and his men had been captured in their beds! Personally, Grant had no affection for Prentiss, but he stood up for his subordinate, pointing out the absurdity of the press reports. Had Prentiss and his command been asleep, "there would not have been an all-day struggle, with the loss of thousands killed and wounded on the Confederate side."

The opening of the battle was nearly catastrophic for the Union, and Confederate Private Stanley can be forgiven for assuming that the fighting was pretty much over. Very quickly, however, he concluded that "it was only a brief prologue of the long and exhaustive series of struggles which took place that day." Having overrun the first Union encampment, the Dixie Greys advanced beyond it until they beheld another "mass of white tents." Almost the very minute they saw this encampment, Stanley recalled, they "were met by a furious storm of bullets, poured on us from a long line of blue-coats, whose attitude of assurance proved to us that we should have tough work here." To Stanley, the world suddenly seemed to be "bursting into fragments. Cannon and musket, shell and bullet, lent their several intensities to the distracting uproar. . . . I likened the cannon, with their deep bass, to the roaring of a great herd of lions; the ripping, cracking musketry, to the incessant yapping of terriers; the windy whisk of shells, and zipping of minie bullets, to the swoop of eagles, and the buzz of angry wasps. All the opposing armies of Grey and Blue fiercely blazed at each other."

His company captain shouted the order to lie down and continue firing. Spying a fallen tree "about fifteen inches in diameter, with a narrow strip of light between it and the ground," Stanley and a dozen others flung themselves behind it. Momentarily, they felt secure—until the "sharp rending explosions and hurtling fragments" of incoming cannonballs, canister shot, and small-arms fire tore through the woods. "I marvelled, as I heard the unintermitting patter, snip, thud, and hum of the bullets, how anyone could live under this raining death."

The projectiles beat "a merciless tattoo on the outer surface of the log" behind which he and his comrades had taken shelter. They thudded "at the rate of a hundred a second. One, here and there, found its way under the log, and buried itself in a comrade's body. One man raised his chest, as if to yawn, and jostled me. I turned to him, and saw that a bullet had gored his whole face, and penetrated into his chest. Another ball struck a man a deadly rap on the head, and he turned on his back and showed his ghastly white face to the sky."

In the midst of this leaden storm of death, the captain ordered his men forward. A young friend of Stanley's, Henry Parker by name, suddenly cried out: "Oh, stop, *please* stop a bit, I have been hurt, and can't move!" He was standing on one leg, his other foot having been smashed by a cannonball. "There was no time to help him."

Many privates, corporals, and sergeants fell—and at about 2:30 in the afternoon, a general, Albert Sidney Johnston, joined them in death. A Minié ball shattered his leg, tearing the femoral artery. He tried to lead on, but soon wobbled in the saddle.

"General," an aide called out to him, "are you hurt?"

"Yes, and I fear seriously."

His high-topped "cavalier" cavalry boot overflowed with blood. His own calm self-assessment of his wound were the last words he spoke.

That Sunday night, the night that ended the first day of the Battle of Shiloh, General Beauregard telegraphed Confederate President Jefferson Davis that A. S. Johnston was dead. He added, however, that victory was certain at Shiloh.

Based on the evidence of the first day of battle, Beauregard was not being unreasonably optimistic. Until nightfall, the Confederates continued advancing in several places, and the company of Dixie Greys Stanley served with took the second line of Union encampments, leaving behind such "ghastly relics" as "a young Lieutenant, who, judging by the new gloss on his uniform, must have been some father's darling. A clean bullet-hole through the centre of his forehead had instantly ended his career." Elsewhere Stanley came across:

> some twenty bodies, lying in various postures, each by its own
> pool of viscous blood, which emitted a peculiar scent, which was
> new to me, but which I have since learned is inseparable from

a battle-field. Beyond these, a still larger group lay, body over-lying body, knees crooked, arms erect, or wide-stretched and rigid, according as the last spasm overtook them. The company opposed to them must have shot straight . . . . I can never forget the impression those wide-open dead eyes made on me. Each seemed to be starting out of its socket, with a look similar to the fixed wondering gaze of an infant, as though the dying had viewed something appalling at the last moment.

By about four in the afternoon, the Confederate private noted that even "the pluckiest" of his company "lacked the spontaneity and springing ardour which had distinguished them earlier in the day. . . . As for myself, I had only one wish, and that was for repose."

And that is what he got, sleeping soundly on the night of April 6 and awakening the next morning believing that the battle was all but won. But the morning roll call revealed that only about half of the Dixie Greys were present. Stanley himself would be captured later in the day as the Union, the Army of the Tennessee now augmented by elements of the Army of the Ohio, counterattacked. Grant's forces were arrayed for battle between Owl Creek and the Tennessee River and were joined on the east by Buell, who crossed the Tennessee at Pittsburg Landing. Lew Wallace closed in from the west. Together, five Union generals under Grant and three under Buell pushed southwestward. By 5 a.m. on April 7, they made contact with Confederate units under Generals Braxton Bragg, Leonidas Polk, John C. Breckinridge, and William J. Hardee. Six hours later, the Union counterattack had forced the entire Confederate line back about half way to Shiloh Chapel, the point from which, on the previous day, the Confederates had routed out Grant's Army of the Tennessee. An hour after this, the rebel line retreated farther, closing back in on Shiloh Chapel. After a two-hour fight on this line, at about two in the afternoon, the Confederate defense broke and withdrew southwest of Shiloh Chapel, falling back toward Corinth, Mississippi. Breckinridge took a blocking position across the Western Corinth Road and the Shiloh Branch. His objective was to cover the retreat of the rest of Beauregard's army. By the night of April

7–8, that army—except for Breckinridge, who lingered across three roads into Mississippi—had withdrawn into Mississippi.

As for the Union forces, exhausted, they did not pursue the retreating Confederates much farther than their own original Shiloh and Pittsburg Landing encampments. Buell, whose Army of the Ohio was far fresher than Grant's Army of the Tennessee, would argue endlessly over what he saw as Grant's "failure" to give chase. As it was, of some 63,000 to 66,000 (estimates vary) Union troops engaged, 1,754 were killed, 8,408 wounded, and 2,885 were captured or went missing. Of roughly 40,000 to more than 44,000 Confederate troops engaged, 1,728 were killed, 8,012 were wounded, and 959 were captured or went missing.

At the time, most Americans found such numbers simply beyond comprehension. Had Lincoln failed to stand behind his general as he endured an assault of public criticism, Shiloh, arguably a pyrrhic victory, might have been counted a massive strategic defeat in the long run. If Lincoln had yielded to popular opinion, Shiloh would have prompted the North to seek a negotiated end to the war. But Ulysses Grant accepted the necessity of his losses, and so did Lincoln. As for the people of the North, they, too, agreed to fight on, even knowing now how determined the Confederacy was and how terrible the cost was certainly going to be. The deadliest battle yet, Shiloh was the prelude to even worse.

15

May 20, 1862

Congress Passes the Homestead Act of 1862

Why it's significant. Despite battlefield disappointments and with no end of the Civil War in sight, President Lincoln affirmed faith in the triumph of the Union by supporting a huge—mostly immigrant—population settlement project, a great national educational initiative, and an epic transportation construction project.

FRANKLIN D. ROOSEVELT signed the G.I. Bill (officially the Servicemen's Readjustment Act) into law on June 22, 1944. Two things were remarkable about it. First, it provided America's returning veterans unprecedented access to low-cost mortgages, business loans, help with tuition (high school, vocational school, and college), a year of unemployment compensation, and other benefits. Second, the law was enacted in the midst of the biggest, most desperately fought war the world had ever known. This second fact proclaimed to the people of America—and the world— that the war *would* end, it would end in an American triumph, and the nation would emerge from the ordeal better and stronger than when it had entered it.

Roosevelt and his advisers could look back to the legislation passed during another immense and desperate war to find a strategic precedent for what the administration was doing. On May 20, 1862, amid heartbreaking battle outcomes and with no end to the Civil War in sight, President Abraham Lincoln signed into law the first Homestead Act, authorizing any citizen (or immigrant who intended to become a citizen) to select any surveyed but unclaimed parcel of public land up to 160 acres, settle it, improve it, and, by living on it for five years, gain title to it. It was legislation that had been promised in the Republican Party platform of 1860.

Like FDR eighty-two years later, Lincoln wanted to show the people of America and the millions of Europeans thinking of immigrating to America that the *United* States had a future. In fact, the Homestead Act of 1862 was just one of four pieces of wartime legislation designed to make this point. The Morrill Land-Grant Act of 1862 created land-grant colleges and universities with agricultural and "mechanical" programs intended to cultivate an educated citizenry throughout the nation, and the Pacific Railroad Acts of 1862 and 1863 promoted the construction of a transcontinental railroad. Like the Homestead Act, the Pacific Railroad Acts would help to settle and bind the nation along its east-west axis even as it was torn apart North from South. All four legislative actions were acts of national faith and defiant statements of the Union's argument against the Confederacy. For these were acts of a nation that envisioned a united future.

Lincoln's forward-looking, future-affirming legislation also looked back to the ideological spirit in which the nation was founded. From colonial days, the "American dream" was based on a free, landholding citizenry. The history of the United States during the eighteenth and nineteenth centuries may be viewed as a succession of American Wests, starting with the trans-Appalachian Ohio Valley and the Old Northwest and moving west to the Mississippi Valley, the settling of the Great Plains, the journey across the wide Missouri, and the settling of the Far West. The westward-moving frontier was a place where families could prosper on their own land, and the acts Lincoln signed into law each affirmed and facilitated this American Dream.

To claim their grant of 160 acres from the surveyed public domain, applicants had to meet an age qualification (twenty-one or older) and be the head of a family (regardless of gender). They were required to sign affidavits certifying their intention to use the land for their individual benefit by settling on it and cultivating it. To obtain full and final title to the land, the settler had to live on the homestead at least five years, make improvements (at least build a house), and pay a nominal registration fee. For those who could pony up $1.25 per acre—no small sum in the 1860s—they could "commute" their claim and obtain title to the land after just six months of residence.

There was a kicker in the affidavit, which required applicants to assert that they had "never borne arms against the United States or aided its enemies." This provision was a legal means of discriminating against Southerners, even those who returned to the North and professed loyalty to the Union. The provision, however, was included less to punish Southerners than to ensure that Northerners and Westerners would settle the new lands, bringing with them the social values of those regions. Indeed, as it began to move through Congress, the Homestead Bill helped to forge a political alliance between the Northeast and the West, which brought further unity to the Union. This alliance grew out of a thirty-year trend; for, when a homestead bill was first discussed in the 1830s, New England abolitionists saw it as a means of settling the Western territories in land packets too small to accommodate plantations. Since slavery was largely a plantation phenomenon—slaves were cheap and abundant labor to work large tracts of agricultural land—ensuring that the West would be settled in family-farm-sized parcels would discourage pro-slavery sentiment in the region.

By the 1860s, the homestead idea was very popular. True, there were some dissenters in the industrialized Northeast, who feared that homesteading would draw away labor from their region, but, by the time the bill was being seriously considered with the approach of the Civil War, a boom in European immigration was supplying the region with all the labor it needed. Moreover, northeastern captains of industry saw in the West a source of mineral wealth that would supply the raw materials for many of their manufacturing operations. At the same time, peopling the West would create whole new markets for the manufactured goods of the Northeast. While passing the Homestead Act in the midst of war was a bold move, it may also have been true that only with the South out of the picture could the act ever have been passed. Throughout the 1850s, Southern members of Congress consistently nipped homestead measures in the bud. Southerners feared—quite rightly—that homesteading would make agriculture in the West a family affair, a business of 160-acre parcels, and that the states that would be created out of the homestead territory would have no incentive *not* to vote themselves free.

Passed in 1862, the Homestead Act went into effect on January 1, 1863, and between 1863 and 1880, nearly 500,000 applications were filed for about fifty-six million acres. A bit more than half of these—257,385 entries—were carried all the way to the issuance of a full title. As impressive as these numbers are, the homestead legislation was responsible for only a sixth of the farms in states and territories where the legislation applied. Homesteaders were obliged to choose from among whatever parcels the government had available. Many of these were in remote locations and even in arid or semiarid regions or regions far from optimal for farming. Settlers who could afford to buy western land privately were often able to obtain the choicest acreage, closer to towns and with more fertile soil. Indeed, the homesteaders—settlers who took advantage of the act—not only had limited choices in where they could stake their claim, but, short on capital, they often were unable to make even the rudimentary improvements required to obtain permanent title to their grant. Even those who managed to build often commanded insufficient means to purchase livestock, machinery, and other requisites of successful farming. Subsequent legislation, after the original 1862 act, addressed some of these deficiencies, but there is no question that the Homestead Act, along with the Morrill Act and the Pacific Railroad Act, made for powerful pro-Union propaganda during the war. They put the United States on the side of those who aspired to the American dream and ensured that it would remain a compelling destination for immigrants from abroad. The legislation made the stakes of the Civil War very personal. For only a great, unified, and free nation could fulfill for each and every citizen the promise of opportunity and the hope for new beginnings.

Indeed, the Homestead Act linked the concept of a democratic American Union with the idea of the American family farm. In contrast to the cruelty of the slave plantation of the Confederate South, the Union farm was pictured as a loving partnership between husband and wife who created a legacy for their children. As the Civil War ultimately perfected the ideals of American independence by liberating those Americans held in bondage, homesteading created in the family farm an enduring national ideal.

For a time following the end of the Civil War, homesteading was also promoted as a way of helping newly free African Americans to live truly independent lives. In 1866, a Southern Homestead Act opened to settlement remaining public lands in the former Confederate states of Alabama, Arkansas, Florida, Louisiana, and Mississippi, specifying the land's availability to African Americans as well as to white Southern loyalists. It was envisioned that the black homesteads would become "cities of refuge" for former slaves. The reality, however, fell far short of the aspiration. The Southern homesteading lands were often ill-suited to agriculture. The soil was of poor quality, and there was an abundance of trees that had to be removed, stumps and all. Add to this the menace of the local and very hostile white population, and it is no wonder that the Freedman's Bureau, which had responsibility for supervising the Southern homesteading program, settled no more than about 4,000 African American families, 75 percent of them in Florida. Only a handful homesteaded in Alabama, and while more families headed for Texas, most of them stopped short and squatted, illegally, in Louisiana without ever filing claims. The Southern Homestead Act was repealed in 1876 when Reconstruction came to an abrupt end in the corrupt bargain that quieted the objections of Democrat Samuel J. Tilden and put Republican Rutherford B. Hayes in the White House in exchange for Hayes's pledge to end Reconstruction and return full sovereignty to the ex-Confederate states. Public lands throughout the South were sold to timber cartels, and African American homesteaders lit out for farms in Oklahoma, Texas, Kansas, and Colorado.

For other American minorities, the homestead movement compiled a mixed record when it came to making the American dream a reality. For Hispanics, homestead laws actually disrupted the old communal ways of farm life lived around villages and shared pastures. On their own, many Hispanic families were too poor to improve their homestead claims, which, as a result, they ultimately forfeited. Native Americans—at least in some cases—did benefit from the homesteading, but relatively few families applied.

Of all the American "minority" groups, women benefitted the most. In contrast to most federal and state laws of the era relating to property, the Homestead Act explicitly allowed women to apply for homesteads. The law did stipulate that female filers had to be single and over twenty-one years of age or the heads of households. For a half-century from implementation of the law in 1863, women homesteaded western lands in unprecedented numbers. In the early years of homesteading, female filers made up just 5 percent of all homesteaders, but the fraction rose to nearly 20 percent by 1900.

Although the Homestead Act of 1862 was an affirmation of national values and the American dream, the life of the homesteader was never easy. As a rule, a family sent the father or the older sons out first to stake a claim and to build at least a crude dwelling on it. This accomplished, the mother and other children soon followed. The plains were far from a uniformly hospitable place. Often compared to a sea of grass, the prairie was solitary and raked by extreme weather—storms, 100-degree-plus temperatures in the summer, and temperatures that could dip into the negative 30s during the winter. Locusts and other destructive pests were prevalent. But the single greatest obstacle to farming was the hard-packed, root-bound soil itself, which had to be broken up before it would yield to the plow's blade. From this, the homesteader earned a new name—sodbuster. And while the sod was an obstacle, in the absence of timber on the thinly forested prairie, sod was also the material from which many homesteaders built their first—sometimes their only—house. Typically, the sodbuster would excavate a rectangular "dugout" about six feet deep and then build it up above the surface of the ground with "bricks" cut from the hard-packed sod. The four walls were roofed with boards, straw, and more sod.

Enacted in the democratic spirit that made the United States what Abraham Lincoln, in his first inaugural address, called the "last best hope of earth," the Homestead Act and subsequent legislation enduringly democratized public land policy—even though only about 10 percent of available Western land actually went to homesteaders. For all its hardships, the cultural and political influence of the homestead movement that was born in the Civil War extended well beyond the span of that war. By bringing families into the West, homesteading fixed in the American imagination the idea of the region as a land of opportunity, enterprise, perpetual renewal and optimism. This enduring Western identity is one of the most important and unexpected legacies of the Civil War.

16

May 2, 1863

Stonewall Jackson Falls to Friendly Fire at Chancellorsville

Why it's significant. December of 1862 brought the Union a catastrophic defeat at Fredericksburg, which was followed in the spring of the next year by an even costlier defeat at Chancellorsville. Celebrated as "Lee's masterpiece," Chancellorsville was, in fact, a pyrrhic victory, gained at the loss of 22 percent of the Army of Virginia, including Lee's greatest general, Thomas J. "Stonewall" Jackson. Whereas the Union could endure two major defeats, Robert E. Lee was convinced that the Confederacy could not long survive another victory like that at Chancellorsville. He therefore decided to invade the North.

N0 GENERAL ENGAGES in battle to lose. The great generals want to achieve not only victory, but to create what military historians call a masterpiece—a tactical and strategic triumph that leverages sacrifice for the greatest, war-winning effect. As they approached the Battle of Chancellorsville (April 30-May 6, 1863), both Joseph Hooker, commanding the Army of the Potomac, and Robert E. Lee, the Army of Northern Virginia, were looking to create just such a masterpiece.

The Union's Joseph "Fighting Joe" Hooker graduated from West Point with the Class of 1837. He served in the Second Seminole War and the US-Mexican War, in which he fought with great gallantry but then testified against his commanding officer, Winfield Scott, in the court martial of another officer. Scott responded to this breach of loyalty by refusing to give Hooker any official assignment during the years following the war with Mexico. This prompted Hooker to resign his commission in 1853, and when, five years later, he wrote to the secretary of war to ask for a position as lieutenant general, his letter went unanswered. For this reason, he became one of many civilian spectators watching the First Battle of Bull Run (July 21, 1861). Afterward, he wrote to President Lincoln: "I was at . . . Bull Run . . . and it is neither vanity nor boasting in me to declare that I am a damned sight better general than you, sir, had on that field." Lincoln must have agreed. He responded to the letter by commissioning Hooker a brigadier general of volunteers.

Hooker's disloyalty to Scott and his unmannerly missive to Lincoln were typical of his brash and grating personality, which would make him one of the most unpopular commanders in the Union army—at least as far as his fellow officers were concerned. He was outspoken in his condemnation of his own commanding general, George B. McClellan, whom he mocked as an "infant among soldiers." There was no happiness in the US Army when, following Ambrose Burnside's tragic failure against Robert E. Lee at the Battle of Fredericksburg (December 11–15, 1862) and the heartbreaking "Mud March" that followed, he was replaced as commanding general of the Army of the Potomac by Hooker.

The public had no particular loyalty to Burnside, but they were disposed to dislike Hooker, who was widely regarded as so ruthlessly ambitious that loyalty to brother officers never entered into his calculations. Still, he had a winning record as a commander, and, even though he was cordially hated by the officer corps, the common soldier had both respect and affection for him. Hooker was, in fact, very effective in restoring the post-Fredericksburg morale of the Army of the Potomac. He did this not with stern speeches, but by obtaining for his soldiers the things they most needed and wanted: better clothing, shelter, and palatable food. Something as simple as replacing the dreaded Union staple, hardtack—a tasteless cracker so hard that it was universally known as "tooth duller"— with freshly baked bread lifted spirits and won the loyalty of soldiers who now had reason to believe that their commanding officer cared about them.

Militarily, Hooker was—at least by comparison with most other Union officers—an innovative thinker. He recognized that Union cavalry was being poorly and inadequately used. Hooker took a new tack and vigorously employed the cavalry for aggressive advanced reconnaissance. Understanding that early intelligence about the enemy was of no use if it could not be conveyed to headquarters quickly, Hooker authorized the creation of the first United States Air Force. He hired civilian balloonists to serve as artillery spotters. Instead of relying on rickety observation towers, he sent them aloft in tethered balloons. A telegraph wire was bound to the tether, running along its length, thereby allowing a Signal Corps telegrapher who accompanied the spotter to tap out in Morse code his observations in real time. Despite his forward thinking, Hooker had the fatal flaw of hubris. In the early spring of 1863, he boasted: "May God have mercy on General Lee, for I will have none."

But, to give Hooker due credit, he meant to use his reinvigorated Army of the Potomac as it had never been used before—as an all-out, go-for-broke, maximum-effort instrument of war. He had nearly 134,000 men, and he knew Lee had 60,000 at most. In contrast to the likes of McClellan, Hooker believed in his vast numerical advantage and intended to use it. In contrast to Burnside, who repeated the same unsuccessful head-on tactics no fewer than fourteen disastrous times at Fredericksburg, Hooker had formulated what he believed would be a military masterpiece. His plan included a diversionary attack by Major General John Sedgwick leading a third of the army across the Rappahannock *above* the Confederate entrenchments at Fredericksburg. Once in position, Sedgwick would attack, forcing Lee to focus his undermanned army against him while he, Hooker, led another third of the army up along the Rappahannock, then wheeled about sharply to fall upon Lee's left flank and rear. The result would be an envelopment in which the Army of Northern Virginia would be crushed between two thirds of the Army of the

Potomac. While this pincers action was under way, Hooker held in readiness the remaining third of his army at nearby Chancellorsville. It would be deployed to reinforce either Sedgwick or Hooker—whichever force required it. Hooker also reserved an ambitious role for the Cavalry Corps, under Brigadier General George Stoneman. Ten thousand troopers would make a series of lightning raids on Lee's lines of communication to Richmond, thereby cutting off the Army of Northern Virginia from both retreat and reinforcement.

The fact was that Fighting Joe Hooker, a talented and competent commander, had created an excellent plan. The only thing he had not counted on was the genius of Robert E. Lee, who instantly comprehended everything that Hooker intended to do and, having comprehended the plan, acted to defeat it. In the process, he created the military masterpiece of Chancellorsville.

Lee's first move was refusing to respond to Stoneman's cavalry. He let the Union troopers raid unmolested while he sent his own great cavalry commander, Jeb Stuart, to take control of the roads in and out of Chancellorsville, thereby bottling up an encampment of some 70,000 Army of the Potomac soldiers. Worse, with Stuart having seized the initiative, Hooker was unable to send out reconnaissance patrols. Suddenly, he was deprived of all situational awareness. He had no idea where Lee's main force was. Lee had thrust upon Hooker the one thing he knew that the Union general could not plan for—the unknown.

George McClellan's great weakness had been that he feared losing more than he craved winning. Hooker suffered from no such flaw—until he was deprived of his eyes and ears. Now he panicked. Effectively tearing up his plan, he abandoned the offensive and groped toward a defensive posture, hunkering down in Chancellorsville. Remarkably, the boastful Hooker let go of the initiative without firing a shot.

With 70,000 Union troops effectively put on ice, Lee listened to Jeb Stuart's reconnaissance report. It revealed that those Army of the Potomac troops who were not idled Chancellorsville were getting ready to attack the flank and rear of the Army of Northern Virginia. They would approach via a dense patch of forest growth called "the Wilderness." Acting immediately to forestall and delay the attack,

Lee deployed Jubal Early with 10,000 men to engage the Federals as they began their advance through the Wilderness. During this delay, Lee intended to strike the Union forces at Chancellorsville. In direct contrast to Hooker, who abandoned offense for defense, Lee gave up his defensive advantages to take the fight to Hooker.

Genius never sleeps. With the battle having begun in earnest on May 1 southeast of Chancellorsville, Lee summoned Stonewall Jackson to his field headquarters shortly after midnight on May 2. Pulling up a couple of cracker barrels, the two men shaped an entirely new plan. At the Second Battle of Bull Run (August 28–30, 1862), Lee had gambled by purposely violating a standard tactical commandment. He divided his army in the presence of the enemy. The risk was being attacked and defeated in detail. The reward was enveloping the enemy. He decided to gamble again.

Lee assigned a command of 26,000 to Jackson, who would lead them in a fierce surprise attack through the Wilderness and directly against Hooker's flank. Hooker would be completely absorbed in defending his flank, which would give Lee, at the head of 17,000 men, the opportunity to attack Hooker's front. While Jackson and Lee were enveloping Hooker at Chancellorsville, Jubal Early would fight a holding action aimed at pinning down the rest of the Army of the Potomac, at Fredericksburg. By dividing in the presence of the enemy, Lee proposed to defeat a divided and diluted Army of the Potomac in detail.

Jackson had the hazardous and demanding mission of advancing—in total stealth—with 26,000 men to positions just two and a half miles from the Union front. He did have an edge in Jeb Stuart's control of the roads in and out of Chancellorsville. Nevertheless, it was supremely difficult to hide the march of so many men. Fortune, however, favored Jackson at this point. Pickets in advance of the Union XI Corps actually detected and reported the movement. Astoundingly, however, the commanding general of the corps, O. O. Howard, considered the movement insignificant. He nevertheless conferred with Hooker, who concurred in his assessment. Thus Jackson's maneuver was ignored.

The day waned—until, just two hours before sunset—a highly unconventional time to initiate an attack—Jackson hit Howard, whose corps formed the entire right flank of the Army of the Potomac. He hit Howard hard, and the surprise was total. The Union troops were at their leisure, engaged in the usual camp activities of eating, swapping stories, playing cards. For the most part, arms were stacked outside of every tent. Most soldiers did not have their rifle muskets to hand when (as one Union man recalled), Jackson's men fell upon them "like a clap of thunderstorm from a cloudless sky."

The Union XI Corps began to melt away under the onslaught. A rout developed, and Hooker gave the command to withdraw from the prepared defenses of Chancellorsville. The Union commander suddenly realized that his only hope of salvation lay in maneuvering. This, as he saw it, would avoid destruction. It was a panic-driven move. As Hooker would later admit, he had "lost his nerve." In leaving the cover of Chancellorsville, he did precisely what Lee and Jackson hoped he would do. He led his men out into the open.

Jackson quickly turned from Chancellorsville proper and engaged some 70,000 Union soldiers on the field. While this was happening, Lee closed in on Hooker's front, but despite the envelopment, the Chancellorsville phase of the battle raged over two days, ending late on May 4. Cut off by Early's control of the road net, Hooker was unable to receive reinforcements. *He,* not Lee, suffered the consequences of having divided his army in the presence of the enemy. As the sun went down on May 4, Hooker and his men made a fighting retreat north of the Rappahannock.

The cost to Hooker of the Chancellorsville phase of the battle was 12,145 men killed, wounded, captured, or missing. The Union general was stunned—as was the whole of the North. Chancellorsville was but a short distance from Fredericksburg, site of the massive defeat of Ambrose Burnside in December 1862. Now, months later, Burnside's replacement, Fighting Joe Hooker, had suffered casualties of the same magnitude—and the battle was not yet over. It was incomprehensible to the Union public, press, and president how Hooker, with more than twice Lee's manpower, was so horrifically defeated.

But, then, the people of the North did not yet know the full extent of Lee's losses. While the final toll of battle would leave the Army of the Potomac with a 13 percent casualty rate and force the army out of Chancellorsville, the victorious Lee would lose nearly one fourth—22 percent—of the Army of Northern Virginia, killed, wounded, captured, or missing.

In fact, Lee would lose even more.

Having opened his assault on Hooker late in the day on May 2, Jackson was compelled to break off the attack before he had finished with his adversary. He therefore decided to scout the front in order to plan a continuation of the battle through the night. After reconnoitering, Jackson and his staff set out to return to their lines via the Plank Road—the very route along which his men had advanced so stealthily to Chancellorsville. Along the road was a picket line from the 19th North Carolina Regiment. These sentries were wound up tight, on the lookout for advancing Federals. The last thing they expected to see was their own commanding general and his aides. So when uniformed figures appeared on the Plank Road, the pickets opened fire—not in a single volley, but in a succession of two. General Jackson was hit three times, twice in the left arm and once in the right hand. Others among those accompanying him were also hit—killed or wounded.

Supported by two of his staff, the stricken general was led to a place where he could be loaded onto a stretcher and carried to the rear. As he was being conveyed, one more shot cracked. The ball struck down one of the stretcher bearers, who lost his grip on the stretcher. The wounded Jackson tumbled onto the ground, hard. Another bearer helped put Jackson on the stretcher again, and the grim party made its way to an ambulance, where Dr. Hunter Holmes McGuire, chief surgeon of Jackson's Corps, knelt to examine his commanding officer.

"I hope you are not badly hurt, General."

"I am badly injured," Jackson replied and, in even more measured words, continued. "I fear I am dying. I am glad you have come. I think the wound in my shoulder is still bleeding." His calm was in sharp contrast to Hooker's panic. The two men were very different generals.

No commander, save Lee himself, meant more to the Confederacy than Thomas J. Jackson, and there he lay, soaked in his own blood. He and the Southern cause were fortunate in just one thing at that moment. McGuire was a first-class physician, who knew exactly what had to be done and did it. Jackson was bleeding out from a major artery in his left arm. McGuire stopped the bleeding by applying hard compression and severely tightening the bandage. He recognized Jackson's icy hands, clammy skin, and colorless lips as the signs of shock caused by massive blood loss. Although the general insisted that he was in no pain, McGuire gave him whiskey and a dose of morphine before sending him to a field hospital. There, the physician made the decision to do one of the few things surgeons of the era could do for a wounded man. He would amputate Jackson's left arm.

"Yes, certainly, Dr. McGuire," Jackson replied without question. "Do for me whatever you think best."

As McGuire gently placed a chloroform-soaked cloth over Jackson's nose and mouth, the general uttered, with gratitude, "What an infinite blessing."

McGuire used the span of Jackson's unconsciousness to attend first to the quick and simple task of removing a musket ball that had burrowed itself under the skin on the back of his patient's right hand after having entered through the palm and fractured two bones. It was a round ball, .57 caliber—nearly three-fifths of an inch in diameter—the old-fashioned ammunition used in so many obsolescent Confederate muskets, not the bullet-shaped Minié ball fired by more modern rifle muskets. This relatively simple operation completed, McGuire swiftly amputated the left arm two inches below the shoulder. He later noted that this limb had been shattered by two musket balls, one having smashed the bone and divided the artery about three inches below the shoulder-joint, the other having torn a wound from the outside of the forearm, an inch below the elbow, through to the opposite side of the arm, exiting just above the wrist. It was the kind of horrific gunshot damage any Civil War surgeon soon became accustomed to treating.

Stonewall Jackson came through the surgery very well, and his chances for recovery seemed promising. True, on regaining consciousness, he was uncharacteristically disengaged from the battle. When Major Sandy Pendleton visited him in the hospital seeking orders to carry to Major General Jeb Stuart, who had assumed command, Jackson replied to his request with "I don't know, I can't tell; say to General Stuart he must do what he thinks best."

With this, he fell asleep and slept until the next morning. By that time, a note had arrived from Lee. Jackson's aide read it to him: "Could I have directed events, I should have chosen, for the good of the country, to have been disabled in your stead. I congratulate you upon the victory, which is due to your skill and energy."

"General Lee should give the praise to God," Jackson told the aide. His faith and humility were also in contrast with the profane bombast of Fighting Joe Hooker.

After passing this day and the night that followed in the field hospital, Jackson, on McGuire's orders, was sent away from the front to Guiney's Station. The doctor explained that he feared Union troops might capture him.

"If the enemy does come, I am not afraid of them; I have always been kind to their wounded, and I am sure they will be kind to me."

He was made comfortable in a private house and even took a crust of bread and cup of tea. Learning that there were men elsewhere in the house who were suffering from erysipelas, a painful and highly contagious skin infection commonly known as Saint Anthony's fire, McGuire moved his patient to an out-building on the property. The next morning brought a cheerful development, as Jackson awakened with a hearty appetite. Better still, on replacing his dressings, Dr. McGuire noted that the wounds were healing well, without any of the telltale indications of infection. The general spoke of soon returning to the field.

About one the next morning, Jackson woke nauseated. He asked a servant for a wet towel, but absolutely forbade him to wake his doctor, noting that the poor man had not slept for three days. When McGuire made his regular visit to his patient later that morning, he diagnosed pleuropneumonia—inflammation of the lungs and the pleura (sacs surrounding the lungs)—on the right side. McGuire speculated that this was caused by Jackson's fall after one of his stretcher bearers had been shot. It could, however, also have been aggravated by the chloroform anesthetic.

Jackson deteriorated through the day, but he seemed to improve that evening and was greatly cheered by the arrival of his second wife, Mary Anna Morrison, who brought with her their infant daughter, Julia Laura.

"I know you would gladly give your life for me," he told Mary Anna, "but I am perfectly resigned. Do not be sad. I hope I may yet recover. Pray for me, but always remember in your prayers to use the petition, *Thy will be done*."

The next morning gave new reason for hope. Jackson's wounds continued to heal satisfactorily, and his pain was fading. Nevertheless, his breathing was becoming progressively more labored, and, as the day wore on, Jackson showed signs of exhaustion as he worked harder to breathe. He made it through another night and, the next day, was sufficiently alert to play with his baby daughter. Later, however, he beckoned to Dr. McGuire: "I see from the number of physicians that you think my condition dangerous, but I thank God, if it is His will, that I am ready to go."

At sunup on Sunday, May 10, Mary Anna sat by her husband's bedside. Dr. McGuire had spoken to her, and now, when Jackson opened his eyes, she told him that the doctor believed his recovery was "doubtful."

"It will be infinite gain to be translated to Heaven," Jackson replied to her. "You have a kind and good father, but there is no one so kind and good as your Heavenly Father."

At about eleven that morning, Jackson tried to calm his wife's fears—"I may yet get well"—and then he asked her to send in Dr. McGuire.

"Doctor, Anna informs me that you have told her that I am to die today; is it so?"

McGuire answered that this was so.

"Very good, very good, it is all right."

By the afternoon, Stonewall Jackson slipped into a strangely calm delirium. He began issuing battlefield orders and then seemingly held mess-table conversation with his staff. When his doctor offered brandy and water, Jackson demurred.

"It will only delay my departure, and do no good. I want to preserve my mind, if possible, to the last."

McGuire told him that he would live, perhaps, another two hours.

"Very good, it is all right."

He sunk deeper into incoherence, but, suddenly, he snapped into something very like full consciousness.

"Order A. P. Hill to prepare for action! Pass the infantry to the front rapidly! Tell Major Hawks——"

At this he stopped, and what Dr. McGuire described as "a smile of ineffable sweetness spread itself over his pale face."

"Let us cross over the river and rest under the shade of the trees," he said. They were his final words. He was thirty-nine.

The Battle of Chancellorsville had ended four days earlier, on May 6, with a final action at nearby Fredericksburg and Salem Church. The Confederate victory was so complete and against such superior numbers that even Northerners admiringly called it "Lee's masterpiece." Yet while Hooker lost 13 percent of the force engaged, Lee lost 22 percent. And the hardest loss of all was Stonewall Jackson.

"I have lost my right arm," Lee said. Realizing that the Confederacy could not replace let alone endure another loss of so many men, including men like Stonewall Jackson, the commanding officer of the Army of Northern Virginia made the fateful decision to try to force a rapid end to the war by bringing the fighting into the North. Battered though the Army of Northern Virginia was, he resolved to invade the Union. He would march into Pennsylvania.

As for Abraham Lincoln, another of his generals having failed him, he could do little more than gasp out his disbelief: "My God! My God! What will the country say? What will the country say?"

17

November 7, 1862

Lincoln Chooses Burnside to
Lead the Army of the Potomac

Why it's significant. Desperate to find a general capable of delivering victory, Abraham Lincoln replaced George B. McClellan with Ambrose Burnside as commanding officer of the Army of the Potomac—even after Burnside twice declined the offer of that prestigious command, protesting that he was not capable of undertaking so great a responsibility. Seven days after hiring Burnside, the president approved his aggressive but ham-handed plan to capture Richmond, the prize that had eluded McClellan. The Battle of Fredericksburg would prove that the desire for victory, no matter how desperate, could not prevail against military genius in the persons of Robert E. Lee and Stonewall Jackson. For the Union, Fredericksburg was sheer heartbreak. For Lee, it was the first of two triumphs—the second was at Chancellorsville (Chapter 16)—that nevertheless failed to bring the North to negotiate a favorable peace with the South.

MOST HISTORIANS—MOST AMERICANS—AGREE that the nation's two greatest presidents were George Washington and Abraham Lincoln. The only disagreement might be over the order of their greatness. Washington first? Lincoln second? Vice versa?

The thing is, although Washington led the nation to victory in the revolution and independence as a result, and while he answered his new nation's call to become its first president, Lincoln redeemed the Union and led America through what was for all intents and purposes a Second American Revolution. So the historical basis for ranking in greatness the first and the sixteenth presidents is not straightforward. Both Washington and Lincoln rendered profound services to the nation. Both proved themselves to be indispensable men.

Viewed from the perspective of popular culture and collective sentiment rather than history, our two greatest presidents are far easier to rank. Congress commissioned Henry "Light-Horse Harry" Lee, brilliant major general in the Continental Army, governor of Virginia, and future father of Robert E. Lee, to write a eulogy on the death of George Washington in 1799. Light-Horse Harry pronounced his subject "First in war, first in peace, and first in the hearts of his countrymen." But, in the farther-seeing eye of history, this magnificent sentence is not quite accurate. Abraham Lincoln, not George Washington, is arguably first in the hearts of his countrymen. To think of Washington is to think of a great figure carved in gleaming marble. To summon up the image of Abraham Lincoln is to recall a Mathew Brady daguerreotype—the face gaunt, rough, gentle, prematurely aged by four years of war. It is the face of a man for whom the nation's greatest office was an honor so burdensome and tragic that the word *bittersweet* is a weak understatement. Lincoln groped his way through the Civil War, desperately seeking a strategy and a military leader to win and end it. He hired and fired one commanding general after another. When Irvin McDowell was defeated at the First Battle of Bull Run (July 21, 1861), he turned to the "Young Napoleon," George Brinton McClellan, who, after frittering away time and lives in his timid Peninsula Campaign (March-July 1862), eked out enough of a victory at the Battle of Antietam (September 17, 1862) to buy the president a platform from which he might publish to America and the world the Emancipation Proclamation. That was a great thing, but, evaluated in strictly military terms, McClellan had delivered in Antietam yet another crushing disappointment.

Militarily, the price paid at Antietam was far too high for the results obtained. Lee had been driven out of Maryland, but his Army of Northern Virginia, though battered, lived to fight another day. Not only had McClellan failed to pursue Lee as he retreated from Antietam, he refused to do much of anything with the Union's flagship force, the Army of the Potomac—prompting the president to complain that its grand name "is a mistake; it is only McClellan's bodyguard."

Lincoln accepted what McClellan had given him at Antietam—the occasion to transform the Civil War into a crusade not only to restore the Union, but to liberate America's enslaved—but then he fired McClellan. For the Young Napoleon had failed to give him and his country nearly enough.

Who could?

Once again, Lincoln found himself forced to choose among candidates of varying degrees of inadequacy. From among these, one stood out—at least more or less—and Lincoln settled on him. His name was Ambrose Everett Burnside, one of those affable and empathetic commanders who naturally express affection for the men they lead and thus receive affection in return. A West Point graduate (Class of 1847), he was deployed to service in the US-Mexican War (1846–1848) too late to see combat, but he did manage to receive an honorable wound after the war in an 1849 skirmish with Apaches in New Mexico when an arrow pierced his neck. He resigned his commission in 1853, devoted himself to perfecting a carbine for cavalry use, and plowed what money he had and could borrow into manufacturing the weapon—only to lose, through the corruption of President James Buchanan's secretary of war, the government contract that should have made him wealthy. Subsequently, he tried politics, running in 1858 for Congress from Rhode Island. After he lost by a landslide, his rifle factory burned to the ground, and he was forced to sell his firearm patents to the highest bidders—who did not bid very high. Desperate, he moved west and found a position as treasurer of the Illinois Central Railroad, the vice president of which was another West Pointer and former US Army officer, George B. McClellan.

The two men became friends, and Burnside would serve under McClellan in the Army of the Potomac. For both McClellan and he answered their country's call at the outbreak of the Civil War. Burnside raised and led the 1ˢᵗ Rhode Island Volunteer Regiment and soon rose to command of a brigade in the Department of Northeast Virginia. His maiden battle was the First Battle of Bull Run (July 21, 1861), in which he performed neither better nor worse than most other unit commanders. Still, McClellan recruited him to train provisional brigades in the emerging Army of the Potomac in August, a job in which he proved his ability to work well with soldiers.

From September 1861 to July 1862, Burnside commanded the North Carolina Expeditionary Force and achieved a series of victories in that state. Although they were minor, they were won against a dreary backdrop of Union defeats and were thus considerably magnified. Besides, Burnside's striking appearance began to command considerable public attention. Trim and broad-chested, he filled out his uniform handsomely. His monumentally high forehead and the stately recession of his hairline, which, joined to magnificent mutton chop whiskers and moustache, dramatically framed his noble features. Those whiskers enjoyed a fame destined to outlive anything else he did. They were so widely emulated that they were called burnsides, a name eventually inverted to sideburns.

Battles won and looks sufficiently distinctive to be considered striking earned Ambrose Burnside good press. Add to this a sincere and highly visible concern for his soldiers, and he shone as one of the few bright lights among the Union's officer corps. His loyal troops lovingly recounted how, after the Battle of New Bern (March 14, 1862), he visited the wounded in a field hospital. There he ran across a soldier named John Hope, whom he recognized as having served in his artillery battery during the US-Mexican War. Seeing that Hope had been badly wounded in the leg, Burnside withdrew a ten-dollar note from his pocket and gave it to the man, along with a friendly command to buy fresh fruit and vegetables. They promoted healing, Burnside assured him. He returned to visit Hope again just before the wounded were scheduled for evacuation. On that occasion, he proffered another five dollars—for the journey, he said.

President Lincoln took Burnside's victories with a grain of salt. They were skirmishes, after all. But he was more impressed by accounts of how soldiers lobbied to serve under him and invariably cheered him wherever he went. It was, according to one officer, a cheer that was first heard at a distance, as Burnside approached, but increased in volume the nearer he came. After North Carolina, Burnside returned to the war's mainstream, as commander of the right wing (I Corps and IX Corps) of McClellan's Army of the Potomac at the Battle of South Mountain (September 14, 1862). In contrast to his earlier battles, this one was major, involving a total of 28,000 Union troops, of whom 2,325 became casualties (killed, wounded, or missing). Still, South Mountain was a Union victory, and Burnside had had a part in it. Days later, he served as left wing (just IX Corps) commander at the far more consequential Battle of Antietam (September 17, 1862). And here he did not perform nearly so well. He failed to make proper reconnaissance and lost both time and men by crossing the Antietam over a very narrow stone bridge that was under fire by Confederate sharpshooters. Burnside's costly delay contributed to McClellan's failures in the battle. Given the Union's more than 2-to-1 numerical superiority, Antietam should have been a decisive victory. Instead, it was a strategic victory but a costly tactical draw—at best.

Why, then, would Lincoln turn from McClellan, who had disappointed him at Antietam, to Burnside, who had materially contributed to that disappointment?

For one thing, Burnside had performed no less competently than other senior commanders at the battle. In addition, he possessed something no other Union Eastern Theater commander possessed: a record of victories. Indeed, Lincoln first offered Burnside the opportunity to replace McClellan as commanding general of the Army of the Potomac on July 27, 1862, *before* Antietam. At that time, Burnside turned down the offer—flat. He told the president that George B. McClellan was simply the better commander. All he needed was "a fair chance" to prove it.

Whatever else Burnside was, he was honorable, and he was loyal. McClellan had given him a good job at the Illinois Central when he desperately needed it, and he had given him every consideration as one of his senior commanders in the Army of the Potomac. But Burnside's demurral was not just the product of loyalty. It was a remarkably frank self-assessment. Many years later, in his

Personal Memoirs, Grant wrote that Burnside "was generally liked and respected," but "was not . . . fitted to command an army." And he added this most telling comment: "No one knew this better than himself. He always admitted his blunders, and extenuated those of officers under him beyond what they were entitled to. It was hardly his fault that he was ever assigned to a separate command"—by which Grant meant command of an entire army.

Lincoln was intent on removing and replacing McClellan. Just before the Battle of Antietam, he summoned Burnside again and, again, offered him command of the Army of the Potomac. This time, Burnside was even more brutally honest about himself. He told the president that he was simply incapable of leading so large an army. Lincoln let it go, until November 5, 1862, after Antietam and after McClellan repeatedly ignored Lincoln's orders to take the battle to Lee. Now, through the War Department, President Lincoln issued General Order No. 182, which was handed to Brigadier General Catharinus Putnam Buckingham for delivery to Burnside, who was with his Army of the Potomac corps in Virginia. Buckingham presented the order to Burnside on November 7. It announced McClellan's relief from command of the Army of the Potomac and the appointment in his place of Ambrose Burnside.

Having twice offered, Lincoln now commanded. Still, Burnside pleaded with Buckingham, telling him that he was incapable of leading 120,000 men and repeating his opinion that McClellan was a well-qualified commander. He also protested that changing generals in the middle of a campaign was potentially disastrous.

Lincoln had made clear to the War Department that he needed Burnside to follow his order, and Buckingham had been thoroughly coached in how to prevail against Burnside's objections and protestations. The brigadier general explained in no uncertain terms that President Lincoln was adamant in his intention to relieve McClellan. The president, he told Burnside, was ordering him to take his place. Of course, he could always resign his commission, but doing so would not save the job for McClellan. Buckingham sympathetically explained that he appreciated the general's self-doubts, but, he continued, if he did not follow orders and take the job, it would almost certainly go to the single senior officer in the entire United

States Army that the universally cordial and popular Burnside actually hated: Joseph Hooker. Hooker was the kind of leader Burnside could not tolerate. He was arrogant, he was a careerist, and he had repeatedly shown himself disloyal to his commanding officers when such disloyalty might gain him a promotion.

The mention of Hooker spurred Burnside to surrender and say yes. With that, Buckingham accompanied him to McClellan's tent. From the strained preliminary courtesies, McClellan must have sensed that something unpleasant was afoot even before Buckingham handed over General Order 182. McClellan read it, laid it down, and locked eyes on Ambrose Burnside. He must have understood that his friend and loyal subordinate had asked for none of this.

"Well, Burnside," he said, "I turn the command over to you."

Poor Burnside! He was absolutely right when he told Lincoln that he was incapable of leading 120,000 men. Lacking any practical idea of how to manage so vast a force, he decided to simplify the organization of the Army of the Potomac by creating three "Grand Divisions" (his term), consisting of two corps each. He put these three immense units under Generals Edwin V. Sumner, Joseph Hooker, and William B. Franklin. It looked like a simple undertaking on paper—but, in the field, it was wholly impractical. There were insufficient levels of command to execute decisions and to provide adequate feedback from the field. Before planning a single battle or firing a single shot, Burnside made his first serious strategic blunder. He had thrown away organizational agility.

Almost immediately after assuming command, Burnside was bombarded by Lincoln and Secretary of War Edwin Stanton with demands that he launch a major offensive against Lee and the Army of Northern Virginia. McClellan would have responded with delaying tactics, including simply turning a deaf ear to Washington. Burnside had a very different personality. He wanted, above all, to please the president. Accordingly, he promised to mount an attack that would accomplish in a single stroke what McClellan had been unable to do over many months. He decided to position the Army of the Potomac north of the Rappahannock River at Warrenton, Virginia, thirty miles from Lee's badly outnumbered Army of Northern Virginia, which consisted of just two corps, commanded by Stonewall Jackson and James Longstreet. From here, he would march on Richmond.

It might actually have worked if Burnside had been a better general or had even taken some time to ponder the position of Lee's army. It was, in fact, quite vulnerable at the moment because it was widely separated into two wings, the corps under Jackson and the corps under Longstreet. The correct move was to attack between the wings, hitting both on their flanks, focusing on one and then the other. Given Burnside's superior manpower, it is likely that he would have thus succeeded in defeating Lee "in detail"—meaning that, by taking on the separated parts of the enemy's forces, it is far easier to destroy them one after the other, than trying to defeat a united force. Pressed by Washington and intent on taking immediate action, however, Burnside blundered. Instead of patiently attacking the two separated wings of his enemy, he decided to advance toward Richmond via Fredericksburg, thereby forcing Lee to make a stand at the town. This relinquished the advantage of attacking a divided army out in the open and instead gave Lee the opportunity to take up a strong defensive position in the hills behind Fredericksburg. Before firing a shot, Burnside had surrendered the high ground, which gave even the outnumbered Army of Northern Virginia a lethal tactical advantage.

All of this said, there was still a way for Burnside to win. By allowing Lee to consolidate his forces, Burnside had given himself a very large bite to chew. What he needed now was to move quickly and attack with a maximum of violence before the consolidation of forces could be completed. Instead, Burnside had a great deal of difficulty moving his unwieldy forces, organized as they were into three ponderous "Grand Divisions." On November 17, 1862, when Sumner's Grand Division arrived on the bank of the Rappahannock River opposite Fredericksburg, Burnside ordered Sumner to wait there until six pontoon bridges could be put in place for the crossing. Incredibly, bumbling staff work managed to delay the arrival of the bridges for a full month. This gave General Longstreet more than enough time to dig elaborate field fortifications into the hills south and west of town. Moreover, it also allowed ample time for Stonewall Jackson to get into well-defended positions. What had been a divided army was now one.

By December 11, as Burnside's engineers labored to assemble the belated pontoon bridges under heavy sniper fire, 78,000 Confederate troops were well entrenched on the south bank of the Rappahannock, with Fredericksburg between their positions and the river. Indeed, Burnside could not have put the Army of the Potomac in a worse spot. He had to cross the Rappahannock to attack, and an even bigger river, the Potomac was at his back, restricting his ability to maneuver.

While Burnside struggled to mount a brute-force head-on attack, Lee had the tactical genius to allow Burnside to do just that. Except for the sniper fire, Lee did very little to contest the enemy's crossing of the Rappahannock during December 11–12. In fact, he allowed Burnside's men to enter and occupy Fredericksburg.

It is difficult to believe that the Union commander did not know he was marching into an ambush. Perhaps he thought that his superior numbers would allow him to overcome even well-entrenched soldiers firing from high ground. Either way, Burnside, a general devoted to his men, was leading them to certain death.

Before occupying the town, Burnside launched an intense artillery barrage against it. To this day, nobody knows why he ordered the massive barrage. Some believe he thought it would suppress sniper fire. But the Union artillerymen did not aim for the hillside entrenchments. They wanted to destroy the town, which had been evacuated of civilians. Thus the barrage of some 5,000 shells was an orgy of property destruction. After Fredericksburg had been reduced to rubble, the soldiers marched in and began looting whatever of value remained.

Watching from their hillside fortifications, the Confederates seethed with rage. When the looting troops temporarily withdrew on the evening of December 12, Stonewall Jackson and an aide surveyed the ruins with disbelief. War was one thing, but wanton, purposeless devastation was the act of a spiteful vandal.

Jackson's aide shook his head and wondered aloud, *What should be done about this?*

Hearing him, Jackson replied under his breath, "Kill 'em. Kill 'em all."

That level of killing began south of town at 8:30 on the morning of December 13 as Major General William Franklin led his Grand

Division through a gap that had opened in Jackson's Corps. Once again, Burnside was presented with an opportunity to do something other than kill and be killed. Had he concentrated more men on exploiting this gap, he might have positioned enough of his troops to direct effective fire against the defenders of Fredericksburg. However, anxious to push the battle relentlessly forward, he began a series of headlong charges against virtually impregnable positions dug into the hills.

This was the beginning of a kind of madness. For there was no strategy, no tactical advantage in this. Burnside hurled his men against the guns of a mostly hidden enemy. He watched as his soldiers fell atop one another, building up a berm of corpses before a stone wall that ran along a sunken road just beneath the Confederates' strongest position at a place the locals called Marye's Heights.

And even as the bodies piled higher and spread wider, Burnside ordered another wave forward, and another, and another.

This is "murder, not warfare," one of Burnside's officers remarked. Later, one of Longstreet's artillerists, perched on Marye's Heights, offered his assessment: "A chicken could not live on that field" once his cannon had opened up on it.

After fourteen furious charges, each a mission of collective suicide, Burnside decided that there was time for just one more charge before the onset of darkness. Openly weeping for men he loved, he announced that he would personally lead this final charge. At this, his staff and others intervened, begging him to withdraw, pointing to the obvious fact that if fourteen frontal assaults had failed, why should a fifteenth suddenly break through?

In the failing light, Ambrose Burnside ordered the buglers to call Retreat. Long accustomed to hearing the cheers of his men, the general heard nothing as he rode among them in the withdrawal back across the Rappahannock. Uncomfortable with the disrespectful silence, his aide-de-camp, riding alongside him, called on the soldiers to raise the traditional three cheers, *Hip, hip* . . . . But there was only more silence by way of response.

Of the roughly 114,000 Army of the Potomac soldiers actively engaged in combat, including the fourteen separate charges against the Confederate entrenchments at Fredericksburg, 12,653 were

killed, wounded, captured, or missing. Of the 78,513 Army of
Northern Virginia defenders, 4,201 were killed, wounded, captured,
or missing.

That night, the reluctant commander of the Union's flagship formation wrote to his commanding officer, Henry Wager Halleck:

> To the brave officers and soldiers who accomplished the feat
> of . . . recrossing the river in the face of the enemy, I owe every-
> thing. For the failure in the attack I am responsible . . . . To the
> families and friends of the dead I can offer my heartfelt sympa-
> thies, but for the wounded I can offer my earnest prayers for their
> comfortable and final recovery.

Ambrose Burnside was a patriot. He wanted to serve. He desperately wanted to give Abraham Lincoln the victory he craved. Heartbroken by the outcome at Fredericksburg, he nevertheless proposed
to General Halleck a new initiative in the hope of redeeming the
disaster he had authored. His plan now was to yet again cross the
Rappahannock for another assault on Lee. Appalled by what they
saw as the certainty of more bloodshed in the cause of utter futility,
a small group of Burnside's commanders sent word of the new plan
to President Lincoln. Whether or not he approved of this mutinous
break in the chain of command, Lincoln ordered Burnside to make
no such attack.

On January 20, 1863, however, Burnside acted on what seemed
a far more feasible tactical plan. This time he would not attack Lee
frontally. Instead, he proposed to envelop the Army of Northern Virginia by marching into position across the Rappahannock at Banks's
Ford, a crossing farther from Lee's position. This would give the
Army of the Potomac more room to maneuver for a flank attack. The
only rub was the long march required to reach Banks's Ford. Still,
the underlying idea was a good one. The weather, however, was far
from favorable. Virginia had been pounded by two days of heavy
sleet followed by a thaw. Combined with the tramping of tens of
thousands of men and horses, the thaw turned the route of the march
into a foul soup. Burnside's bold advance, his shot at redemption,
degenerated into the infamous "Mud March." It was a supremely

humiliating spectacle—the Union's greatest army, the Army of the Potomac, bogged down in knee-deep mud.

The Mud March and what it seemed to symbolize were too much for Abraham Lincoln. On January 26, 1863, the president relieved Ambrose Burnside of command of the Army of the Potomac and replaced him with the very man Brigadier General Buckingham had threatened Burnside with, Joseph "Fighting Joe" Hooker.

The president sent Hooker a detailed personal letter laying out his rationale for having chosen him to command the Army of the Potomac. He closed with a brutally frank statement of the reservations he entertained about his own choice. Lincoln criticized Hooker for failing to support Burnside, and he firmly admonished him over a rash remark Hooker had made to the press. "Both the Army and the Government need a dictator," Hooker had proclaimed. Lincoln now wrote, "Only those generals who gain success can set up dictators. What I now ask of you is military success, and I will risk the dictatorship. . . . Beware of rashness, but with energy and sleepless vigilance go forward and give us victories."

To his credit, Fighting Joe set about reinvigorating his army. Then he led it to a town not far from Fredericksburg. Called Chancellorsville, it would be the site of an even more catastrophic Union defeat (Chapter 16).

18

August 28–30, 1862

Lee Divides and Conquers
at the Second Battle of Bull Run

Why it's significant. Outnumbered two to one, Robert E. Lee and his corps commanders Stonewall Jackson and James Longstreet outgeneraled the Union's pompous and unpopular John Pope at the Second Battle of Bull Run. The reputations of three Confederate generals rose to mythic proportions as yet another Union military leader—Lincoln's latest candidate for top command—suffers not merely defeat but humiliation. The outcome was another blow to Northern morale and a grave political threat to Abraham Lincoln. At this point, the Union was losing the Civil War.

GEORGE B. MCCLELLAN, the vaunted "Young Napoleon" on whom Abraham Lincoln relied to redeem the Union Army from the humiliation of the First Battle of Bull Run (July 21, 1861), had promised to capture Richmond in what he called the Peninsula Campaign, a name that echoed Napoleon's "Peninsular War," fought for possession of the Iberian Peninsula in 1807–1814. It was not the best Napoleonic parallel to evoke. The Peninsular War was one of the defeats from which Napoleon could not recover.

McClellan's Peninsula Campaign spanned March to July 1862, culminating in the so-called Seven Days Battles (June 25-July 1, 1862), the last of which was Malvern Hill (July 1). That battle ended in a tactical victory for McClellan, but a victory fought not on ground to which he had advanced, but to which he had retreated. Having set out to capture Richmond, the Young Napoleon ended up farther from the Confederate capital than he had been at the start of his endeavor. Moreover, while McClellan defended his high ground position expertly at Malvern Hill, bombarding Robert E. Lee's attacking forces with fire from massed cannon that were positioned nearly wheel to wheel, he refused his field officers' pleas to seize the initiative, hold Malvern Hill, and counterattack Lee. This might have revived and redeemed the Peninsula Campaign. Certainly, it would have taken a greater toll on Lee than the mere defense did. But George B. McClellan was completely cowed by the Confederate general, even when, as now, Lee committed a great blunder in fruitlessly attacking uphill. No sooner did Lee break off his attack than McClellan completed his withdrawal from the campaign against Richmond by returning to Harrison's Landing, the location on the James River from which the Army of the Potomac had originally embarked.

Commanding a larger army than Lee, McClellan had failed in his mission. Nevertheless, his 16,000 casualties (killed, wounded, captured, or missing) were 4,000 fewer than what he had inflicted on the Army of Northern Virginia. Tactically, the Union forces had come out ahead. Strategically, they were humiliated. As if to certify his failure, Major General McClellan sent an abject telegram to the War Department on July 2, 1862: "I now pray for time. My men have proved themselves the equals of any troops in the world—but they are worn out. Our losses have been very great. I doubt whether more severe battles have ever been fought—we have failed to win only because overpowered by superior numbers."

The telegram did not appease Abraham Lincoln. Astoundingly, McClellan assessed Lee's strength at almost 200,000 men. It was actually between 55,000 and 65,000. Feeling that McClellan was not just making poor use of the magnificent army he had built, but virtually no use of it, Lincoln summoned Major General John Pope to a conference. He assigned him to command a force to be known as the Army of Virginia. It would consist of numerous units in and around Virginia that had been slated for incorporation into the Army of the Potomac. As if this weren't a sufficient demonstration of Lincoln's loss of confidence in McClellan, who seemed not only unwilling but incapable of leaving Harrison's Landing, Lincoln ordered him to return to northern Virginia and detach three Army of the Potomac corps to be put under Pope's command and used in coordination with the Army of Virginia.

From today's perspective, few would argue that Lincoln was wrong to shift the initiative away from McClellan; however, he could hardly have chosen a less popular officer to turn to. Pope had shown a certain brilliance as commanding general of the Army of the Mississippi against Confederate General Sterling Price in Missouri and in the capture of Island No. 10 on the Mississippi River (February 28-April 8, 1862). His far greater military talent, however, was his unerring ability to alienate virtually everyone in the army, both officers and enlisted men. When he assumed command of the Army of Virginia in July 1862, he addressed his soldiers with a level of condescension that makes one cringe even to read it:

> Let us understand each other. I have come to you from the West, where we have always seen the backs of our enemies; from an army whose business it has been to seek the adversary and to beat him when he was found; whose policy has been attack and not defense. In but one instance has the enemy been able to place our Western armies in defensive attitude. I presume that I have been called here to pursue the same system and to lead you against the enemy. It is my purpose to do so, and that speedily. I am sure you long for an opportunity to win the distinction you are capable of achieving. That opportunity I shall endeavor to give you . . .

Amazingly, Pope also provoked a special outrage from the enemy. The Army of Virginia occupied a sliver of northern Virginia. Instead of trying to win over the populace there, Pope tyrannized them. He seized from the people whatever food supplies he wanted, and he repeatedly threatened to hang civilians as well as prisoners of war and traitors. Robert E. Lee found Pope's conduct so unbecoming a military officer that he condemned him as no better than a "miscreant" in need of being "suppressed."

It was not idle trash talk. Lee saw Pope as an inept and bombastic commander who was supplanting a timid one, McClellan. This made both the Army of Virginia and at least the three corps of the Army of the Potomac that were assigned to Pope's command especially vulnerable—provided that Lee could strike before those three corps could link up with the Army of Virginia. Accordingly, on August 9, 1862, Lee dispatched Stonewall Jackson to attack a portion of the Army of Virginia at Cedar Mountain, near Culpeper. The resulting Battle of Cedar Mountain (August 9, 1862) was a minor Confederate victory that did no more than force Pope to withdraw to the north bank of Rappahannock River. But that was precisely where Lee wanted him. Lee could now attack before the reluctant, petulant, and slow-moving McClellan arrived with his three Army of the Potomac corps.

For the first time in his military career, Lee decided to violate a very basic tenet of military practice in the field. He put half the Army of Northern Virginia under Major General James "Old Pete" Longstreet, charging him with the mission of occupying Pope's front. The other half Lee gave to Stonewall Jackson, ordering him to lead his wing on a roundabout march to the northwest, so that he could hit the rear of the Army of Virginia with a surprise attack as Longstreet attacked Pope's front. It was a strategy Lee would use again in the Battle of Chancellorsville (April 30–May 6, 1863). The idea was to hold the enemy by the nose while kicking him in the rear.

Pope observed the movement of Longstreet and Jackson, but he did little enough about it, except to launch a harassing raid on the encampment of Confederate cavalryman Jeb Stuart. The aim of the raid was to capture or kill Stuart. While the raiders did manage to bag the cavalryman's adjutant, Stuart himself got away. In his haste to leave, he forgot to take with him his trademark ostrich-plumed hat and crimson-lined cape. Pope's raiders took these items as prizes—something that delighted them almost as much as having captured Stuart himself.

Jeb Stuart was outraged. Bad enough that his adjutant had been taken, but the raiders went too far when they stole that hat and cape. Duly provoked, on August 22, Stuart and a small raiding party rode full gallop into Major General Pope's headquarters camp at Catlett's Station. They captured 300 prisoners and "appropriated" $35,000 in Union army payroll money. Worse, perhaps, they rifled through Pope's personal baggage, taking his dress uniform coat and also his battle plans. Four days later, on August 26, Stonewall Jackson attacked and destroyed Pope's supply depot at Manassas Junction, Virginia, very near the site of the First Battle of Bull Run. As serious as the loss of supplies was, Jackson's raid did far worse by severing Pope's telegraph and rail lines. This partially cut off rapid communications to and from the field and greatly limited Pope's ability to transfer large numbers of men rapidly. The Union commander pursued Jackson, but was unable to locate him—at least until Jackson *wanted* to be found.

On August 28, Stonewall suddenly materialized. He attacked a Union brigade under Brigadier General Rufus King at Groveton. The skirmish was intense. Not only were two of Jackson's division commanders seriously wounded, but King's "Black Hat Brigade" (later called the "Iron Brigade") fought with a fervor Jackson had never before seen in a Union military unit. While King took a toll on Jackson, however, he also suffered heavy losses. Nearly a third of his brigade were killed, wounded, captured, or missing.

Together, the Manassas raid and the Battle of Groveton were overtures to the Second Battle of Bull Run (August 28–30, 1862). For all the problems Jackson had caused him, Pope was actually given an important advantage. The Confederate commander had revealed himself and thereby sacrificed the element of surprise. Pope knew exactly where he was, and he began concentrating his forces accordingly, deploying near Groveton with the intention not only of defeating Stonewall Jackson, but boasting that he would "bag the whole crowd."

Pope did what McClellan seemed unable to do. He took the initiative, and he attacked Jackson on August 29. The trouble was that the attacks came piecemeal. I Corps, under Franz Sigel, started in on Jackson, and then the Pennsylvania Reserves under John Reynolds joined in. Pope ordered Major General Fitz John Porter's V Corps, Army of the Potomac, to get between Jackson's Corps and Long- street's—but it was too late. Longstreet had already made contact with Jackson on his right. Porter was stymied, not knowing where to attack.

Another of Pope's commanders, Major General Samuel P. Heintzelman, bore down on Jackson with his corps, as did elements of Major General Jesse L. Reno's IX Corps and two divisions under Irvin McDowell, the Union commander defeated at the *First* Battle of Bull Run. Despite this impressive array of forces, Pope proved utterly unable to coordinate them. Individual Army of Virginia and Army of the Potomac units made inroads against Jackson's line here and there, but, lacking effective overall command, were unable to consolidate any of their gains. Each Union attack was repulsed in turn, and, after heavy fighting, Jackson remained in control of his position by the end of the day on August 29, while Longstreet, on his right, actively extended the Confederate line. Noting Longstreet's advantage, Lee urged him to attack, but, always cautious, Longstreet declined, protesting that he had no idea of Pope's strength to his right and front. Longstreet did launch a reconnaissance in force to ascertain what lay ahead. This resulted in some confused nighttime skirmishing, which prompted Longstreet to recall his brigades to their starting positions.

Although Longstreet had not intended this withdrawal to deceive Pope, Pope was nonetheless deceived. At daybreak on August 30, he assumed that both Jackson and Longstreet were in full and final retreat. He assumed that the Second Battle of Bull Run was over and that he had won. When it became evident that the Confederate com- manders were not giving up, Pope was confused. Unsure what to do, Pope launched a massive attack against Jackson's front. Porter's V Corps attacked just after three in the afternoon. Although the attack was bold, it discounted the presence of Longstreet, who used his artillery to enfilade the attackers, firing along the length of Porter's advance and cutting his men down like reaped wheat.

Lee was quick to take advantage of Porter's repulse. He ordered Longstreet to make a general advance, and, this time, Longstreet did so wholeheartedly and with absolute confidence. His troops surged forward, smashing into Union positions on much the same ground that had been contested at the First Battle of Bull Run. Still, two Union corps managed to hold out, and federal troops were able to hold a position on Henry House Hill. This made it possible that the tide of battle could still be turned in the Union's favor. But Pope had lost both situational awareness and the will to fight on. He saw only that his forces were being mauled and generally driven back. He did not grasp the significance of the action on and around the high ground of Henry House Hill. Accordingly, he ordered a general retreat back across Bull Run. Longstreet rushed in to take over Henry House Hill, and Pope continued to fall back, withdrawing the combined Army of Virginia and Army of the Potomac to the outer defenses of Washington itself. Of the 75,696 troops under John Pope's command, 1,724 were killed, 8,372 wounded, and 5,958 went missing. It was a devastating 21 percent casualty rate. Lee had a total of 48,527 men engaged, of which he lost 1,481 killed, 7,627 wounded, and 89 missing, making for a casualty rate almost as heavy as Pope's—19 percent.

President Lincoln wasted no time in disposing of a general he hoped could have effectively replaced McClellan. Three short days after the Second Battle of Bull Run, Pope was ordered to service in the Department of the Northwest, where he was tasked with battling the Santee Sioux, who had staged an uprising in Minnesota. In effect, Lincoln exiled him, altogether removing him from the Civil War. His Army of Virginia was dissolved, and most of its units and personnel incorporated into the Army of the Potomac, whose three corps were also returned, all under the command of George B. McClellan—at least for the time being. McClellan was apparently rehabilitated, but—at this point—the Union was losing the Civil War.

19

October 16–18, 1859

John Brown Raids Harpers Ferry

Why it's significant. John Brown's raid on the federal armory and arsenal at Harpers Ferry in an attempt to arm and incite a slave rebellion, together with his subsequent trial and execution, hardened abolitionist forces in the North. Less well recognized is the effect Brown had on the South, which reorganized its militias for greater efficiency, thereby laying the foundation for the rapid creation of a Confederate army. Although many abolitionists denounced the raid at the time, many historians regard it as the spark that ignited the Civil War.

JOHN BROWN BEGAN fighting the Civil War in 1856, five years before the firing on Fort Sumter. He was born in 1800, at Torrington, Connecticut, of early American Puritan stock, and he held the immutable religious, moral, and ideological conviction that slavery was an evil and an abomination that could be ended only by armed insurrection. His first field of battle was Kansas.

Civil war erupted in Kansas even earlier, in 1854, with passage of the Kansas-Nebraska Act that year. The guerrilla violence there between pro- and anti-slavery factions became a national disgrace

called "Bleeding Kansas." Its cause, ultimately, was the failure of
the founding fathers of the United States to resolve the issue of slavery before the Articles of Confederation and then the Constitution
were ratified in 1781 and 1788, respectively. From that point on, the
addition of each new state threatened to upset the balance between
the representation of slave and free states in Congress, especially in
the Senate. The prospect of each new addition to the Union threw
the nation into crisis. A series of legislative compromises were cob-
bled together in an effort to defuse national disputes that threatened
to escalate into civil war.

In 1802, the Louisiana Purchase added a vast territory to the
United States, destined eventually to be divided into states. In 1818–
19, a portion of the purchase, the Missouri Territory, petitioned for
statehood as a slave state. At the time, the Senate consisted of twenty-two senators from northern states and twenty-two from southern states. Adding a new slaveholding state would have shifted the
balance. Seeking to blunt the impact of Missouri statehood, Representative James Tallmadge of New York introduced an amendment
to the statehood bill calling for a ban on the further introduction of
slavery into the state, while maintaining all slaves there in their current status. As for slaves subsequently born in the state, they would
be automatically emancipated at age twenty-five. Thus slavery
would gradually disappear in Missouri through natural attrition. The
House passed the Tallmadge Amendment, but the Senate rejected
it, setting off a tortured debate that produced, in March 1820, the
Missouri Compromise. The compromise provided for the admission
of Missouri as a slave state, but, at the same time, Maine (hitherto
a part of Massachusetts) would enter as a free state, thereby maintaining the slave-free balance in Congress. Looking to the future,
the Missouri Compromise also drew a line across the territory of the
Louisiana Purchase at latitude 36 degrees, 30 minutes. North of this
demarcation, slavery would be permanently banned—except in the
case of Missouri.

Nobody much liked the Missouri Compromise, but it postponed
civil war until victory in the US-Mexican War (1846–1848) brought
both more new territory and a new crisis to the United States. During
the war, in 1846, Congress hoped to hasten the end of the conflict

by appropriating $2 million to *pay* Mexico for what were termed "territorial adjustments." Anti-slavery Pennsylvania Representative David Wilmot introduced an amendment to the appropriation bill, the "Wilmot Proviso," barring the introduction of slavery into any land acquired as a result of the Mexican War. This proposal provoked South Carolina's John C. Calhoun to counter with four resolutions of his own: first, that all territories, including those acquired as a result of the war, were to be regarded as the common and joint property of the states; second, that Congress acts as an agent for the states and therefore can make no law discriminating among the states or depriving any state of its rights with regard to any territory; third, that the enactment of any national law regarding slavery violates the Ninth Amendment and its implied doctrine of states' rights; and, fourth, that the people have the right to form their state governments as they wish. Having promulgated these resolutions, Calhoun warned that if they were rejected, civil war would result.

In the event, not only did the purchase of the Mexican land fail to take place, but the Wilmot Proviso was also defeated. Nevertheless, the Missouri Compromise began to break down, and Senator Lewis Cass of Michigan sought to replace it with the full implementation of a doctrine called "popular sovereignty." This would remove federal authority over slavery altogether by providing for the organization of new territories without mention of slavery one way or the other. Only when the territory subsequently applied for statehood would the people of the territory itself vote the proposed state slave or free. The federal government would be obliged to abide by the decision of the people—their "popular sovereignty." As for California, acquired as a result of the US-Mexican War, it would be admitted to the Union directly instead of going through the customary interim territorial status. Southerners objected, arguing that California would vote itself free, as would New Mexico, another territory acquired as a result of the war. To resolve these objections, Senators Henry Clay of Kentucky and Daniel Webster of Massachusetts proposed a whole new compromise. California would be admitted as a free state, but all of the other territories acquired as a result of the Mexican War would be subject to popular sovereignty. Clay and Webster added a provision closing the slave market in the

District of Columbia, an international embarrassment in the nation's capital, but to make this so-called Compromise of 1850 easier for the South to swallow, a new fugitive slave law was included, barring individuals and states from giving refuge to escaped slaves.

The Compromise of 1850 greatly diluted the Missouri Compromise and bought a few more years of uneasy peace. But in 1854, when Nebraska and Kansas applied for statehood, Congress repealed the Missouri Compromise altogether, replacing it with the Kansas-Nebraska Act, which extended popular sovereignty to all new territories, not just those acquired from Mexico. The 1820 boundary between slavery and freedom was erased. In this way, legislators hoped to remove the federal government from the slavery issue once and for all.

That hope died aborning. Popular sovereignty was sure to result in a free state of Nebraska, but Kansas, to its south, could go either way. Thus the act was an open invitation to conflict, which came immediately in the form of a bloody guerrilla war within the territory of Kansas between pro-slavery and anti-slavery factions.

"Bleeding Kansas" triggered debate throughout the country as proslavery Missourians and antislavery Iowans rushed across the Kansas territorial line in an effort to tilt the popular sovereignty majority one way or the other prior to the statehood vote. In the end, the incoming Missourians outnumbered the Iowans and installed a proslavery territorial legislature. Having done this, most of them returned to their permanent homes in Missouri whereas the Iowa newcomers remained in Kansas. The guerrilla war therefore escalated, and it was at this time that John Brown became the leader of an armed band calling itself the "Free Soil Militia."

Born in Connecticut, Brown grew up in Ohio. His father was a tanner by trade, but John felt a religious calling and wanted to become a Congregationalist minister. Lacking the money for the required study and afflicted by a painful chronic inflammation of the eyes, Brown tried the tannery and farming instead. Failing at both, he began to drift—until he read of the death of one Elijah P. Lovejoy, a Presbyterian minister and passionate abolitionist who was killed by a pro-slavery mob in Alton, Illinois in 1837. Brown swore what he deemed a public oath: "Here, before God, in the presence of these witnesses, from this time, I consecrate my life to the destruction of slavery!"

But cruel fate seemed to conspire against him. A federal court's declaration of his bankruptcy in 1843 was followed by the deaths of four of his eleven children, from dysentery, during a few terrible days of that same year. After another failed farming venture, he moved with his family in 1848 to the Adirondack town of North Elba, New York, where a wealthy abolitionist, Gerrit Smith, was granting land to poor black men. Deciding to settle among them, Brown got by as a subsistence farmer until early in 1856, when he received a letter from his four adult sons, who had moved to Kansas. They wrote that they and their families were menaced daily by marauding proslavery gangs, who not only terrorized anti-slavery locals, but had also raided, pillaged, and burned Lawrence, the center of abolitionist activity in Kansas.

Galvanized into action, Brown moved out to Kansas to join his sons. He rose to leadership of the abolitionist Free Soil Militia there. He recruited his sons and two other militiamen, armed them with cavalry sabers, and set out on the night of May 24, 1856, to make a bloody raid against proslavery settlers along the Pottawatomie River. Brown and the others used their sabers to hack five unarmed settlers to death. This done, they rode back triumphantly to Lawrence, where John Brown claimed full responsibility for having avenged the "sack of Lawrence."

From this point on, Brown built a reputation as an abolitionist crusader who would stop at nothing in the name of the cause. In the meantime, the so-called Topeka Constitution of 1855, which purported to create Kansas as a free state, was challenged in 1857 by a constitutional convention convened at Lecompton. The Lecompton Constitution proclaimed Kansas a slave state. Although the Free Soilers boycotted the ratification vote, President James Buchanan urged Kansans to ratify and Congress to approve the Lecompton Constitution and duly admit Kansas as a slave state. Neither the Senate nor the House meekly complied, however. Legislators ordered another vote. This one was boycotted by the proslavery faction. With both the Topeka and Lecompton Constitutions dead, a new document, the Wyandotte Constitution, was offered for ratification in 1859. It made Kansas a free state and was ratified by a margin of two to one. It was the constitution with which Kansas entered the Union on January 29, 1861, as a free state. Guerilla violence continued sporadically in Kansas throughout the Civil War.

While Kansas bled, another battle—this one bloodless yet just as bitter—was fought in the Supreme Court in the case of *Dred Scott v. Sandford*. Scott was a Virginia-born slave who had been sold to Dr. John Emerson of St. Louis, a US Army surgeon. Transferred by the army to Illinois and then to Wisconsin Territory, Emerson took Scott with him to each new post. After Emerson's death in 1846, Scott returned to St. Louis and, aided by lawyers in the employ of an abolitionist group, he sued Emerson's widow, in a Missouri court, for his freedom. He claimed that he was now a citizen of Missouri, a slave state that nevertheless had a long-standing practice of freeing slaves who had been longtime residents of free states. Because he had been a resident of Illinois, where slavery had been banned by the Northwest Ordinance of 1787, and also of Wisconsin Territory, where the provisions of the Missouri Compromise (in effect during his residence there) had made slavery illegal, he argued for his emancipation. When the Missouri court decided against him, Scott's lawyers appealed to the Supreme Court. The chief justice, Roger B. Taney, was a pro-slavery Virginian, and a majority of the court were Southerners. Unsurprisingly, the court upheld the verdict of the Missouri court and decided against Dred Scott, Taney writing the majority opinion.

The major premise on which Taney denied the appeal was his contention that neither a free "Negro" nor a slave was a citizen of the United States and therefore had no legal standing to bring suit. This decision should have closed the case, but Taney was interested in doing much more than settling a particular case involving a particular fugitive slave. The decision he wrote went on to hold the Missouri Compromise unconstitutional. True, Congress had already repealed it, but, as Scott's attorneys had argued, it was the law of the land when their client was transported to free territory. Taney decided that the Missouri Compromise violated the Fifth Amendment's prohibition against the government's depriving persons of "life, liberty, or property" without due process of law and that, therefore, it was unconstitutional, null, and void even prior to its repeal. In effect, the Supreme Court decided that the Missouri Compromise never lawfully conferred the authority to exclude slavery from the territories or anywhere else. "The right of property in a slave is distinctly and expressly affirmed in the Constitution," Taney wrote. "It is the opinion of the court that the [Missouri Compromise,] which prohibited a citizen from holding and owning property of this kind in the territory of the United States north of the line therein mentioned, is not warranted by the Constitution, and is therefore void." This meant that the federal government had no authority to limit, much less abolish, slavery, which was protected by the Fifth Amendment as a property right subject to due process.

The Dred Scott decision outraged abolitionists and others as well. Many Americans were aghast that the highest court in the land had used the Bill of Rights to ensure that a class of human beings remained in chains. That was bad enough. But the decision did even worse. By declaring the Missouri Compromise unconstitutional, it foreclosed all federal legislation that sought to limit slavery. Worse still, by defining slavery as strictly a property issue and therefore protected by the Fifth Amendment, the Taney opinion lawfully required every official of every state to actively protect the ownership of slaves. In short, the Taney opinion took slavery beyond the possibility of compromise—at least until such time as the Constitution was amended to abolish slavery in the United States. The likelihood of Congress passing such an amendment was near zero. The possibility that such an amendment, even if passed, would be ratified by three-fourths of the state legislatures or by special ratifying conventions in three-fourths of the states was precisely zero. In the end, the Dred Scott decision meant that the only way the slave states would agree to abolishing slavery was if they were forced to do so by violence.

There was talk of war, but for the most part, it was just talk. However, one man, John Brown, had stopped talking. The Dred Scott decision had the force of law, but the law, Brown held, was immoral, a violation of higher law, God's law. In Kansas, he had proved himself willing to spill blood to achieve justice in the eyes of God. He would do it again. Recruiting the backing of six prominent abolitionists—Samuel Gridley Howe, Thomas Wentworth Higginson, Theodore Parker, Franklin Sanborn, George L. Stearns, and Gerrit Smith (on whose land Brown lived)—Brown financed a plan to seize the federal armory and arsenal at Harpers Ferry, Virginia (today West Virginia), obtain guns and ammunition from it, and use them to arm local Virginia slaves. They would rise up, and their uprising—Brown convinced himself—would incite many other slaves to do likewise. With a general slave insurrection under way, people of conscience across the nation would join with their black brothers and act to crush the slaveholders once and for all. The uprising would not stop until the South had renounced slavery.

"One man and God can overturn the universe," John Brown proclaimed. And, on October 16, 1859, he led a party of sixteen whites and five blacks in a nighttime raid on Harpers Ferry. The armory, almost entirely unguarded, was readily overrun, as was the nearby Hall's Rifle Works. Brown was well aware that the government would soon act to recover its stronghold. He therefore took hostage some sixty residents of Harpers Ferry, among them the great-grandnephew of George Washington. As he, the hostages, and most of his raiders holed up in the arsenal, Brown assigned two of his African American raiders to rouse the slaves in the vicinity of the town. Brown had no doubt that he would soon be at the head of an army of many thousands.

The two men rode off, and the hours ticked away. Yet no slaves rallied to the cause. Sometime before daybreak, numerous residents of Harpers Ferry took up positions around the arsenal and began opening fire. When Brown's men returned fire, the first man they hit was a free black resident of the town. He succumbed to his wounds.

Throughout the morning and afternoon of October 17, Brown, his followers, and his hostages lay under siege by the townspeople. After two of Brown's sons were killed, the surviving raiders betook themselves and their hostages to the firehouse adjacent to the armory. It was a good place from which to mount a defense.

President James Buchanan was about as far from being a man of action as one could possibly be. At a loss as to how he should cope with the raid, he summoned the army's top general, Winfield Scott, who told him that Lieutenant Colonel Robert E. Lee was nearby, at Arlington, attending to his late father-in-law's estate. Acting on Scott's advice, Buchanan gave Lee command of the nearest available troops. They were militiamen, a handful of regular army soldiers, and a company of US Marines dispatched from their barracks at Eighth and I Streets in Washington. Lee's second in command of this ad hoc force was an army cavalry lieutenant, James Ewell Brown "Jeb" Stuart.

Lee and his command arrived at Harpers Ferry on the evening of October 17. He found the townspeople frantic, fearing a massive slave rebellion, and clamoring for immediate action. Lee, who had not had time to change out of his civilian clothes and into a uniform, looked more like a distinguished professor than a military officer. He did not allow the anxious citizens to pressure him into imprudent action. With the evening light failing, he did not want to risk storming the arsenal in the dark and quite likely shooting hostages by accident. He decided to wait until first light, at which time he would send Lieutenant Jeb Stuart under a flag of truce to talk with Brown and demand his surrender. Lee instructed Stuart to wave his hat if Brown refused to surrender.

The next morning, Stuart bravely walked toward the arsenal and armory, flag in hand. He entered the fire house, spent some time there, and then reemerged. His broad-brimmed cavalry hat was in his hand, held by the crown. Lee watched as he lifted it above his head and waved it in a broad arc. With that, the lieutenant colonel ordered his men to charge. The marines went directly for the firehouse door, smashing it in, and then storming through the shattered doorway. On entry, they skewered two of the raiders with their bayonets. They acted as quickly as they could to save the hostages, but four, including the mayor, were killed, as was one marine. Brown and his men got much worse. Only four, including Brown, escaped death. Brown himself suffered a deep gash from a marine saber. Among the dead were two of the three Brown sons who participated in the raid, twenty-one-year-old Oliver Brown and twenty-four-year-old Watson Brown. Both were mortally wounded, Oliver dying on October 19, Watson on October 22.

Predictably, President Buchanan refused to treat the attack on a federal facility as a crime against the United States. Instead, he let the state of Virginia prosecute the surviving raiders. Happy to oblige, the state charged all with "treason against Virginia," murder, and conspiracy to incite "servile insurrection." The state's justice was carried out swiftly. Ten days after their capture, the men were tried. Found guilty, the four survivors were sentenced to death by hanging.

The public spectacle on December 2, 1859, was very well attended. Acting on orders of Virginia Governor Henry A. Wise, Thomas Jonathan Jackson—soon to enter history as Stonewall Jackson—a professor at the Virginia Military Institute (VMI), led a detachment of youthful cadets to the place of execution, not merely to observe the proceedings, but to assist, if necessary, in maintaining public order. Also present among the spectators that day was an actor from Maryland, a darkly handsome matinee idol who enjoyed particular popularity with female audiences south of the Mason-Dixon Line. His name was John Wilkes Booth.

If Virginia authorities believed that the executions would edify the public and discourage rebellion against the laws protecting slaves and slavery, they were sorely mistaken. Brown was not only unapologetic, he faced his end without a visible trace of fear. At his sentencing, he did not curse, and he did not threaten. He merely recited to judge and jury the words of Christ: "Remember them that are in bonds, as bound with them." After this, he addressed the court and jurors more personally: "Now, if it is deemed necessary that I should forfeit my life for the furtherance of the ends of justice, and mingle my blood further with the blood of my children and with the blood of millions in this slave country whose rights are disregarded by wicked, cruel, and unjust enactments—I submit; so let it be done."

The truth was that Virginia gave to the abolitionist movement what that movement most craved: a martyr. Many abolitionists viewed Brown this way and said that his execution proved that the South could protect the manifest evil of slavery only through the force of "bayonet rule." Yet Brown's raid and his subsequent execution did little to prepare the North for civil war, whereas many Southern governors took note of the antiquated condition and inefficiency of their militias. This led to a reorganization of the militia throughout the region, and the result produced an important basis for quickly building a Confederate army. As for Brown himself, he had no doubt about what his actions portended. The morning of his execution he asked for pen and paper. "I John Brown am now quite *certain* that the crimes of this *guilty* land will never be purged *away;* but with Blood," he wrote.

20

March 8, 1862

The Ironclads Clash at Hampton Roads

Why it's significant. The Battle of Hampton Roads (March 8–9, 1862) between the Confederate ironclad *Virginia* (ex-*Merrimack*) and the Union proto-battleship *Monitor* revolutionized naval warfare. Even more significantly, it revealed the Civil War as a new kind of war, a war driven by industrial civilization, a war with outcomes determined at least as much by technology and technological innovation as by manpower, strategy, and national will. The Battle of Hampton Roads raised the curtain on modern warfare, destined to evolve rapidly through the Russo-Japanese War (1904–05), World War I (1914–18), World War II (1939–1945), and the ever-present threat of worse to come.

As NARRATED IN Chapter 10, William Tecumseh Sherman was enjoying a pleasant dinner with one of his academic colleagues at Louisiana State Seminary of Learning & Military Academy when news reached him that South Carolina had seceded from the Union. Laying down knife and fork, Sherman immediately predicted not only a bloody war, a massive war, and a long war, but a war that would be driven by industry. "The North can make a steam engine, locomotive or railway car; hardly a yard of cloth or a pair of shoes can you make," he scolded his Southern dinner companion. "You are rushing into war with one of the most powerful, ingeniously mechanical and determined people on earth—right at your doors. You are bound to fail."

Sherman was being hyperbolic, but he wasn't lying. In 1858, South Carolina's Senator James Henry Hammond had famously pronounced cotton "king" of the Southern economy, and indeed much of the arable land in South Carolina, Georgia, Alabama, Mississippi, Tennessee, Arkansas, upper Louisiana, the eastern half of Texas, and even the Florida Panhandle was devoted to the cultivation of that single crop. Where cotton wasn't being grown, rice, tobacco, and sugar were. Large-scale agriculture employing slaves made a relatively few Southerners very wealthy, but these plantation owners invested their money in their own plantations, not in industrial enterprises. By 1860, the South had just 18,000 manufacturing establishments employing 111,000 workers. By that same year, the North had 111,000 factories, employing 1.3 million workers. In 1860, approximately 90 percent of the nation's manufacturing was in the North. In fact, it was thanks to manufacturing that Northern farmland was actually much more productive, acre for acre, than that in the overwhelmingly agricultural South. In the year before the outbreak of the Civil War, the average Northern farmer owned $0.89 worth of farm machinery per acre, compared to $0.42 per acre for the average plantation owner. Thanks largely to mechanization, Northern farming was more efficient, which made Northern farmland more productive, thereby increasing its value. On average, an acre of farmland was worth $25.67 in the North, but less than half that in the South, $10.40.

There were far-seeing Southern men who counseled the wealthy to invest beyond their plantations and put money into mining, manufacturing, and railroad building in order to diversify and strengthen the economy and civilization of the region. Such advice was largely ignored. As a result, the South went to war as a net exporter of its major slave crops and a net importer of manufactured goods. Before the war, Southerners imported most of their manufactured needs from the North. During the war, they turned of necessity to Europe—mostly England and France—for the bulk of their weapons. They supplemented imports with some locally manufactured arms in addition to whatever they had managed to seize at the outbreak of the war from federal arsenals located in the South and, throughout the war, whatever they could capture.

The Confederate military managed to obtain sufficient arms and ammunition that no Southern army ever avoided or lost a battle for want of materiel. Nevertheless, not surprisingly, Confederate soldiers were typically armed with obsolescent weapons. They often used smoothbore muskets instead of more modern and more accurate rifle-muskets. Their ammunition often consisted of old-fashioned round ball shot instead of the bullet-shaped Minié ball, which was fired from weapons with rifled barrels and was therefore capable of greater range and accuracy. Neither side in the conflict used a great many breech-loading long arms or rapid-fire repeating rifles; however, the Union army was equipped with many more of both than the Confederate army. When it came to artillery, the North had many more cannon of all calibers, and what it had was more modern, accurate, and reliable than what the Confederate army was equipped with.

There is no denying that the South was at an industrial disadvantage compared with the North. That is what makes it all the more remarkable that weapons innovation was far from dead in the South. While it is true that the region could not manufacture sufficient numbers of infantry weapons—rifle-muskets, especially—to equip its army with the latest in long arms, it did produce highly innovative naval weapons, which, by their nature, were manufactured in small, sometimes one-of-a-kind quantity. The most innovative was undoubtedly CSS *H. L. Hunley,* a submarine intended to be a prototype of a submersible vessel capable of destroying the surface ships of the ever-expanding Union naval blockade that was strangling the Confederate economy. On February 17, 1864, the *Hunley* actually succeeded in attacking and sinking one of the blockade ships, the Union screw sloop USS *Housatonic*, in Charleston's outer harbor. That victory, however, also sank the *Hunley* and cost the lives of its eight-man crew. After successfully ramming the *Housatonic* with an explosive spar torpedo, the submarine disappeared. (The wreck of the *Hunley* was discovered in 1995 and raised in 2000. It is believed that the crew was knocked unconscious or even killed when its spar torpedo exploded a mere twenty feet from the submarine, which drifted under the surface, eventually took on water, and settled to the bottom.)

The *Hunley* was built to disrupt the Union blockade of the South. Earlier, the Confederacy had also turned to another innovation in warships to fight that blockade. At the very beginning of the war, in 1861, the Union's general-in-chief, Winfield Scott, ordered a naval blockade of Southern ports. Throughout 1861 and well into 1862, Union ships on blockade duty managed to stop fewer than one out of every ten Confederate "blockade runners," privately owned crafts manned by daring crews who specialized in slipping past the Union patrols.

Even the loss of one in ten cargoes was a heavy cost to the Confederate economy and war effort. Confederate military planners were also well aware that Northern shipyards were turning out Union naval vessels at a remarkable rate. New ships were being continually added to the blockade fleet. Moreover, the Confederate strategy during the first months of the war was not to engage the Union ships in combat, but simply to evade them. So the blockading fleet kept growing and became increasingly effective. By the close of the war, the Union navy was bagging one of every three blockade runners.

The Confederacy could not afford to build or buy a large navy. Most of the warships it was acquiring were so-called commerce raiders, fast vessels designed to operate in distant waters, where they preyed upon the North's commercial ships carrying goods to or from Europe. It was not feasible for the Confederates to confront the Union blockade on a ship-for-ship basis, but what if a new kind of ship could be designed, one capable of striking at the blockade vessels with relative impunity?

At the outbreak of the Civil War, the US Navy's Gosport Navy Yard, on the south shore of Hampton Roads, Virginia, was quickly evacuated. In the frenzy to avoid capture of personnel and the most important warships, there was neither sufficient time nor manpower to move every vessel out of Gosport and back to the safety of

Northern ports. Among the ships left behind was the screw frigate USS *Merrimack.* Not wanting to relinquish the ship to the Confederates, Union sailors burned it to the waterline and then scuttled the hull.

What was to the North a burned-out, sunken hulk was to the needy Confederate navy the makings of a secret weapon. The severely damaged vessel was refloated and towed to a "graving dock"—a dry dock—at the Gosford yard, which was now occupied by Confederate navy personnel. After inspection, they concluded that the lower hull was intact and most of the ship's machinery capable of restoration. Confederate Secretary of the Navy Stephen Mallory decided on July 11, 1861, to convert the *Merrimack* into an ironclad—a steam-propelled warship built of wood but clad in armor plates made of iron. A design was quickly worked up for a so-called casemate ironclad, a vessel that sat very low in the water, with an iron-reinforced prow and ram. Rising from its deck was a low superstructure built as a casemate, an armored enclosure inside which guns were mounted. The casemate was designed with sloping sides all around. These would deflect most cannonballs and other projectiles. The casemate's sides were pierced by narrow openings to accommodate cannon. The ship was designed to be armed with four new muzzle-loading Brooke rifles and six smoothbore nine-inch Dahlgren guns, the latter salvaged from the *Merrimack.* Two of the rifled weapons, seven-inchers, were used as pivot guns at the fore and aft ends of the casemate, and two 6.4-inch Brookes were added to the broadside array, along with the salvaged Dahlgrens. The steam engines, gears, and screw (propeller) of the *Merrimack* were also salvaged and restored.

While the vessel would be built—or rebuilt—at the graving dock, the Brooke rifles and the large number of iron plates required were ordered from Richmond's celebrated Tredegar Iron Works. Although it was one of the very few industrial-scale foundries in the South, Tredegar was a modern plant on a par with the best of major foundries in the North. The plant supplemented its paid workforce with slave labor in order to cast the required cannon, numerous iron fittings, and armor plates as quickly as possible.

Rechristened CSS *Virginia*, the salvaged and rebuilt vessel was commissioned on February 17, 1862, and fully completed and fitted out on March 7. The next day, Franklin Buchanan took command of CSS *Virginia*. Formerly commandant of the Brooklyn Navy Yard, Buchanan resigned his commission in the US Navy at the outbreak of the war and defected to the Confederate service. He now steamed the *Virginia* into Hampton Roads for her maiden battle with the vessels of the Union blockading fleet, some powered exclusively by sail, others by a combination of sail and steam, all with hulls of timber.

Those Union sailors who saw the approach of CSS *Virginia* were bewildered by the appearance of the strange craft. One took it for a huge, half-submerged crocodile. Another described it as "the roof of a very big barn belching . . . smoke." But as the warship closed in, her guns became visible, protruding slightly through the narrow ports of the casemate. It was the Union commanders who ordered their own guns into action first. When he observed this, the commanding officer of the adjacent Union shore batteries also opened fire. The barrage directed against the *Virginia* was intense and created a great deal of smoke, which blended with the black billows pouring out of the *Virginia*'s stack. As the smoke cleared somewhat during a pause in the bombardment, the harbor pilot aboard USS *Cumberland* was horrified to see that not a single shot had penetrated the enemy's hull. He later remarked that the cannonballs had bounced "upon her mailed sides like India-rubber."

Now at close range, CSS *Virginia* opened up with a broadside against the *Cumberland*. In this first fusillade, five US Marines were killed instantly by shrapnel and splintered timber. The two ships exchanged broadsides until the guns of the *Cumberland* suddenly fell silent. The absence of return fire was a signal to Captain Buchanan, who ordered his engine room to make all possible steam. Those aboard USS *Cumberland* must have heard the enemy's boilers and machinery roar as CSS *Virginia* maneuvered to drive her iron ram into the hull of the Union vessel. Forwarded by its propeller, the iron-heavy ship—displacing some 4,000 long tons—staved in the enemy's hull as if it were built of nothing more than matchwood. Since the *Virginia* rode so low in the water, its iron ram penetrated the Union ship well below the waterline. Instantly, the *Cumberland* took on water and heeled over sharply. With capsize imminent, her commander made for the sandy shallows just beyond the Roads, hoping to beach his heavily listing, rapidly sinking ship. He partially succeeded. Although the hull went under and the decks were awash, the masts, still mostly undamaged, remained well above the waterline and the waves. Even Old Glory still flapped in a stiff gale. Sailors clambered up ratlines and ropes, deploying themselves along the yardarms in an effort to keep from drowning.

Most of the other Union warships nearby were support vessels and did not engage in the fight, but another frigate, USS *Congress,* made for the shallows in search of a position from which to train close fire on the enemy. Alas, the *Congress* maneuvered too far into the shallow water and ran aground. Unable to move, captain and crew could do nothing but await their fate.

They did not have to wait long. CSS *Virginia* steamed close to *Congress* and let loose a broadside that included hot shot—cannon balls heated red hot before firing and used as incendiary ammunition. The Union ship caught fire and quickly "struck its colors," lowering its flag as a token of surrender. Buchanan immediately dispatched a rescue party from another Confederate vessel nearby. Unfortunately, the commander of the Union shore batteries did not interpret this as a rescue, but as a boarding expedition. The Union batteries opened fire on the *Virginia*, whereupon Captain Buchanan took up a rifle and began firing at the artillerists. Provoked, a Union sharpshooter targeted Buchanan, who was hit in the leg. Disabled, he turned over command to his first officer, Lieutenant Catesby ap R. Jones and allowed himself to be lifted below deck to have his wound attended to.

Although the *Virginia* emerged from the battle still seaworthy, her bow was leaking because part of the ram had been damaged in the attack on the *Housatonic*. Moreover, severe damage to her smokestack diminished the boilers' draft. This made the stokers' fires smaller, diminishing steam pressure and substantially slowing a ship that, at best, could make no more than six knots. Two of her broadside cannon had also been hit and put out of action. Despite this, Buchanan ordered Jones to turn his attention to the

USS *Minnesota*, which, frantically trying to evade the ironclad, had run aground on a sandbar in the shallows. That sandbar was sufficiently large, however, to prevent the *Virginia* from approaching *Minnesota* closely enough to cause serious damage. Moreover, the sun was low in the sky, and Jones decided to pull back for the evening and, in the morning, return to find a way to finish off both the *Congress* and the *Minnesota*.

Many onlookers had watched the action of March 8 from shore, and newspaper correspondents were transmitting detailed reports by telegraph. Washington buzzed with rumors of an indestructible Confederate ironclad that was preparing to steam up the Potomac and fire on the Capitol and the White House. There were fears that Washington would be bombarded with incendiaries and burned as it had been by the British during the War of 1812. Even President Lincoln was sufficiently alarmed to convene an emergency Cabinet meeting. The result was quite unsatisfactory, however. No one present could think of any expedient more useful than earnest and immediate prayer.

Nevertheless, although the appearance of CSS *Virginia* had baffled Union sailors, this was not the first that Union navy brass had heard of the vessel. Months earlier, Union spies in Virginia had reported on the work being done to salvage and reconfigure USS *Merrimack*. In October 1861, Congress responded by appropriating funds for a contract with John Ericsson, a Swedish-born New York mechanical engineer who specialized in designing and building steam locomotives and steamships. His commission was to build an iron steamship—not a wooden ship clad in iron. It was to be a warship capable of sinking a similar vessel. The Navy and Congress were aware that Ericsson had already designed such a ship, which he had tried (without success) to persuade Napoleon III to let him build for the French navy. They were confident that he knew what to do. The thing is, they wanted him to do it in just 100 days, from design to launch.

Ericsson labored day and night, but the vessel was not yet ready to launch on day 100. When Washington sent him secret intelligence that the Confederate ironclad was very near completion, however, he redoubled his efforts and managed to launch USS *Monitor* on March

6 from New York. There was no time for testing or troubleshooting. The vessel's shakedown cruise would be its voyage down the coast to do battle in Hampton Roads.

Monitor may have been the ugliest warship ever created. It rode even lower in the water than the much larger *Virginia,* and instead of a casemate with multiple guns rising from its deck, it had a single cylindrical object that made the vessel look like what some derided as a "tin can on a shingle" and others as a "cheesebox on a raft." But this ungainly looking "can" or "cheesebox" was actually the most innovative and remarkable feature of the *Monitor.* It was something never before seen on a ship—or on land, for that matter. Ericsson had invented the revolving gun turret, which held two massive eleven-inch smoothbore Dahlgrens. Thanks to the turret's steam-powered gearing, they could be rotated into any direction for firing. Whereas conventional warships—even the *Virginia*—had to be sailed and maneuvered in order to bring their guns to bear as desired on a target, the guns of USS *Monitor* could be aimed 360 degrees independently of the ship's direction and orientation. The time and exposure to enemy fire this saved were incalculable.

True, much like the *Virginia,* the *Monitor* was not a "handy" ship. She was not agile. In fact, she was barely seaworthy. Moreover, her top speed was six knots, no better than her adversary—though *Virginia* had been compromised and slowed by battle damage. If *Virginia* rode very low in the water, the *Monitor* rode even lower, so low that any moderate swell, let alone a really rough sea, threatened to swamp her.

Despite *Monitor*'s shortcomings, the untested vessel, under Lieutenant John L. Worden, arrived in Hampton Roads on the morning of March 9. Call it what it was: the nick of time. Worden immediately grasped that the grounded *Minnesota* was the ship in greatest immediate danger, and so he steamed into a position covering it and then lay in wait for the anticipated appearance of CSS *Virginia.* The Confederate ship heaved into sight at nine.

We don't know if the captain and crew of the Confederate vessel had any advance knowledge of the Union's iron ship of war, but there was no sign that anyone aboard the *Virginia* was shocked. The Confederate ship opened fire on the *Monitor* immediately, and for the next three hours the ironclad and the iron ship rained down upon one another a storm of iron.

The two vessels were not precisely matched. *Monitor* was smaller and, while far from highly maneuverable, was considerably more maneuverable than CSS *Virginia*. This advantage was multiplied by its rotating turret, which could keep its adversary in the line of fire at virtually all times. Nevertheless, the contenders landed blows that *seemed* to have no permanent effect—at least not on the hulls of the ships. What the combat did to the human beings aboard those ships was something else however. The crash of iron projectiles against iron plate was relentless. The ears of crew members on both ships bled as eardrums burst. But it was not just these delicate human membranes that tore. The multiple shockwaves assaulted the entire body, beginning with the soles of the men's feet, which were in contact with the deck. They ached and bled copiously, even though the skin was unbroken. Some crew members found themselves wading in the blood that filled their shoes.

Prior to this three-hour combat, naval battles constituted a history of captain against captain, crew against crew. The contest between *Monitor* and *Virginia* was very different. It was a fight of machine against machine, of iron against iron. The flesh-and-blood beings who were in nominal control of the battle were really at the mercy of their relentless machines. Lieutenant Worden occupied the *Monitor*'s cramped iron pilot house. There were no windows to the world outside, just narrow observation slits sliced through the iron. Amid the pounding, Worden would press his eye against one of the slits, as if he were a jousting knight squinting through the visor of his unwieldy helmet. At about noon, one of *Virginia*'s shells exploded against the pilot house wall, throwing Worden back from his observation slit in excruciating pain. He was blinded—temporarily, it turned out—but he was deprived of sight for the remainder of the battle. He turned over command to his first officer, Lieutenant Samuel Dana Greene, who later recalled that Worden "was a ghastly sight, with his eyes closed and the blood apparently rushing from every pore in the upper part of his face."

Greene's first task was to get USS *Monitor* back under control. "In the confusion of the moment resulting from so serious an injury to the commanding officer, the *Monitor* had been moving without direction." Greene could see, however, that CSS *Virginia* was taking on water—"leaking badly"—and was therefore withdrawing toward the Elizabeth River. Greene did not want to break off the fight, and so he continued to fire "at the retiring vessel." But the *Virginia* was making for Norfolk and the safety of Confederate shore batteries. Not wanting to get within their range, Greene, like it or not, concluded that the "fight was over."

Historians assess the two-day Battle of Hampton Roads as a draw, although it was the *Virginia* that suffered the greater damage, the *Virginia* that withdrew, and the *Virginia* that left the grounded *Minnesota* without delivering the *coup de grâce*. Both vessels were products of new developments in industrial technology. The difference was that *Virginia* had been built on the salvaged foundation of an earlier period of naval warfare, whereas the *Monitor* was the product of entirely new invention and innovation. This gave it an edge, however narrow.

Neither ship went on to a history of further glory. USS *Monitor* served as a gunboat on the James River at the Battle of Drewry's Bluff (May 15, 1862), providing naval artillery support to the Army of the Potomac. But that, its second battle, was also its last. The ship was lost at sea in a storm off Cape Hatteras, North Carolina on New Year's Eve 1862. The *Virginia* did not even last as long as the *Monitor*. She ran aground on May 11, 1862. Unable to break her free, her crew set her aflame.

The brevity of the combatant vessels' lives notwithstanding, their duel at Hampton Roads profoundly transformed naval warfare. What is more, the transformation began almost immediately. Before the war ended, the US Navy built and deployed some twenty-nine "monitors," as the new class of ship was called. The Confederate Navy purchased (from Britain and from France) or built at least thirty-one "ironclad batteries." Like the *Virginia,* these were wooden-hull vessels clad with iron or steel plates. They were not intended for high seas use, but as maneuverable, steam-powered floating gun batteries for shore defense. But it was the *Monitor* and the "*Monitor* class" of vessels it inspired that, by the end of the nineteenth century, evolved into the modern battleship, with multiple arrays of turreted guns. The battleship spelled an end to the era of wood and sail and became the symbol of the global projection of military power through the mid-twentieth century. During World War II, however, the battleship itself was supplanted by the submarine and the aircraft carrier. Of these two innovations in naval warfare, the submarine had made a brief and tragic appearance in the Civil War as the doomed *Hunley*.

The Civil War's most profound impact on the future of warfare was not, of course, limited to naval innovations. But what ships like the *Hunley, Virginia,* and *Monitor* represented was radical innovation driven by technological economies. The wars of the twentieth and twenty-first centuries would be, like the Civil War, the products of industrial civilization.

21

Lest We Forget

T WENTY IS AN arbitrary number of "most significant" events. Why not twenty-five? Twenty-three? Well, why not twenty + ten? In my judgment, the following ten events may not have had as great an impact on the Civil War and American history as the preceding twenty, but they are highly significant nevertheless and should not be forgotten. They are discussed in chronological order.

South Carolina Secedes from the Union, December 20, 1860

With the highest percentage of slaves among the Southern states—57 percent of the population owned by 46 percent of white families—South Carolina was more invested than any other state in slavery as the foundation of an economy and a way of life. Prior to the election of 1860, a South Carolina politician named Alfred P. Aldrich proclaimed: "If the Republican party with its platform of principles, the main feature of which is the abolition of slavery and, therefore, the destruction of the South, carries the country at the next Presidential election, shall we remain in the Union, or form a separate Confederacy? This is the great, grave issue. It is not who shall be President, it is not which party shall rule—it is a question of political and social existence." It was this mindset that equated secession with survival for the South, and it prompted passage, on November 9, 1860, three days after the election of Republican Abraham Lincoln as president, a South Carolina General Assembly "Resolution to Call the Election of Abraham Lincoln as US President a Hostile Act." The very next day, November 10, the Assembly called for a secession "Convention of the People of South Carolina," which was convened on December 17 and voted unanimously to leave the Union. Three days after this, the state formally enacted an ordinance of secession.

This sequence of events is remarkable for four things:

- Its assertion of life-or-death stakes for the state, the Southern economy, and the Southern way of life.
- Its absolute assumption that, under a Republican administration, no compromise on slavery was possible.
- The speed with which secession proceeded.
- The unanimity driving secession.

Just as remarkable was the response of the federal government under lame-duck President James Buchanan. Declaring the secession ordinance illegal, he did nothing to act against it. From this, the South concluded that, while the federal government objected to secession, it would—perhaps could—do little to stop it. The example of South Carolina, together with Buchanan's feckless response to it, inspired the eventual secession of six more states—Mississippi (January 9, 1861), Florida (January 10), Alabama (January 11), Georgia (January 19), Louisiana (January 26), and Texas (February 1; referendum, February 23)—prior to the inauguration of Abraham Lincoln on March 4, 1861. After the attack on Fort Sumter (April 12–14, Chapter 3) and Lincoln's call for volunteers (April 15), four more states seceded: Virginia (April 17; referendum, May 23), Arkansas (May 6), Tennessee (May 7; referendum, June 8), and North Carolina (May 20). South Carolina took secession from a *doctrine* to an *action*, which, on May 20, 1861, became the *fact* of the eleven Confederate States of America.

The United States Sanitary Commission Is Authorized, June 8, 1861

Although the Civil War tore the nation apart, it also elevated the federal government to unprecedented supremacy in American life. Indeed, historians have often argued that the Civil War was the Second American Revolution, the revolution that transformed what had been a federation of separate states into a true nation, a place in which people no longer identified themselves as Ohioans or Virginians, but as Americans. Nevertheless, the demands of the war on both sides also revealed the limits of the central government's power and competency. In both the Union and the Confederacy, recruitment and mobilization efforts were overwhelmingly the responsibility of the states. It was the states that took primary responsibility for raising and, to a large extent, training and equipping the needed regiments.

Where both the central governments and the state governments fell short in these tasks, the Civil War brought out the power of collective and individual civilian volunteerism. Both the national and state governments turned to newly created charitable and civic organizations in part simply to help feed and clothe the troops, but, far more extensively, to care for them when they were sick or wounded. Mid-nineteenth-century industrial technology and mass production had produced weapons, both shoulder arms and artillery, of unprecedented efficiency and destructive power. The wounds these weapons produced were of an abundance and severity that far outstripped the capacity of mid-nineteenth-century medicine to cure, treat, or even palliate adequately. Military medicine, in particular, was hardly up to the monumental task the war represented.

In the Confederacy, civic organizations such as Association for the Relief of Maimed Soldiers (which furnished prosthetics to Confederate amputees), the Georgia Relief and Hospital Association (furnished medicines, bandages, and other supplies to military hospitals and subsidized the services of civilian physicians), the Richmond Ambulance Committee (supported, fed, and transported wounded Confederate soldiers from the battle front to hospitals in the rear), and hundreds of small, local women's relief organizations (which collected clothing, food, and medical supplies and provided volunteer female nursing services) did their best to fill a huge gap in medical and basic humanitarian aid to wounded troops.

Although the Union Army's medical department was better equipped and more adequately staffed than its Confederate counterpart, it was nevertheless inadequate to care for the massive numbers of wounded and sick soldiers the war produced. The principal civilian aid organization in the North was the United States Sanitary Commission. It was established by federal legislation on June 18, 1861, but it was a totally private organization, founded by a prominent clergyman, Henry Whitney Bellows, and the great American landscape architect Frederick Law Olmsted, who modeled the organization on the British Sanitary Commission, which had been created during the Crimean War (1853–56). Like the American Civil War, it was a conflict that produced wounded and sick soldiers in numbers beyond the ability of the army and the government to care for them.

The remarkable United States Sanitary Commission operated using funds raised by public contributions, often obtained through public "Sanitary Fairs" the organization staged. Organization volunteers inspected Union camps and hospitals with an eye toward improving sanitary conditions. The commission collected clothing, food, medicines, and medical supplies and subsidized civilian nursing care for the sick and wounded. The Commission inspired the creation of other private aid organizations, most notably the United States Christian Commission (an activity of the YMCA of New York, which became famous for the food and coffee wagons it sent to the front) and the Western Sanitary Commission (established in St. Louis in 1861, it addressed the often-neglected problems of the war's "Western Theater" and set up hospital kitchens, furnished medical supplies, and even outfitted a paddle steamer, the *City of Louisiana,* as a hospital ship). Without the efforts of private citizens on both sides of the Civil War, the conflict would have been even more brutal and barbaric than it was.

Confederate "Diplomats" Mason and Slidell Are Seized from the British-flagged *Trent,* November 8, 1861

Confederate President Jefferson Davis, anxious to hammer out an alliance with England and France, appointed James M. Mason of Virginia minister to England and John Slidell of Louisiana minister to France. He sent the pair to Europe and assigned them to negotiate both diplomatic recognition of the Confederate States of America and formal alliances.

Getting them safely to Europe was not easy. The pair slipped out of Charleston on a blockade runner in October and made it to

Havana. There, Mason and Slidell boarded a British mail packet, the *Trent,* which was headed for England. Officially, Great Britain was neutral in the American Civil War—though various English manufacturers and shipbuilders began covertly supplying the Confederacy with arms and vessels in violation of British neutrality laws. Under universally accepted international law, the US could not touch Mason and Slidell as long as they were on board a neutral vessel, which offered them protection.

As luck would have it, the USS *San Jacinto*, under Captain Charles Wilkes, was in Havana on its way back from patrol on the African coast to take its place in the Union naval blockade. Receiving word of Mason and Slidell's departure from Havana, Wilkes steamed out and intercepted the *Trent* on November 8. He fired two warning shots across her bow, which forced the British ship to admit a boarding party. Slidell and Mason were arrested and bundled aboard the *San Jacinto*, which deposited the pair at Fort Warren in Boston Harbor, where they were confined. The British government responded with outrage at such a seizure on the high seas. Eleven thousand British soldiers were dispatched to Canada, and the Royal Navy was put on war alert. The prime minister demanded an apology from the Lincoln government, as well as the release of Mason and Slidell.

President Lincoln's secretary of state, William Seward, advised the president to make no apology. He actually believed that provoking a war with Great Britain would unite South and North against a common foe. President Lincoln sensibly disagreed, replying to Seward with the admonition, "One war at a time." At this, Seward came to his senses, backed down, and ordered the release of Mason and Slidell. He did not, however, apologize on behalf of the government, but, on December 26, presented to Lord Richard Lyons, British minister to the United States, a note justifying the boarding and the seizure of Mason and Slidell while asserting that Captain Wilkes had acted without permission from the government.

The "*Trent* affair" might well have touched off a war with Great Britain, which would have almost certainly benefitted the Confederacy and quite possibly cost the Union the Civil War. As events ultimately developed, neither the British nor French governments could ever bring themselves to ally with a slave nation— although, on May 13, 1861, Queen Victoria herself conferred on the Confederacy the only international recognition it was to gain. Her government treated it as a "belligerent" entity, using a term reserved for sovereign nations at war.

The Dix-Hill Prisoner Exchange Is Signed, July 22, 1862

Historians often compare the Civil War to twentieth-century warfare in two respects. First, there is the historical status of the Civil War as the first war in history to be driven so extensively and ferociously by industrial technology. Mass-produced, advanced weaponry capable of an unprecedented volume and degree of devastation, transportation by railroad, and communication via telegraphy, all of these played key roles in the war and foreshadowed even greater reliance on industrial technology and innovation in World War I and World War II during the next century.

The second point of comparison is the mass incarceration and inhumane treatment of prisoners of war, a phenomenon that not only seemed to predict the manner in which POWs would be abused in the twentieth century but, by extension, how the British (in the Second Boer War of 1899–1902) and the Germans (in World War II, 1939–1945) would confine civilian populations to concentration camps. In the case of the Nazis, the concentration camps became places of genocidal mass murder.

Mention prisoners of war and the Civil War, and the horrors of Andersonville in the South or Elmira (called "Hell-mira") in the North become the focus of conversation. Daguerreotypes of liberated prisoners show men reduced to living skeletons and invite comparison today with the horrors of World War II's Auschwitz and Dachau. Though less infamous than Andersonville, the Elmira camp, near the upstate New York city of that name, was even more deadly. Its thirty acres had thirty-five barracks that held half of the camp's 10,000 prisoners. The rest were assigned to tents or left to shift for themselves in the open, even during the frigid upstate winters. As guards, Union authorities assigned ex-slaves, who openly abused their charges. Nearly a quarter of the prisoners confined at

Elmira—24 percent—died there, a mortality rate even higher than that at Andersonville.

Yet POWs were not always treated this way during the Civil War, which began at a time in the nineteenth century when most Western nations were making earnest efforts to treat military prisoners humanely. Indeed, most warring nations exchanged rather than confined prisoners. At the outbreak of the Civil War, both the Union and Confederacy followed this model. There was no formal exchange agreement between the belligerents because President Lincoln refused to make any treaty or even quasi-treaty with an entity his administration did not want to legitimize by implying diplomatic standing. Instead, exchanges were negotiated ad hoc by the field commanders involved. In some cases, only sick or wounded captives were exchanged.

At last, on December 11, 1861, the US Congress passed a joint resolution calling on Lincoln to introduce "systematic measures" for prisoner exchange. But it was not until July 8, 1862, that his secretary of war, Edwin Stanton, appointed Major General John A. Dix to negotiate standard terms for prisoner exchange with a representative from the Confederacy. For the Confederacy, Robert E. Lee named Major General Daniel Harvey Hill to this position on July 14. The two men worked out a scale of equivalents by which a captain captured by one side would be exchanged, say, for a captain captured by the other, or a POW colonel could be redeemed by exchanging him for fifteen privates, and so on.

Enactment of the so-called Dix-Hill Cartel suggested that the Civil War could be fought with a degree of humanity after all. In fact, the cartel functioned quite smoothly until December 1862, when Confederate President Jefferson Davis suspended it. Earlier that year, the Union's Major General Benjamin F. Butler, as military governor of Union-occupied New Orleans, ordered the execution of one William Mumford, a civilian resident of New Orleans, for tearing down the Stars and Stripes from the flagpole at the US Mint in that city. Davis retaliated by suspending prisoner exchange. Union Secretary of War Edwin M. Stanton issued a similar suspension order. The cartel broke down even further after the Davis government refused to exchange captured African-American soldiers on the grounds than some were fugitive slaves. By early June 1863, the prisoner exchanges and the cartel were effectively dead.

Attempts were made to resume prisoner exchange, but the idea became decreasingly popular among Northern military commanders. They believed that the Confederacy, with its smaller population, was always hungry for manpower, whereas the Union had a much larger pool of military-age men on which to draw. Exchange, Northern generals concluded, benefitted the South, not the North, and so the large and squalid POW camps multiplied, grew, and became places of extreme misery and deliberate brutality on both sides. The cartel's fleeting promise of humane warfare vanished.

The Great Santee Sioux Uprising Begins in Minnesota, August 17, 1862

For most Americans, the Eastern Theater, especially the southeast, was the focus of attention during the Civil War. Nevertheless, the so-called Western Theater—Alabama, Georgia, Florida, Mississippi, North Carolina, Kentucky, South Carolina, Tennessee, and Louisiana east of the Mississippi River—was also crucial. But there was yet another "Western" Theater, whose combatants did not participate directly in the Civil War, yet were strongly affected by it. This was the military theater of the Plains Indian Wars, and what happened there beginning on August 17, 1862, demonstrated that the Union, full as its hands were fighting the Confederacy, had another war ongoing along with it.

In the mid-nineteenth century, the Santee Sioux, now more usually referred to as the Dakota people, a cultural subdivision of the Great Sioux Nation, initially acquiesced in the federal government's policy of concentrating them on government reservations. In this, the Santee, who lived in the eastern Dakotas and central Minnesota, differed from the Apaches and Navajos of the Southwest, tribes that violently resisted confinement to reservations. But by the start of the 1860s, as the Santee suffered from crop failures and found themselves increasingly hemmed in by an influx of Scandinavian and German immigrant settlers, discontent with reservation life quickly grew. It was aggravated by the corruption, incompetence, indifference, and, sometimes, outright cruelty of a federal Indian agency system whose white officials often diverted funds and stole supplies and food provisions promised by treaty.

During the drought-ravaged summer of 1862, the Santees repeatedly petitioned for the release of rations and cash that local agents withheld. Their petitions went unanswered or were rebuffed. At last, Little Crow, chief of the Mdewakanton villages, put the desperate situation of his people this way: "We have no food, but here are these stores, filled with food. We ask that you, the agent, make some arrangements by which we can get food from the stores, or else we may take our own way to keep ourselves from starving. When men are hungry they help themselves."

Andrew Myrick, a prominent local trader, replied to the chief that he and his people could, if they were truly hungry, "eat grass."

With tensions at the boiling point, on August 17, four young Mdewakanton men, returning from a futile hunting trip, stopped at a white family's farm. One suggested stealing eggs from the chicken coop. This set off a dispute among the four concerning fear of white men. The young man escalated the issue at hand from egg stealing to a resolution that the four should kill the very next white man they encountered. With that, they murdered the farmer and his family. Having done this deed, the next day, they stormed the trading post of Andrew Myrick, whom they shot dead—and then stuffed his mouth with the grass he had told them to eat.

Soon, much of the Santee tribe was at war. Before the Civil War, the tiny United States Army had chiefly served to police Indian country. The demands of the war drew down the soldiers available for that police work, and, taking advantage of the paucity of troops, the Santee rapidly spread war throughout the region.

The effect was devastating. New Ulm, an immigrant village, was laid under siege on August 20 and 23. Thirty-six residents were killed, twenty-three were wounded, and the town was razed to the ground. Its two thousand settlers, homeless, fled to Mankato. By August 27, virtually all the Dakota people in Minnesota were at war with the whites. Before it ended, between 350 and 800 settlers had been killed, many victims of torture.

About half the state's population became refugees from the uprising—and there were rumors that it was not abuse and deliberate starvation, but Confederate agents, who had incited the Santee. These rumors were unfounded, but the uprising did indirectly benefit the Confederacy. Minnesota Governor Alexander Ramsey had to ask President Lincoln for permission to delay sending his state's quota of enlistees east to fight the Civil War. Lincoln replied by telegraph: "Attend to the Indians. If the draft cannot proceed of course it will not proceed. Necessity knows no law."

The uprising ended on September 23, 1862, at the Battle of Wood Lake. Little Crow fled westward, but he returned to Minnesota the following year. He and his son were ambushed and killed on July 3, 1863. They were picking raspberries, even as, in Gettysburg, 15,000 Confederate soldiers charged Union positions on Cemetery Ridge.

CSS *Alabama* Is Commissioned by the Confederate States Navy, August 24, 1862

Much derided by both the Northern and Southern press and public as "Scott's Anaconda," the naval blockade the Union army's first general-in-chief, Winfield Scott, initiated in an attempt to close Southern ports to commerce and military operations became increasingly effective as the Union Navy grew. From the beginning, however, the Confederacy was determined to defy the blockade, and the tiny Confederate States Navy, as well as intrepid civilian mariners, honed "blockade running" into a maritime military art.

The most famous and effective of the Confederate blockade runners was Raphael Semmes. He was a commander in the US Navy until he resigned his commission in February 1861 to serve the Confederacy as an agent for the covert purchase of arms from foreign powers. Quickly restless in this job, Semmes lobbied for a command in the Confederate navy, and was given the CSS *Sumter,* which the Confederates had converted the from *Habana,* a commercial steamer that happened to be tied up at New Orleans at the outbreak of the war. Under Semmes, CSS *Sumter* became the first Confederate warship to successfully run the Union blockade, on June 30, 1861. After steaming into the open Atlantic via the Gulf of Mexico, Semmes spent the next six months preying upon Northern commercial vessels, capturing eighteen of them, together with their cargoes.

Semmes left CSS *Sumter* at Gibraltar, where he boarded a ship called the *Agrippina*, which rendezvoused with a vessel built in England as the *Enrica*. The ship was refitted for combat and, rechristened CSS *Alabama*, became, in Semmes's hands, a veritable scourge. Commissioned in the Confederate Navy on August 24, 1862, *Alabama* stalked shipping lanes from September 1862 to June 1864. During this long period, Semmes seized or sank sixty-five—perhaps sixty-nine—Northern commercial vessels. It was not just a matter of looting cargoes. Semmes conducted a military campaign of terror that took a crippling toll on Northern financiers and insurance underwriters. Strategically, he presented such a menace that the US Navy was compelled to remove a number of ships and crews from blockade duty to find, engage, and destroy him and his ship. For this reason, Semmes's military achievement as a commerce raider cannot be calculated solely on the number of ships he captured or sank. The effect his operations had on reducing the strength of the Union blockade cannot be estimated by numbers alone.

The months passed, and the toll taken by CSS *Alabama* continued to multiply until USS *Kearsarge* was pulled off blockade duty and, under Captain John A. Winslow, sent in pursuit of Semmes. *Alabama* displaced 1,050 tons, and its steam engine, with the aid of auxiliary sails, could make 13 knots, carrying six thirty-two-pound cannons, one sixty-eight pounder, and one 110 pounder. *Kearsarge* was bigger, displacing 1,570 tons, and far better armed with more modern artillery: two eleven-inch smoothbore Dahlgren guns, four thirty-two pounders, and one thirty-pound, highly accurate Parrott rifle.

Kearsarge was anchored off the Dutch coast on Sunday, June 12, 1864, when Captain Winslow received a report that the *Alabama*, which he had been chasing for almost a year, was just seen in the port of Cherbourg, France, where it was unloading prisoners and taking on coal. Winslow immediately weighed anchor and steamed toward Cherbourg, taking up a position just outside of the three-mile French territorial limit, at the southern mouth of the English Channel. He waited for CSS *Alabama* to appear.

Learning of Winslow's proximity, Semmes was faced with an unpalatable choice. He could either try to wait Winslow out, or he could venture out himself and fight him. He knew that he had long been the object of Winslow's pursuit, so he assumed that the Union commander would have no problem lying in wait for a long time. This in itself would be a victory for Winslow, since it would keep *Alabama* out of action. For this reason, Semmes decided to fight. He would pit what he believed was his superior seamanship and the modest speed advantage of his vessel against Winslow's superior firepower.

Semmes quietly left port at 9:45 on Sunday morning, June 19. His departure was spied by Winslow's lookout, who announced that *Alabama* was heading straight for *Kearsarge*. Winslow, who had been conducting Sunday religious services, calmly dismissed those attending and ordered "beat to quarters," the traditional call to battle stations. He also ordered full steam ahead and moved rapidly out of the English Channel and into open waters. He knew he had no time to waste. The important thing was to bring his heaviest guns to bear on *Alabama* as quickly as possible. The best chance he had of preventing the wily Semmes from eluding him yet again was to destroy him—fast. Captain Winslow conceded that *Alabama* was faster, but it also had a deeper draft, riding four feet lower in the water than *Kearsarge*. This would give Winslow an advantage in maneuverability.

By 10:57, Winslow and Semmes were just one mile apart. *Alabama* opened fire first, with her heaviest gun, the 110 pounder. Instead of attempting to withdraw out of range, Winslow bore down on *Alabama* with all the steam he had. Semmes fired every gun he could bring to bear, but Winslow kept coming on, so fast that Semmes's gunners were unable to land a single shot. At a half-mile range, Winslow finally opened fire—methodically, endeavoring to make each shot count. He fired only about a third of the rounds that Semmes had gotten off, but he was much more accurate. Although both ships were damaged, the *Alabama* was fatally wounded and began to sink. She did not surrender, but when Winslow saw her crew abandoning ship, he called out to the crew of a nearby British yacht to "do what you can to save" the *Alabama*'s survivors. *Kearsarge* itself picked up seventy Confederate sailors before the raider disappeared under the waves at 12:24 p.m. Semmes and forty others did succeed in evading Winslow, but the career of CSS *Alabama* was at an end.

The 54th Massachusetts Infantry Regiment Assaults Fort Wagner, July 18, 1863

The Emancipation Proclamation officially made the abolition of slavery one of the Union's war aims in fighting the Civil War (Chapter 4). This did not mean that a majority of Northerners were abolitionists or even believed that black people were in any way equal to whites. The New York Draft Riots (Chapter 8) revealed the extent of resentment among many Union men at being required to lay down their lives to liberate people they not only believed were inferior to them, but were also after their jobs. A freed slave, after all, would work for the lowest of wages.

For their part, many African American men yearned for the opportunity to join in the fight, to take responsibility for helping to win their own freedom. In March 1863, while Lincoln and his cabinet were still arguing over how to bring black troops into the army, Massachusetts Governor John A. Andrew authorized raising a "colored" regiment. It became the 54th Massachusetts.

From the beginning, the regiment made national news as the first "colored" regiment raised in the North. Before this, the few black units that existed in the Union army had been slaves liberated by Union forces occupying portions of Southern states. But while the 54th was unique in having been recruited from free Northern black men and slaves who had escaped to the North, it was in every other way typical of a black unit in a white American army. It consisted of African American enlisted men commanded by Caucasian officers. In this case, Robert Gould Shaw, the twenty-six-year-old man Governor Andrew appointed as colonel, was a prominent young abolitionist.

On May 13, 1863, the regiment mustered with a strength of 1,100 and set off from Boston, bound for Union-occupied Beaufort, on the South Carolina coast. Although the troops had been promised pay and allowances equal to those of white soldiers, $14 a month, they were notified on arrival in Beaufort that their gross pay would be just $10 per month and that $3 would be taken out for clothing—

an expense that was not deducted from the pay of white soldiers. By way of quiet protest, the soldiers of the 54th, together with their white officers, refused to accept *any* pay until they received equal pay. (That would not happen until March 3, 1865.)

For the most part, the 54th was given minor assignments, typically involving manual labor rather than combat. Then came July 18, 1863, when Colonel Shaw volunteered elements of his regiment to lead an assault on Fort (or Battery) Wagner, a Confederate stronghold protecting the entrance to Charleston Harbor.

The mission he and his men accepted was close to suicidal. They were to make a frontal assault via an extremely narrow beach that passed below the fort, where cannon fire as well as rifle fire would be poured down on them. It seemed a hopeless endeavor, but, remarkably, the 54th ultimately succeeded in breaching small portions of the fort's wall. Nevertheless, the Union brigades that followed this initial attack were forced to withdraw.

Six hundred of the 54th Regiment's total strength of 1,007 black enlisted men (all thirty-seven officers were white) participated in the attack, of whom 272 were killed, wounded, or captured. Shaw, in the first wave, was among those who fell. The Confederates sought to disgrace him by throwing his body into a common grave with the bodies of the black men he had led. When he was told of this, Shaw's father spoke on behalf of his son's entire family: "We can imagine no holier place than in which he is."

The valiant record of the 54th paved the way for creation of the United States Colored Troops (USCT) on May 22, 1863. Some eighty years would pass before the US military was racially integrated, but African Americans now had a permanent place in the Army and, by war's end, African American soldiers made up 10 percent of the Union's military forces.

Nathan Bedford Forrest Leads the Fort Pillow Massacre, April 12, 1864

In contrast to most of the principal generals who fought in the Civil War, on both sides, Lieutenant General Nathan Bedford Forrest not only lacked a West Point education, he had very little education of any kind. Yet he was a born genius when it came to combat, a warrior fierce and wily. William Tecumseh Sherman called him a "devil," who "must be hunted down and killed if it costs ten thousand men and bankrupts the Federal treasury." Sherman also pronounced him "the most remarkable man our Civil War produced on either side."

Forrest's philosophy of war can be summed up in a single sentence he once uttered: "War means fightin', and fightin' means killin'." On April 12, 1864, he sent one of his divisions under Brigadier General James R. Chalmers to Fort Pillow, an earthwork fort on a high bluff overlooking the Mississippi. It had been built by a Confederate general, Gideon Pillow, but it was now held by a Union garrison, which manned it with the purpose of protecting Union supply lines. Forrest's assignment was to disrupt those supply lines, and so he resolved to re-take Fort Pillow.

It was garrisoned by 262 black soldiers and 295 whites. Chalmers attacked, forcing the Union pickets (advance guard) to take refuge inside the fort. At this point, Forrest arrived on the scene and took over command from Chalmers. His first act was to demand that the Union garrison immediately surrender. When the demand was rejected, he ordered his men to charge the fort. A fully manned division consists of as many as 8,000 soldiers. The 1st Division of Forrest's Cavalry Corps mustered anywhere between 1,500 and 2,500. In either case, the numbers overwhelmed the small Fort Pillow Garrison.

Everyone agrees on that. But where accounts differ, South from North, is on just how the attack proceeded. We do know the result: 231 men of the garrison were killed and another hundred wounded. Additionally, 168 whites and fifty-eight African Americans were captured, and many of those died in captivity. Forrest explained the heavy losses he inflicted as the result of the Union commander's foolishly stubborn refusal to surrender. Northern survivors claimed that the garrison *did* surrender—immediately after the fort had been breached. But instead of accepting the surrender, the attackers yelled out: "No quarter! No quarter! Kill the damned niggers; shoot them down!" And then they proceeded to do just that.

Witnesses insisted that Nathan Bedford Forrest led the whole "massacre." These charges were sufficient reason for the Congressional Committee on the Conduct of the War to investigate. The committee concluded that Forrest and his troops had indeed committed atrocities, chief among which was the murder of men after they had surrendered. The stories that emerged from the battle are lurid. Forrest's men, it was said, buried "colored" troops alive, and they set fire to hospital tents where Union wounded lay.

For many Northerners, the Fort Pillow Massacre made the fight for the end of "Southern tyranny" and slavery even more urgent. As for Forrest, he survived the war, was never called to account for Fort Pillow, and he even rebuilt the fortune that the war had cost him. He also became a founding member and Grand Wizard of the original Ku Klux Klan—which even he renounced some years after the war, when the violence it directed at African American Southerners, former slaves, transformed the former Confederacy into a land of terror.

Congress Passes the Wade-Davis Bill, Mandating a Punitive Reconstruction Policy, July 2, 1864

"Reconstruction," they called it—putting the country back together after the war. President Lincoln wanted to make the process quick and simple. All he intended to require was a loyalty oath to be administered in each of the former Confederate states. When 10 percent of voters in a state had taken the oath, the state would be readmitted to the Union and its population and leaders would be granted a full and complete amnesty. Indeed, even before the war ended, new state governments were created for Louisiana, Tennessee, and Arkansas, as they came under Union military control.

Congress, particularly the faction called the Radical Republicans, did not want to let the South off so easily. Senator Benjamin Wade of Ohio and Representative Henry Winter Davis of Maryland presented a bill that required not just 10 percent, but a simple majority of voters in each state to take an "ironclad" oath that not only affirmed their loyalty to the United States but also swore that they had never in the past supported the Confederacy. This effectively excluded Confederate political leaders, government officials, military officers, and even common soldiers. The Wade-Davis Bill also required that each state constitution explicitly abolish slavery, repudiate secession, and bar all former Confederate officials from ever holding office or even from voting.

President Lincoln believed this punitive approach would doom the nation so many had fought and died to restore. When the bill nevertheless passed both houses of Congress on July 2, 1864, Lincoln used a political and legal maneuver called a pocket veto in an effort to kill it. Per Article 1, Section 7 of the Constitution, if the president does not sign or veto a bill within ten days after it is presented to him, it becomes law, even without a presidential signature—unless, that is, "the Congress by their Adjournment prevent [the bill's] return." The Wade-Davis Bill was passed at the end of the congressional session. Lincoln simply did not sign it before adjournment. It was as if he had "pocketed" the document, and so it did not become law.

For his pocket veto, Lincoln was strongly attacked by the Radical Republicans. Union victories in Atlanta and elsewhere, however, helped propel him to a landslide reelection in November 1864, and subsequent passage of the Thirteenth Amendment, making slavery unconstitutional, blunted the perceived need for the stringent loyalty requirements. It is likely that the bill, when resubmitted after Congress returned, would either have been modified or would have failed to survive a formal veto. But President Lincoln was assassinated on April 14, 1865 (Chapter 1), before this could take place. The bill was therefore resubmitted to President Andrew Johnson when Congress reconvened. Johnson demanded important revisions. He called for dropping the oath concerning past conduct and, instead, demanded that amnesty be granted to anyone who took an oath to be loyal to the Union going forward. While Johnson required states to ratify the Thirteenth Amendment as a condition for readmission to the Union, he did not want to make readmission contingent on the majority of the population taking the loyalty oath. Finally, he required states to forbid slavery in their own constitutions, to repudiate debts incurred during the rebellion (thereby relieving the federal government of responsibility for them), and to declare secession null and void both in fact and in theory.

Ultimately, Wade-Davis failed to pass, but the friction between Andrew Johnson and Congress escalated when he did not wait for Congress to approve his changes to Wade-Davis before he issued, on his own authority, executive proclamations of amnesty for all of the Confederate states and proclamations prescribing provisional governments for each of the former Confederate states. Congress impeached Johnson on February 24, 1868. Although finally acquitted by a single vote, his executive authority was, as a practical matter, neutralized as the Radical Republicans in Congress imposed on the former Confederacy a Reconstruction scheme so punitive that it effectively extended the bitterness of the Civil War even after Reconstruction was formally ended in 1876. Economic, cultural, and political division, as well as the organized repression of African Americans, persisted into the mid-twentieth century.

Bloody Bill Anderson Leads the Centralia Massacre, September 27, 1864

As summer turned to fall in 1864, the Confederacy was rapidly losing its grip on the West. Major General Sterling Price responded by leading his Missouri State Guard in an invasion of northern Missouri, with the objective of capturing St. Louis and, he hoped, thereby sufficiently undermine Northern confidence that President Lincoln would lose his bid for reelection. An important element in Price's plan was guerrilla warfare, and for this he turned to William T. "Bloody Bill" Anderson.

Before the Civil War, Anderson had made his living as a trafficker in stolen horses along the Santa Fe Trail. When the war started, he joined Quantrill's Raiders, a Confederate guerrilla band led by William Quantrill and including among its number the future outlaws Frank and Jesse James. After compiling a record of mayhem throughout Missouri, the Quantrill band broke into several smaller groups, one of which was led by Bloody Bill, who took Jesse and Frank James with him.

Anderson's guerrillas, about eighty in number, were terrorists who exuberantly tortured, scalped, and even decapitated their victims—sparing only women. (Three of Bloody Bill's sisters had been killed when Union forces jailed them and others in a ramshackle building that collapsed on its inmates.) On September 27, 1864, Anderson led his eighty guerrillas on a raid to cut the North Missouri Railroad in Centralia as part of Price's invasion. Many disguised themselves in Union uniforms taken from troops killed earlier.

After looting the town, Anderson's men piled obstacles on the rail line. An approaching train stopped, and the blue-uniformed guerrillas swarmed it. Of 125 passengers, twenty-three were Union soldiers. At gunpoint, they were ordered to strip. Anderson called for an officer to step forward. Sergeant Thomas Goodman responded, offering himself as a sacrifice in the hope that the others might be spared. Instead, Anderson and his men gunned down the soldiers, mutilated their bodies, and took their scalps as the civilian passengers looked on. Sergeant Goodman was taken prisoner. (He would manage to escape ten days later.)

That afternoon, Union Major A.V.E. Johnston, leading the 155 men of the 39th Missouri Infantry Regiment (Mounted), rode into Centralia, was told what had happened, and set out in pursuit of Anderson. He caught up with the guerrillas, but his regiment, raw recruits all, was outgunned and defeated. Of 155 Union troops, 123 were killed or wounded. Major Johnston was among the slain, gunned down, according to Frank James, by his brother Jesse.

Anderson himself met his own death on October 26, 1864, at the hands of 33rd Regiment of the Missouri State Militia in a firefight at Albany, Missouri. But his career of terror lives on as an example of what the Civil War might have become had a few men of noble goodwill and common sense not prevailed after the Confederate government collapsed and the formally constituted armies departed the field. Robert E. Lee's surrender at Appomattox Court House on April 9, 1865 (Chapter 5), where Ulysses S. Grant offered terms both honorable and humane and Lee accepted them with dignity and good faith, created the model on which this most terrible of American wars was ended.

The 20 Most Significant Civil War Books

Ira Berlin, et al, eds., *Free at Last: A Documentary History of Slavery, Freedom, and the Civil War* (New York: The New Press, 1992).

A trove of original documents that reveal the course of slavery and abolition up to and through the Civil War.

David Blight, *Race and Reunion: The Civil War in American Memory* (Cambridge, MA: Harvard University Press, 2002).

A study of the Civil War in American popular culture and the popular conception of history.

Michael Burlingame, *Abraham Lincoln: A Life,* 2 volumes (Baltimore: Johns Hopkins University Press, 2008).

A superb biography of the Union's Civil War president.

Bruce Catton, *The Centennial History of the Civil War, 1861-65,* 3 volumes (Garden City, NY: Doubleday, 1961. Includes all three volumes of *the* classic Civil War trilogy, *Mr. Lincoln's Army*, 1951; *Glory Road*, 1952; and *A Stillness at Appomattox*, 1953.

To this day, these books remain among the most widely read works on the Civil War.

Alice Fahs. *The Imagined Civil War: Popular Literature of the North & South, 1861-1865* (Chapel Hill: The University of North Carolina Press, 2002).

This survey and study of the popular literature of the Civil War period provides a window into prevailing public sentiment about the war in the North and the South.

Shelby Foote. *The Civil War: A Narrative*, 3 volumes (1958-1974; reprint ed., New York: Vintage, 1986).

Excellent history as written by a noted historical novelist.

Douglas Southall Freeman. *Robert E. Lee: A Biography,* 4 volumes (New York: Scribner's, 1947).

Both exhaustive (2,445 pages) and immensely readable, this biography of perhaps the most-admired general in military history will never be surpassed.

Doris Kearns Goodwin. *Team of Rivals: The Political Genius of Abraham Lincoln* (New York: Simon & Schuster, 2006).

A study of the Civil War president in the context of his contentious yet often brilliant cabinet.

Ulysses S. Grant, *Personal Memoirs of U. S. Grant* (1885-1886; reprint ed., New York: Da Capo, 1982.)

A great work of military autobiography that is also a notable work of American literature.

William C. Harris, *With Charity for All: Lincoln and the Restoration of the Union* (Lexington: University Press of Kentucky, 1997).

The story of how Lincoln began Reconstruction—he called it "Restoration"—before the Civil War ended.

William Marvel. *Andersonville: The Last Depot* (Chapel Hill: University of North Carolina Press, 1995).

The best and most complete historical treatment of the Civil War's most notorious POW camp.

James McPherson. *Battle Cry of Freedom* (New York: Oxford University Press, 1988).

Certainly the best and most authoritative one-volume history of the Civil War.

James McPherson, *For Cause and Comrades: Why Men Fought in the Civil War* (New York: Oxford University Press, 1997).

The title and subtitle perfectly define the subject of this extraordinary work of history.

Allan Nevins, *The War for the Union*, 4 volumes (New York: Scribner's, 1959-1971).

This is the most complete treatment of the Civil War from a Union perspective.

David M. Potter, *The Impending Crisis, 1848–1861* (New York: Harper, 1976).

A study of the political causes of the Civil War, beginning with the end of the US-Mexican War.

Charles Royster. *The Destructive War: William Tecumseh Sherman, Stonewall Jackson, and the Americans* (New York: Knopf, 1992).

An unflinching look at the two fiercest warriors of the Civil War—advocates not merely of victory, but extermination.

Michael Shaara, *The Killer Angels* (1974; reprint ed., New York: Modern Library, 2004).

This masterpiece of Civil War fiction focuses on the commanders instrumental in the Battle of Gettysburg.

Harriet Beecher Stowe, *Uncle Tom's Cabin; or Life Among the Lowly* (Boston: John P. Jewett, 1852).

When Abraham Lincoln met the author of this enormously popular antislavery novel, he greeted her with "So this is the little lady who started this great war."

Russell F. Weigley. *A Great Civil War: Military and Political History, 1861-1865* (Bloomington: Indiana University Press, 2000).

The dean of historians of American military doctrine and policy studies the strategy and tactics that dominated the Civil War.

Bell Irvin Wiley. *The Life of Johnny Reb* (1943; reprinted, Baton Rouge: Louisiana State University Press, 2008) and *The Life of Billy Yank* (1952; reprinted, Baton Rouge: Louisiana State University Press, 2008).

Lovingly researched and compassionately written, this is the classic study of the common soldier in both the Confederate and Union armies.

Index

Author Biography

Alan Axelrod is a popular military historian, whose Civil War books include *The Real History of the Civil War: A New Look at the Past* (2012), *Generals South, Generals North: The Commanders of the Civil War Reconsidered* (2011), *The Horrid Pit: The Battle of the Crater, the Civil War's Cruelest Mission* (2007), *Complete Idiot's Guide to the Civil War* (1998; Second Edition, 2003), and *The War between the Spies: A History of Espionage During the American Civil War* (1992). He has also written widely on the American Revolution, World War I, and World War II, and is the author of biographies of George S. Patton Jr. and Omar Bradley, as well as the co-author of a biography of George C. Marshall.

A former university professor and publishing executive, Alan Axelrod is president and CEO of the Ian Samuel Group, Inc., a creative services firm. He has been a creative consultant (and on-camera personality) for *The Wild West* television documentary series (Warner Bros., 1993), *Civil War Journal* (A&E Network, 1994), "The American Experience" series (PBS, 2016), and The Discovery Channel, and he has appeared on MSNBC, CNN, CNNfn, CNBC, Fox Network affiliates in Philadelphia and Atlanta, and numerous radio news and talk programs, including National Public Radio.

He and his wife, the artist Anita Arliss, make their home in Atlanta.